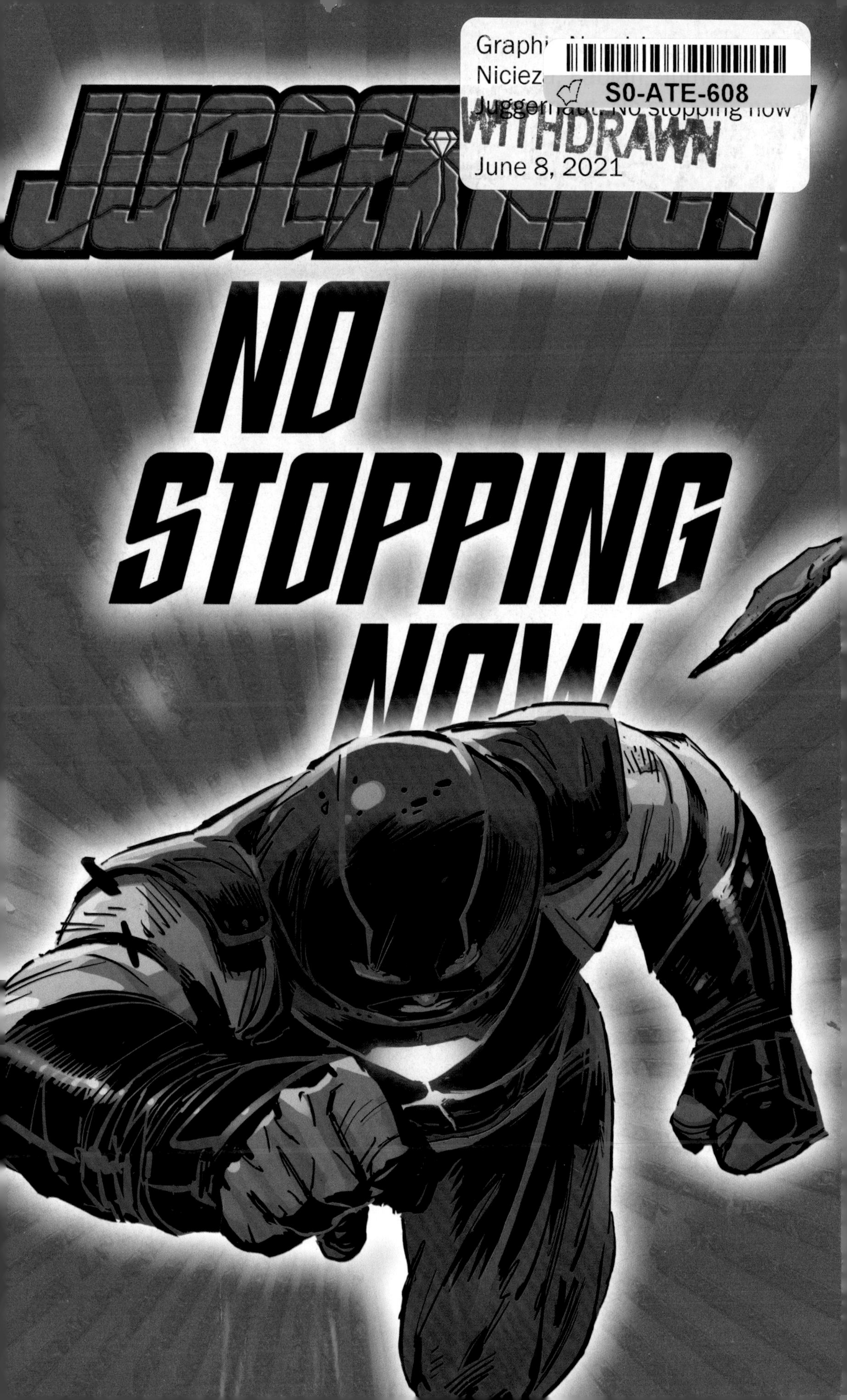
JUGGERNAUT
NO STOPPING NOW

A mystic gem. A force of overwhelming power.
Nothing can stop the JUGGERNAUT. Except himself.
Another building falls. Another building falls. Another building falls.
CAIN MARKO is done letting others pick up the pieces of the things he has destroyed.

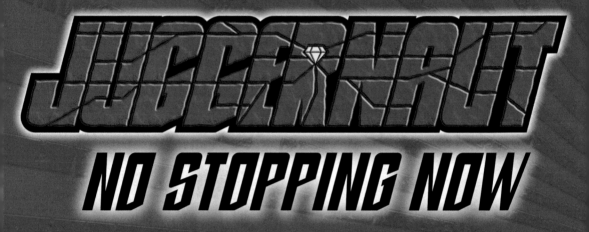

JUGGERNAUT

NO STOPPING NOW

WRITER: FABIAN NICIEZA
ARTIST: RON GARNEY
COLOR ARTIST: MATT MILLA

LETTERER: VC's JOE SABINO
COVER ART: GEOFF SHAW & MATT MILLA

ASSISTANT EDITORS: CHRIS ROBINSON & ANNALISE BISSA
EDITOR: JORDAN D. WHITE

JUGGERNAUT CREATED BY STAN LEE & JACK KIRBY

COLLECTION EDITOR: JENNIFER GRÜNWALD ASSISTANT EDITOR: DANIEL KIRCHHOFFER
ASSISTANT MANAGING EDITOR: MAIA LOY ASSISTANT MANAGING EDITOR: LISA MONTALBANO
VP PRODUCTION & SPECIAL PROJECTS: JEFF YOUNGQUIST BOOK DESIGNER: JAY BOWEN
SVP PRINT, SALES & MARKETING: DAVID GABRIEL EDITOR IN CHIEF: C.B. CEBULSKI

JUGGERNAUT: NO STOPPING NOW. Contains material originally published in magazine form as JUGGERNAUT (2020) #1-5. First printing 2021. ISBN 978-1-302-92450-8. Published by MARVEL WORLDWIDE, INC., a subsidiary of MARVEL ENTERTAINMENT, LLC. OFFICE OF PUBLICATION: 1290 Avenue of the Americas, New York, NY 10104. © 2021 MARVEL. No similarity between any of the names, characters, persons, and/or institutions in this magazine with those of any living or dead person or institution is intended, and any such similarity which may exist is purely coincidental. **Printed in Canada.** KEVIN FEIGE, Chief Creative Officer; DAN BUCKLEY, President, Marvel Entertainment; JOE QUESADA, EVP & Creative Director; DAVID BOGART, Associate Publisher & SVP of Talent Affairs; TOM BREVOORT, VP, Executive Editor; NICK LOWE, Executive Editor, VP of Content, Digital Publishing; DAVID GABRIEL, VP of Print & Digital Publishing; JEFF YOUNGQUIST, VP of Production & Special Projects; ALEX MORALES, Director of Publishing Operations; DAN EDINGTON, Managing Editor; RICKEY PURDIN, Director of Talent Relations; JENNIFER GRUNWALD, Senior Editor, Special Projects; SUSAN CRESPI, Production Manager; STAN LEE, Chairman Emeritus. For information regarding advertising in Marvel Comics or on Marvel.com, please contact Vit DeBellis, Custom Solutions & Integrated Advertising Manager, at vdebellis@marvel.com. For Marvel subscription inquiries, please call 888-511-5480. **Manufactured between 1/22/2021 and 2/23/2021 by SOLISCO PRINTERS, SCOTT, QC, CANADA.**

10 9 8 7 6 5 4 3 2 1

1

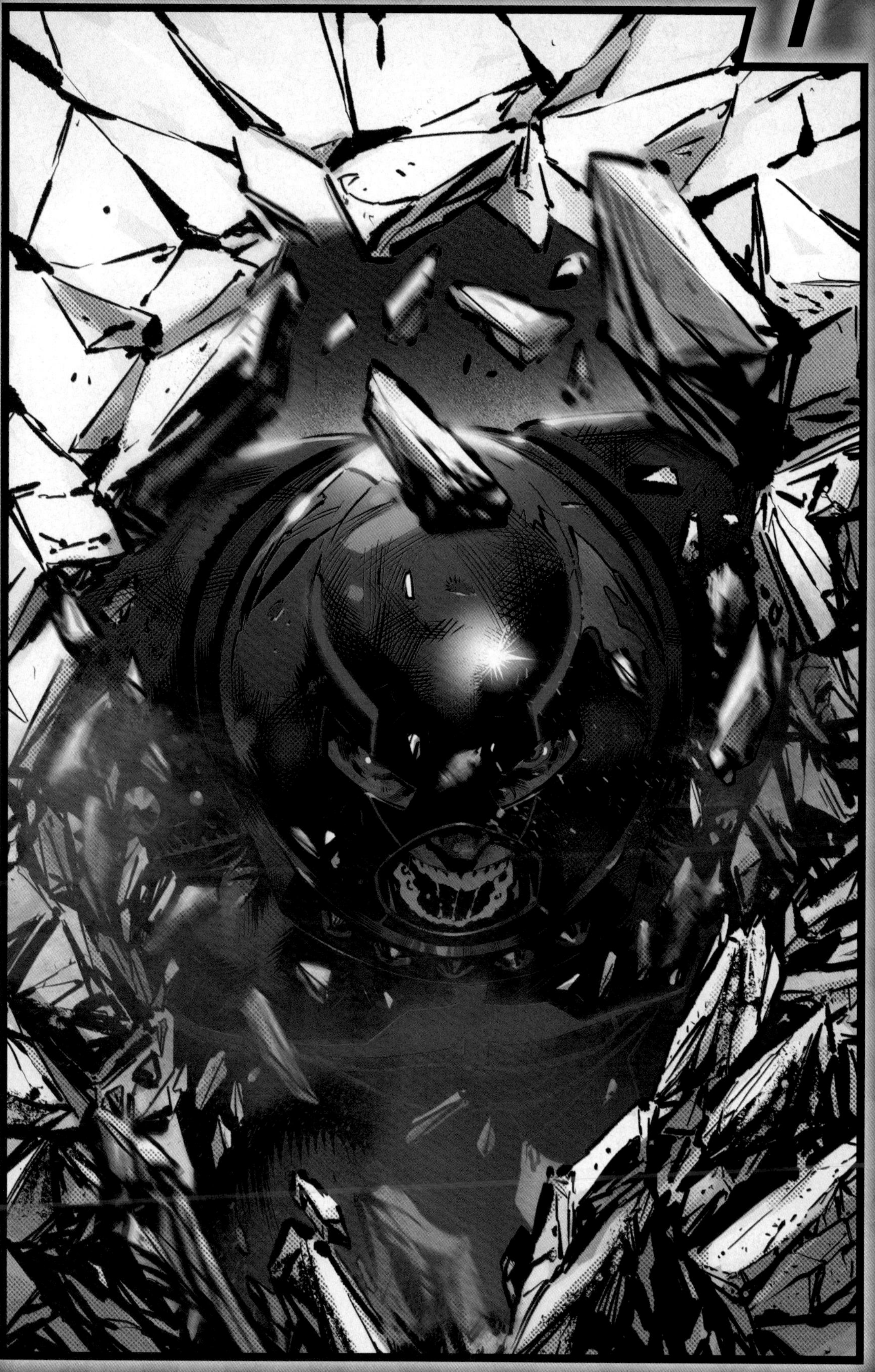

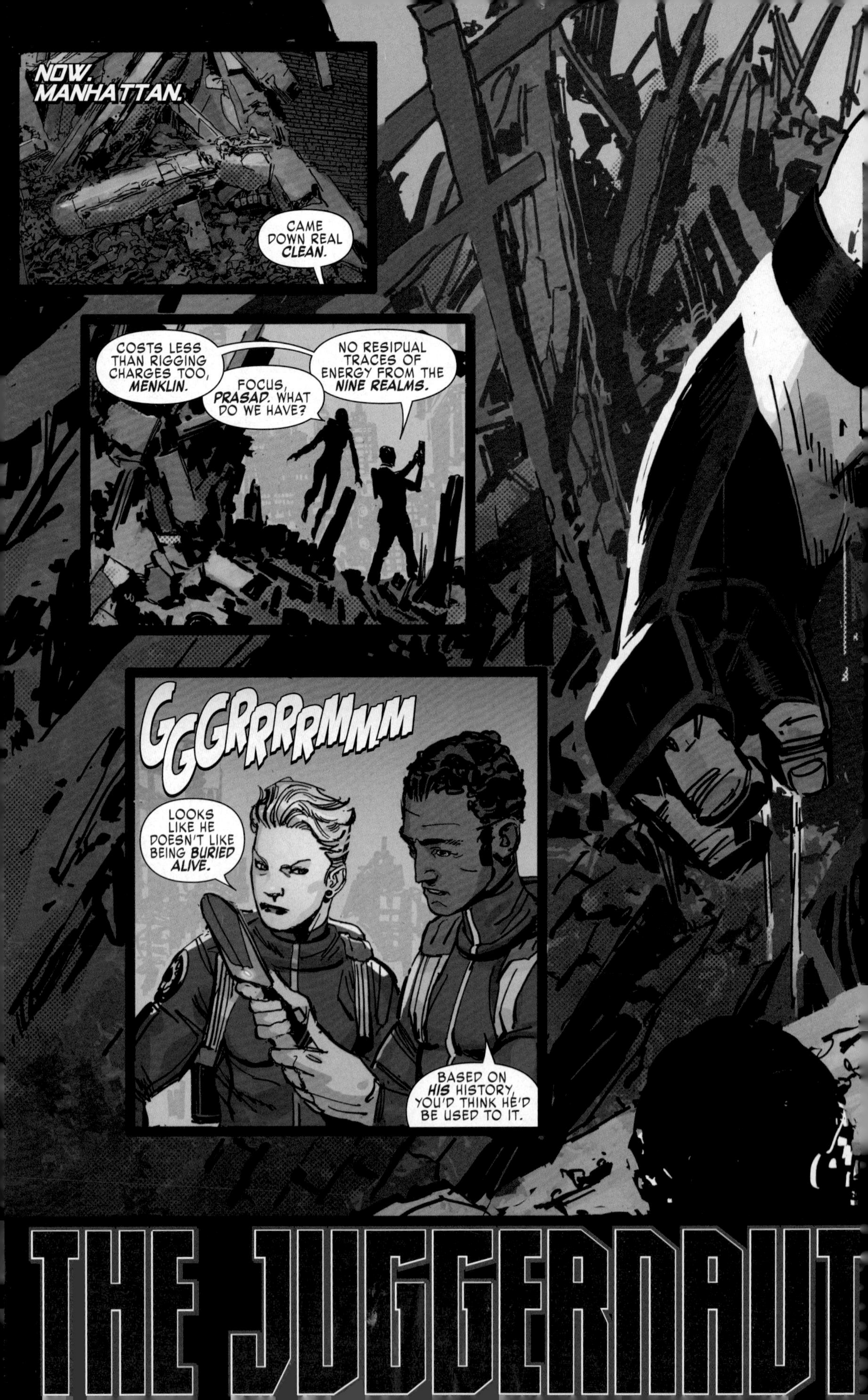
NOW. MANHATTAN.
CAME DOWN REAL CLEAN.
COSTS LESS THAN RIGGING CHARGES TOO, MENKLIN.
NO RESIDUAL TRACES OF ENERGY FROM THE NINE REALMS.
FOCUS, PRASAD. WHAT DO WE HAVE?
GGGRRRRMMMM
LOOKS LIKE HE DOESN'T LIKE BEING BURIED ALIVE.
BASED ON HIS HISTORY, YOU'D THINK HE'D BE USED TO IT.
THE JUGGERNAUT

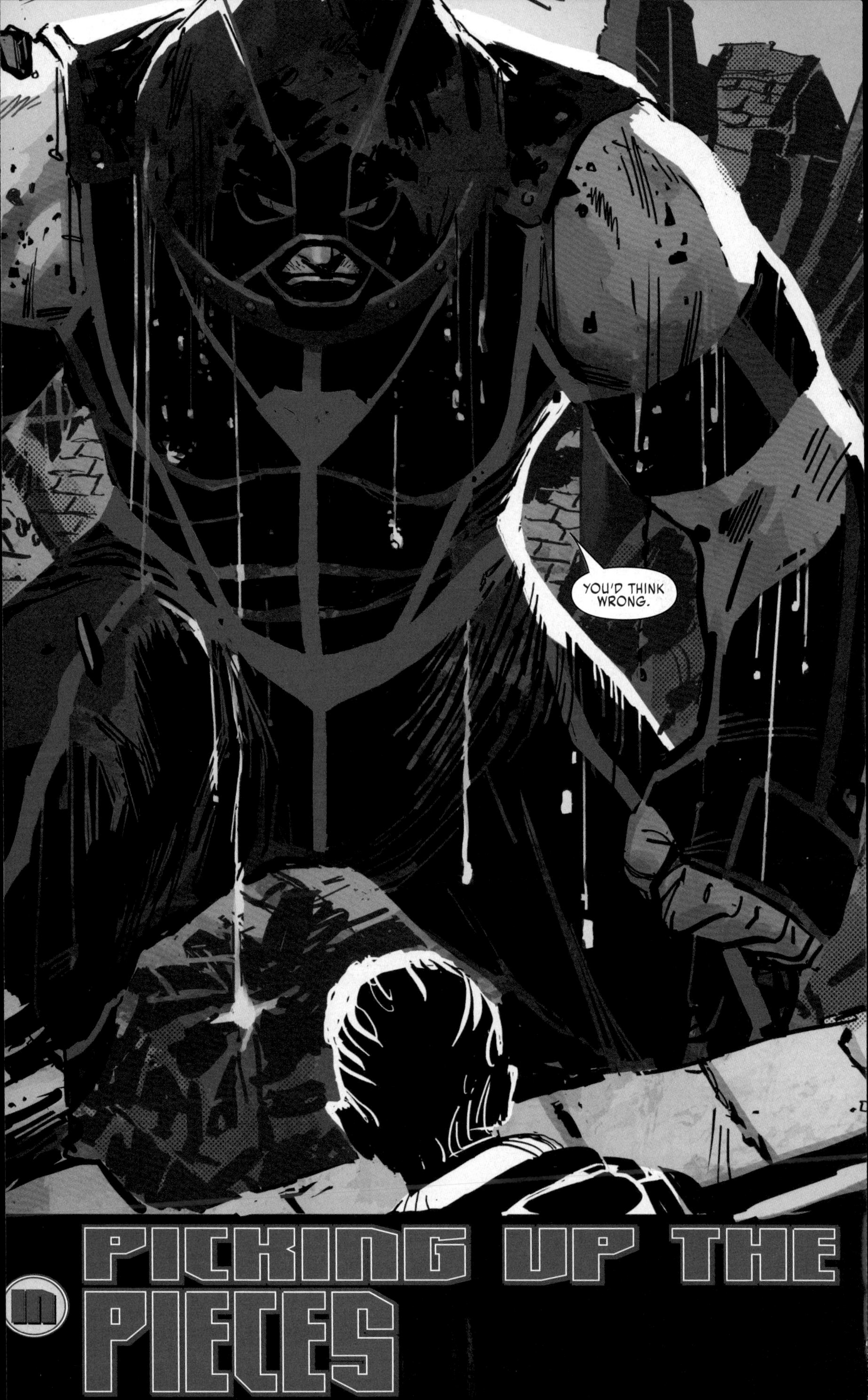
YOU'D THINK WRONG.
in
PICKING UP THE
PIECES

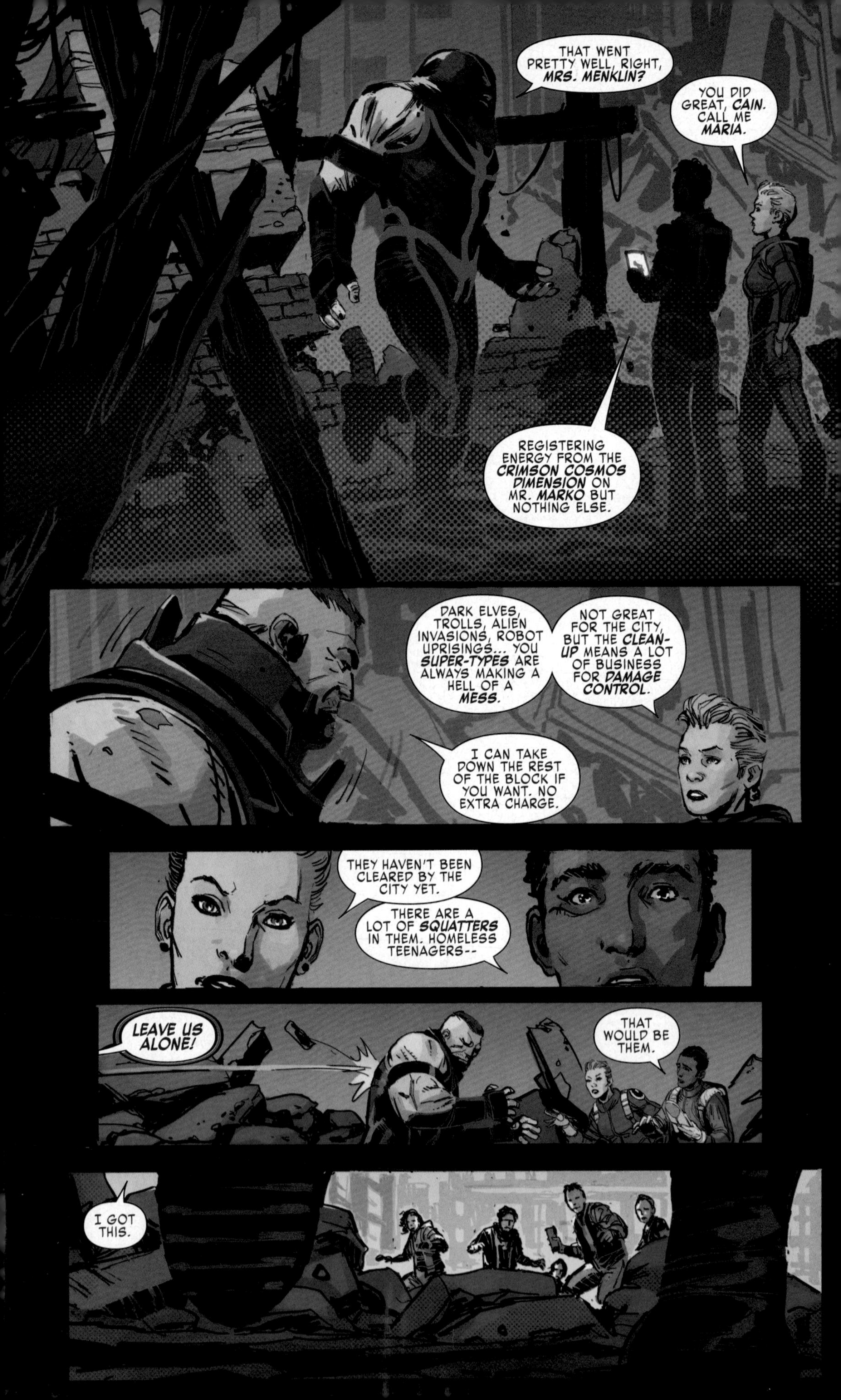
THAT WENT PRETTY WELL, RIGHT, MRS. MENKLIN?
YOU DID GREAT, CAIN. CALL ME MARIA.
REGISTERING ENERGY FROM THE CRIMSON COSMOS DIMENSION ON MR. MARKO BUT NOTHING ELSE.
DARK ELVES, TROLLS, ALIEN INVASIONS, ROBOT UPRISINGS... YOU SUPER-TYPES ARE ALWAYS MAKING A HELL OF A MESS.
NOT GREAT FOR THE CITY, BUT THE CLEAN-UP MEANS A LOT OF BUSINESS FOR DAMAGE CONTROL.
I CAN TAKE DOWN THE REST OF THE BLOCK IF YOU WANT. NO EXTRA CHARGE.
THEY HAVEN'T BEEN CLEARED BY THE CITY YET.
THERE ARE A LOT OF SQUATTERS IN THEM. HOMELESS TEENAGERS--
LEAVE US ALONE!
THAT WOULD BE THEM.
I GOT THIS.

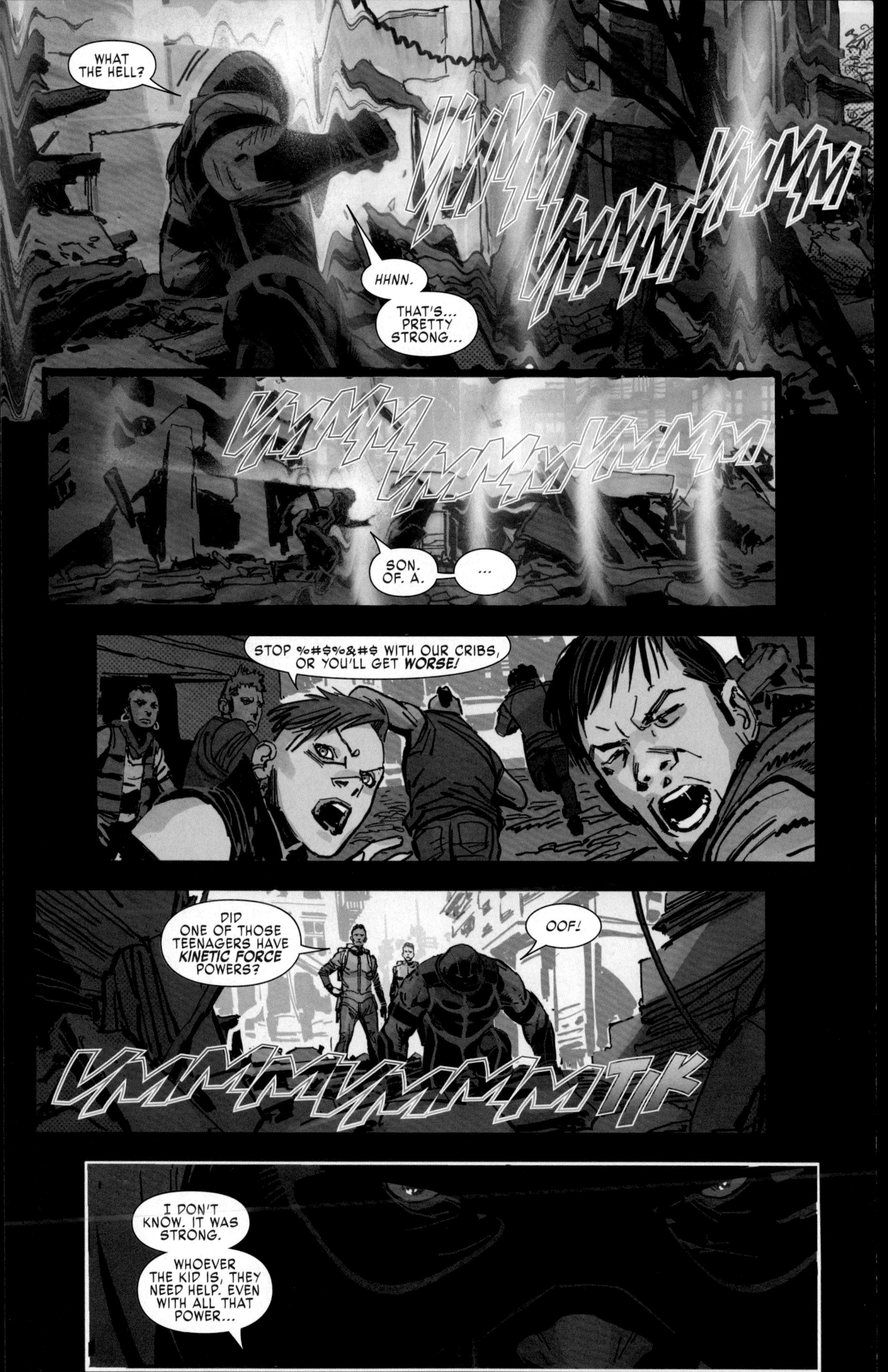
WHAT THE HELL?
VMMM VMMM VMMM
HHNN.
THAT'S... PRETTY STRONG...
VMMM VMMM VMMM
SON. OF. A.
...
STOP %#$%&#$ WITH OUR CRIBS, OR YOU'LL GET WORSE!
DID ONE OF THOSE TEENAGERS HAVE KINETIC FORCE POWERS?
OOF!
VMMMMMMMMMM TIK
I DON'T KNOW. IT WAS STRONG.
WHOEVER THE KID IS, THEY NEED HELP. EVEN WITH ALL THAT POWER...

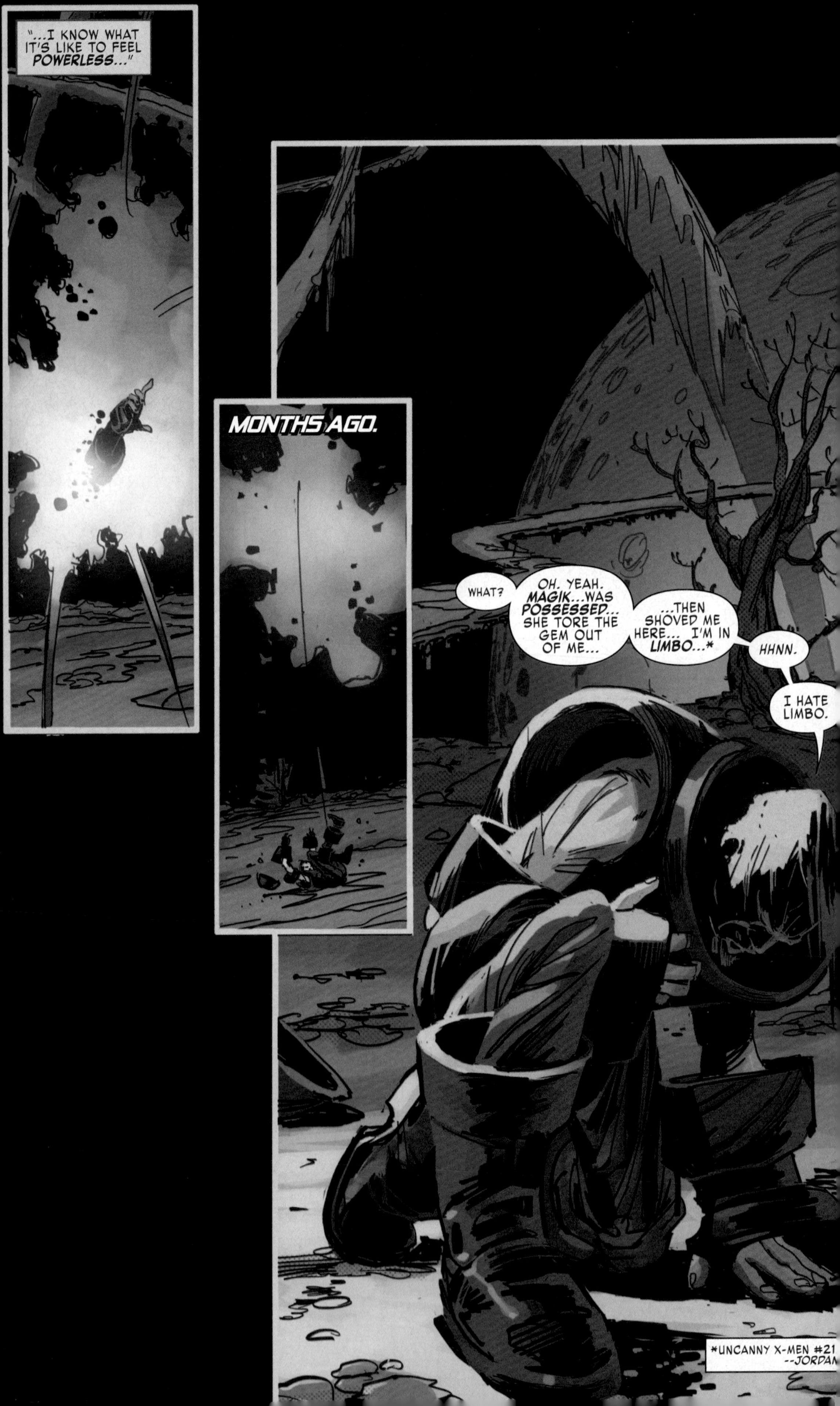

"...I KNOW WHAT IT'S LIKE TO FEEL POWERLESS..."
MONTHS AGO.
WHAT?
OH. YEAH. MAGIK...WAS POSSESSED... SHE TORE THE GEM OUT OF ME...
...THEN SHOVED ME HERE... I'M IN LIMBO...*
HHNN.
I HATE LIMBO.
*UNCANNY X-MEN #21
--JORDAN

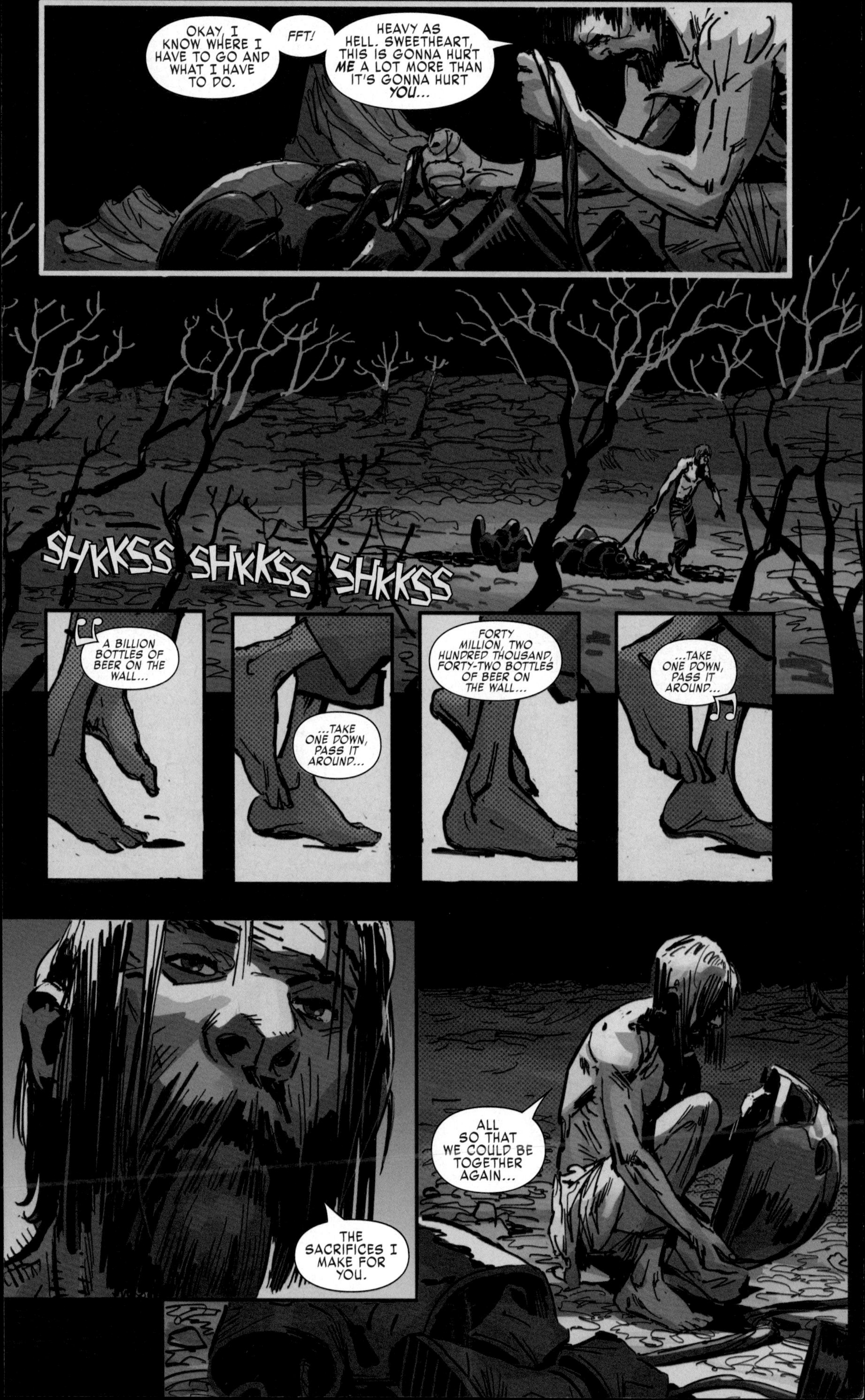
OKAY, I KNOW WHERE I HAVE TO GO AND WHAT I HAVE TO DO.
FFT!
HEAVY AS HELL. SWEETHEART, THIS IS GONNA HURT ME A LOT MORE THAN IT'S GONNA HURT YOU...
SHKKSS SHKKSS SHKKSS
A BILLION BOTTLES OF BEER ON THE WALL...
...TAKE ONE DOWN, PASS IT AROUND...
FORTY MILLION, TWO HUNDRED THOUSAND, FORTY-TWO BOTTLES OF BEER ON THE WALL...
...TAKE ONE DOWN, PASS IT AROUND...
ALL SO THAT WE COULD BE TOGETHER AGAIN...
THE SACRIFICES I MAKE FOR YOU.

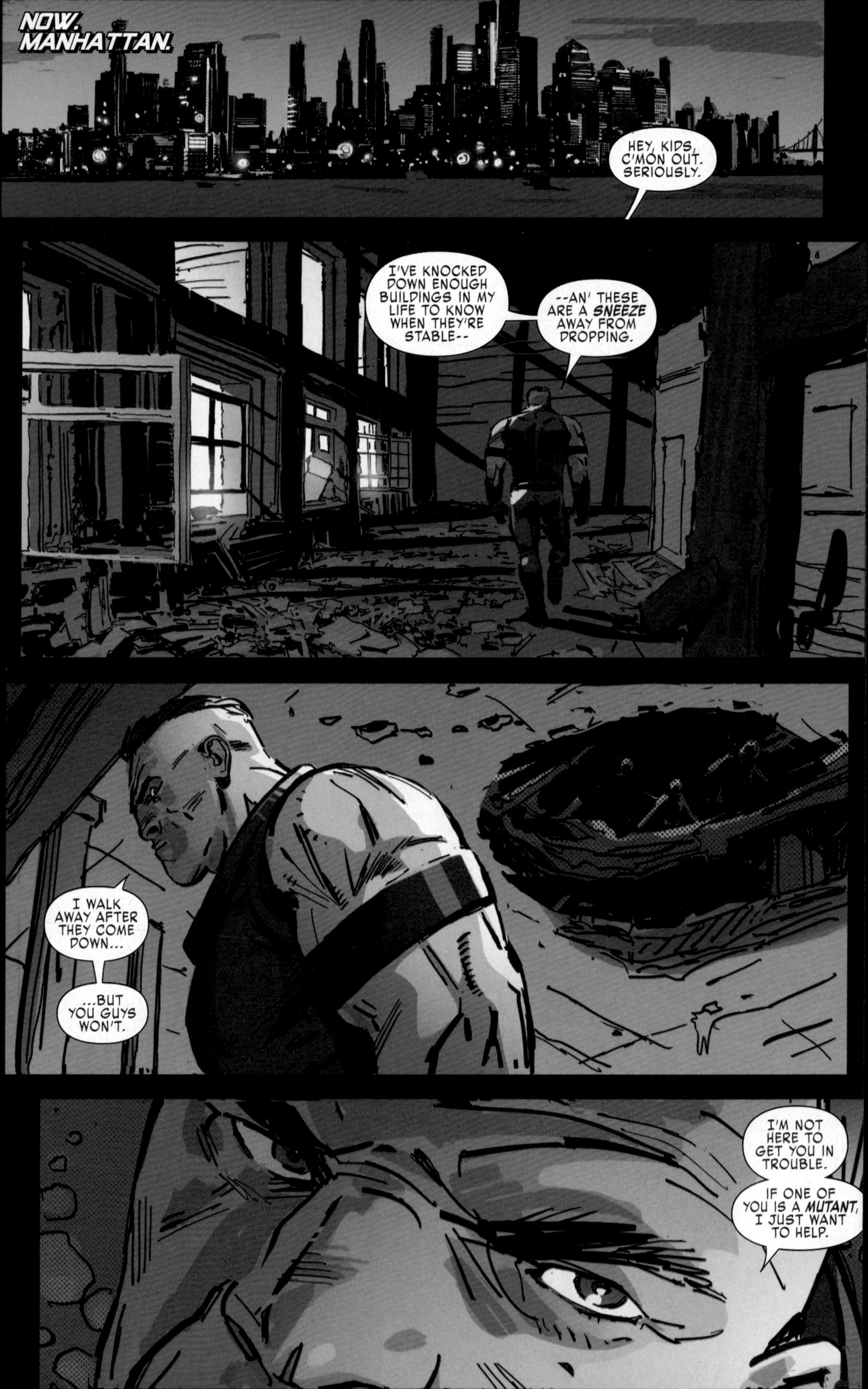
NOW. MANHATTAN.
HEY, KIDS, C'MON OUT. SERIOUSLY.
I'VE KNOCKED DOWN ENOUGH BUILDINGS IN MY LIFE TO KNOW WHEN THEY'RE STABLE--
--AN' THESE ARE A SNEEZE AWAY FROM DROPPING.
I WALK AWAY AFTER THEY COME DOWN...
...BUT YOU GUYS WON'T.
I'M NOT HERE TO GET YOU IN TROUBLE.
IF ONE OF YOU IS A MUTANT, I JUST WANT TO HELP.

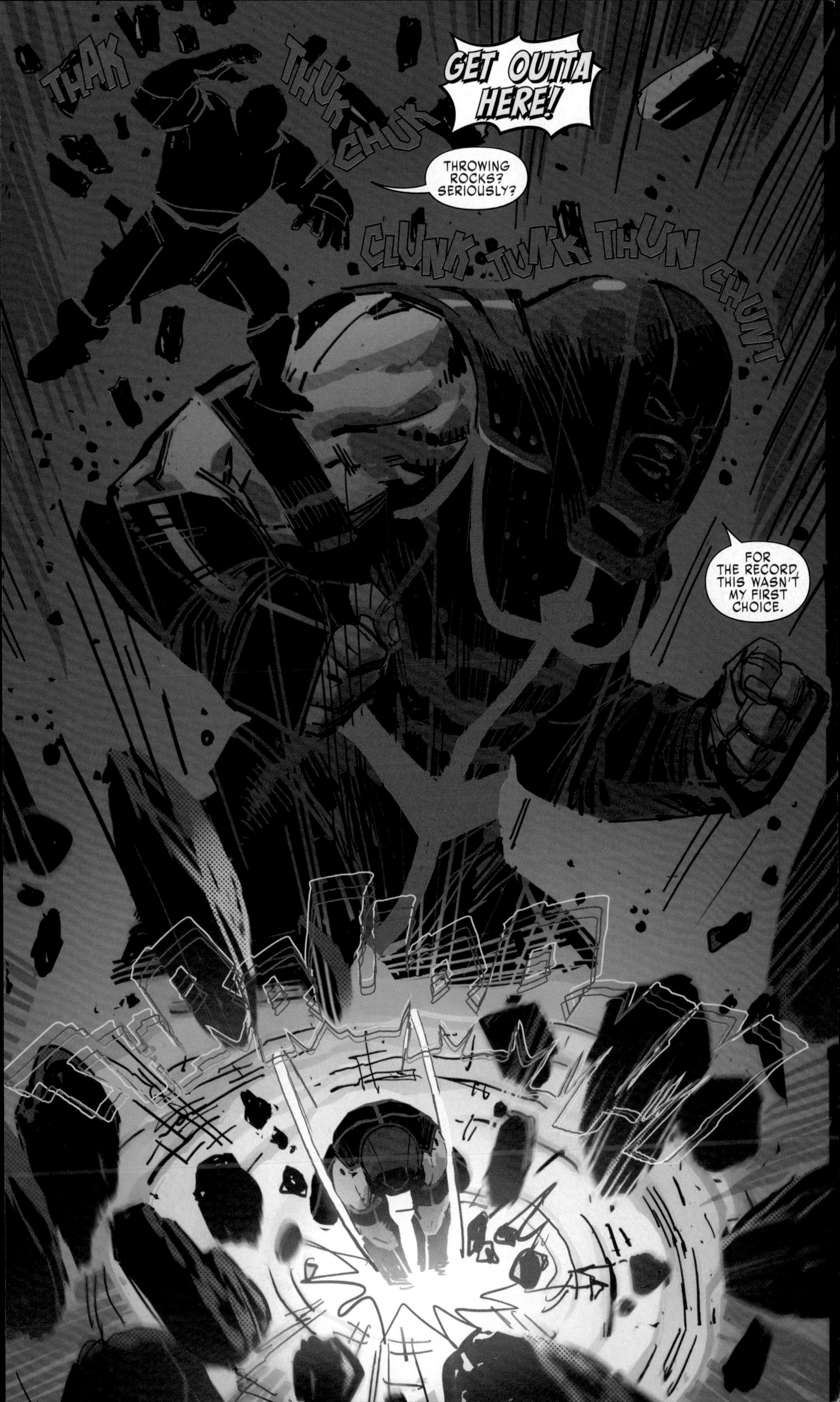
THAK
THUK CHUK
GET OUTTA HERE!
THROWING ROCKS? SERIOUSLY?
CLUNK TUNK THUN CHUNT
FOR THE RECORD, THIS WASN'T MY FIRST CHOICE.

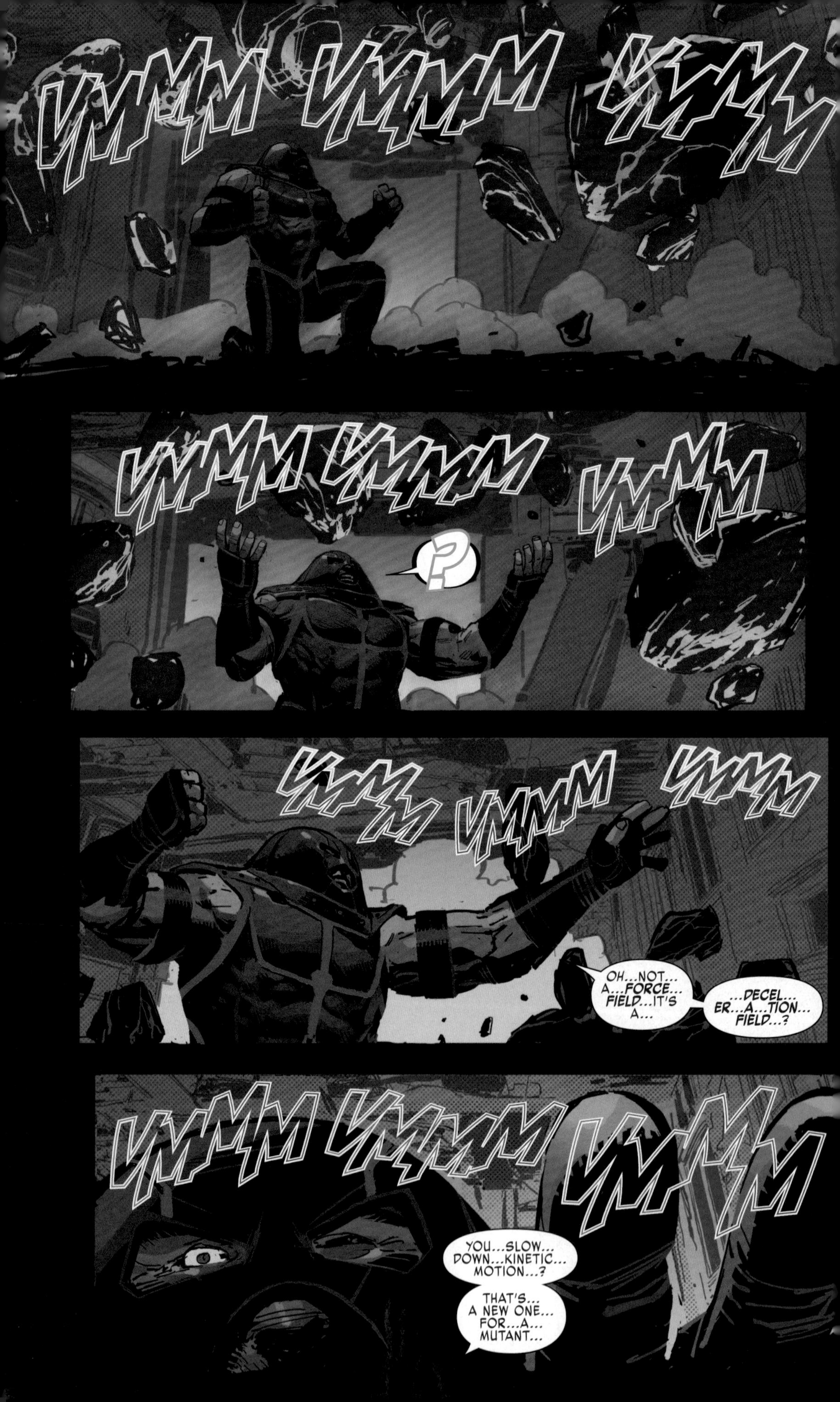
VMMM VMMM VMMM
VMMM VMMM VMMM
?
VMMM VMMM VMMM
OH...NOT... A...FORCE... FIELD...IT'S A...
...DECEL... ER...A...TION... FIELD...?
VMMM VMMM VMMM
YOU...SLOW... DOWN...KINETIC... MOTION...?
THAT'S... A NEW ONE... FOR...A... MUTANT...

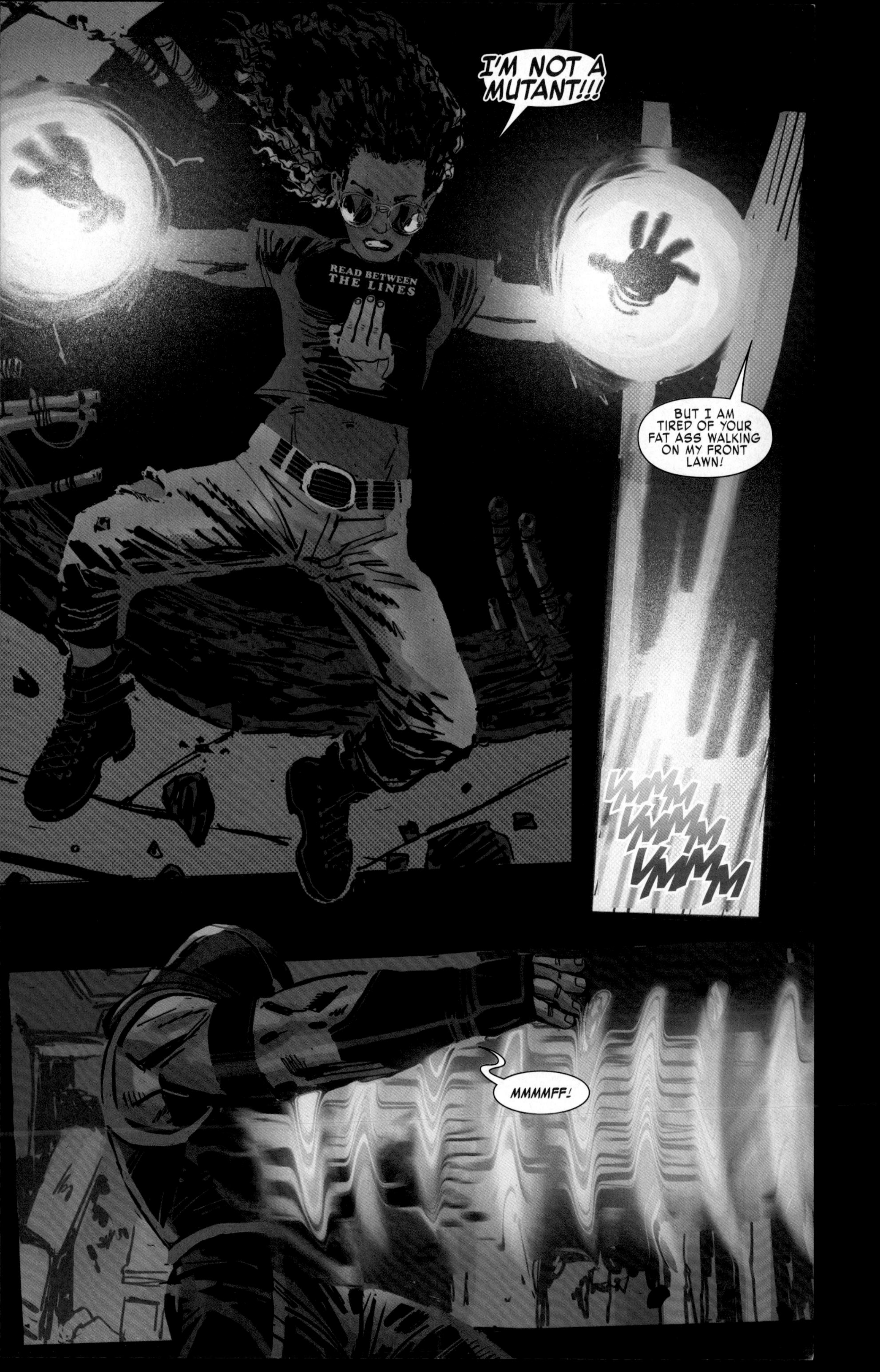
I'M NOT A MUTANT!!!
READ BETWEEN THE LINES
BUT I AM TIRED OF YOUR FAT ASS WALKING ON MY FRONT LAWN!
VMMM VMMM VMMM
MMMMFF!

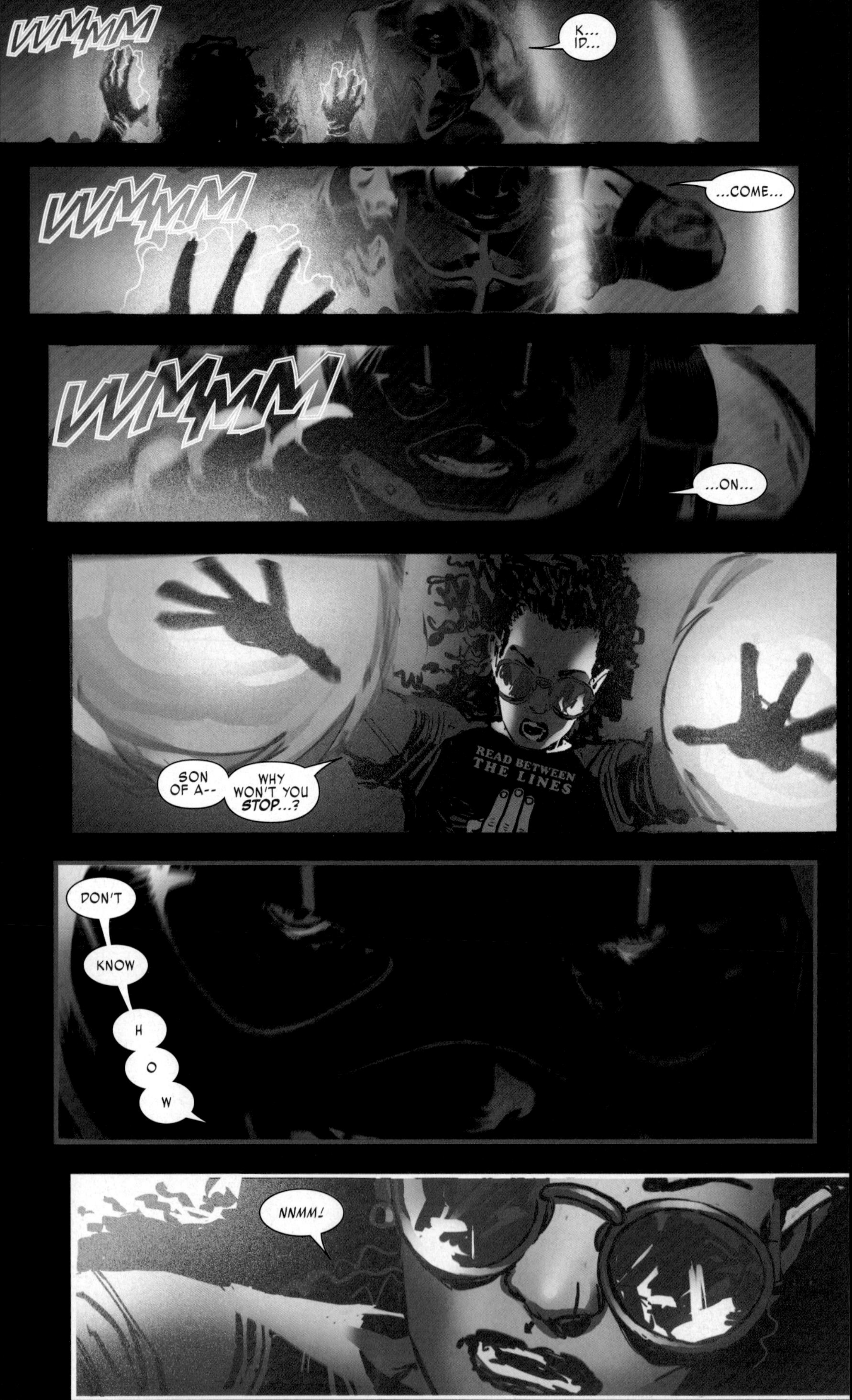
VVMMM
K... ID...
VVMMM
...COME...
VVMMM
...ON...
SON OF A--
WHY WON'T YOU STOP...?
READ BETWEEN THE LINES
DON'T
KNOW
H
O
W
NNMM!

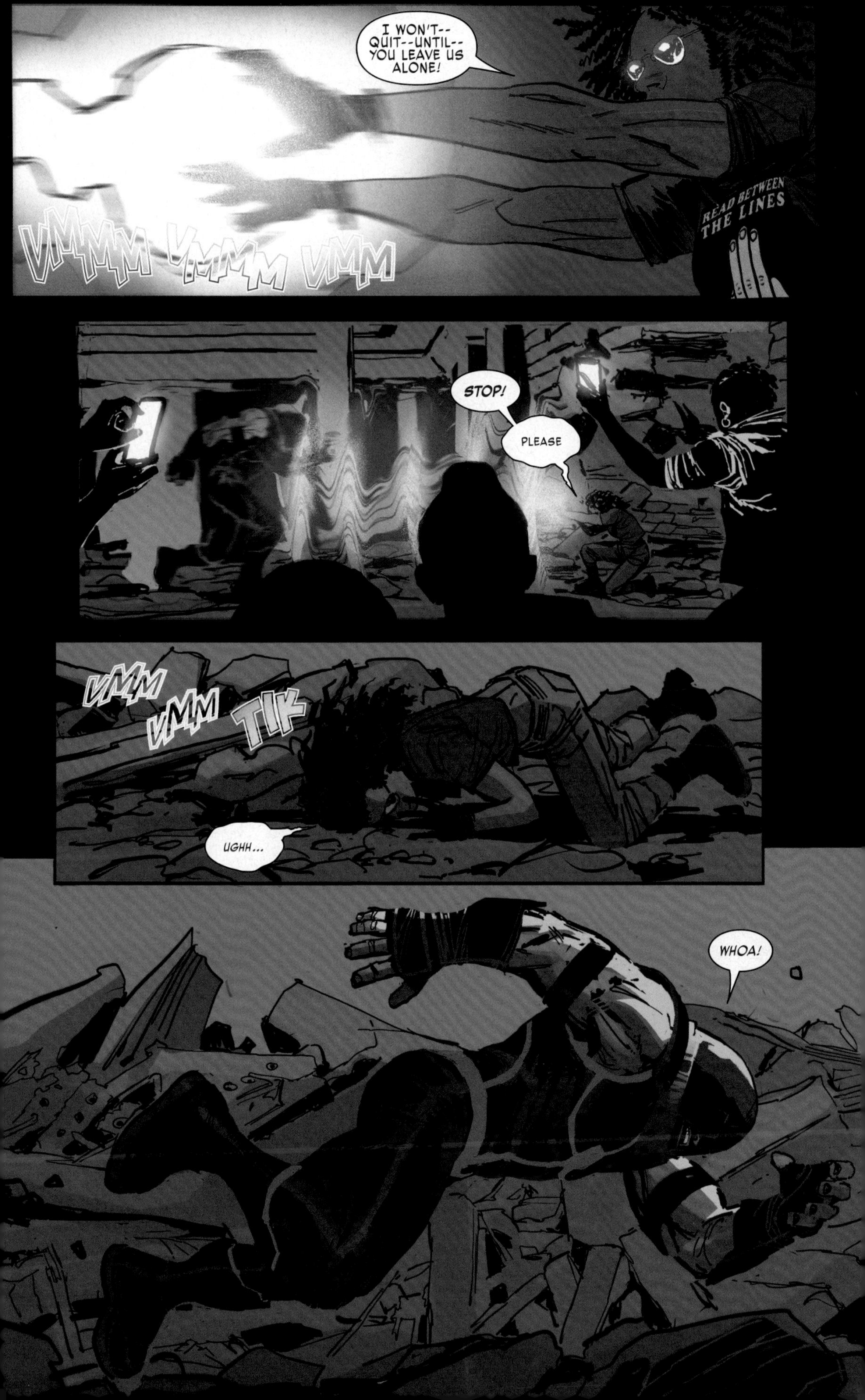
I WON'T--
QUIT--UNTIL--
YOU LEAVE US
ALONE!
VMMM VMMM VMM
READ BETWEEN THE LINES
STOP!
PLEASE
VMM
VMM
TIK
UGHH...
WHOA!

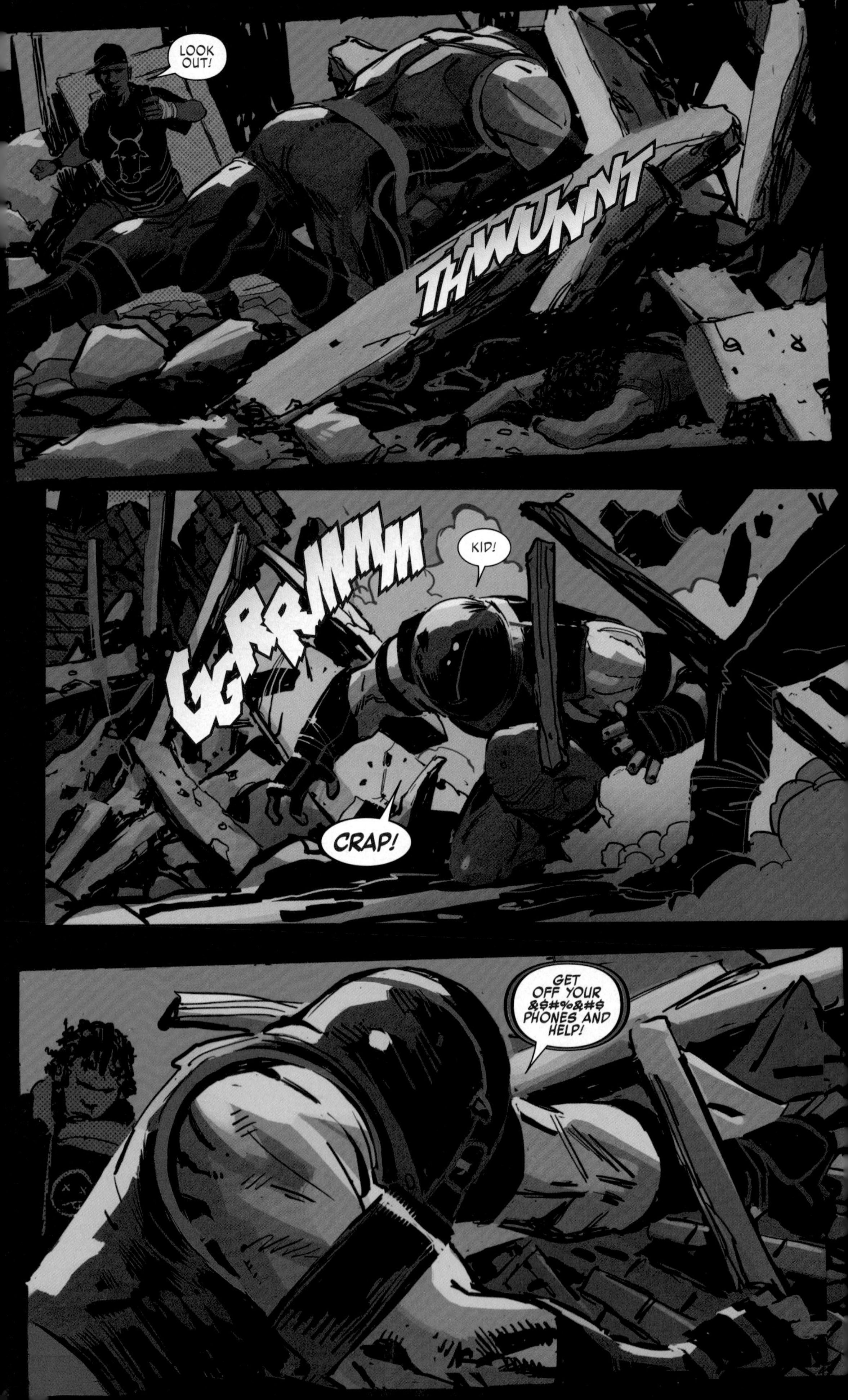
LOOK OUT!
THWUNNT
GGRRMMMM
KID!
CRAP!
GET OFF YOUR &$#%&#$ PHONES AND HELP!

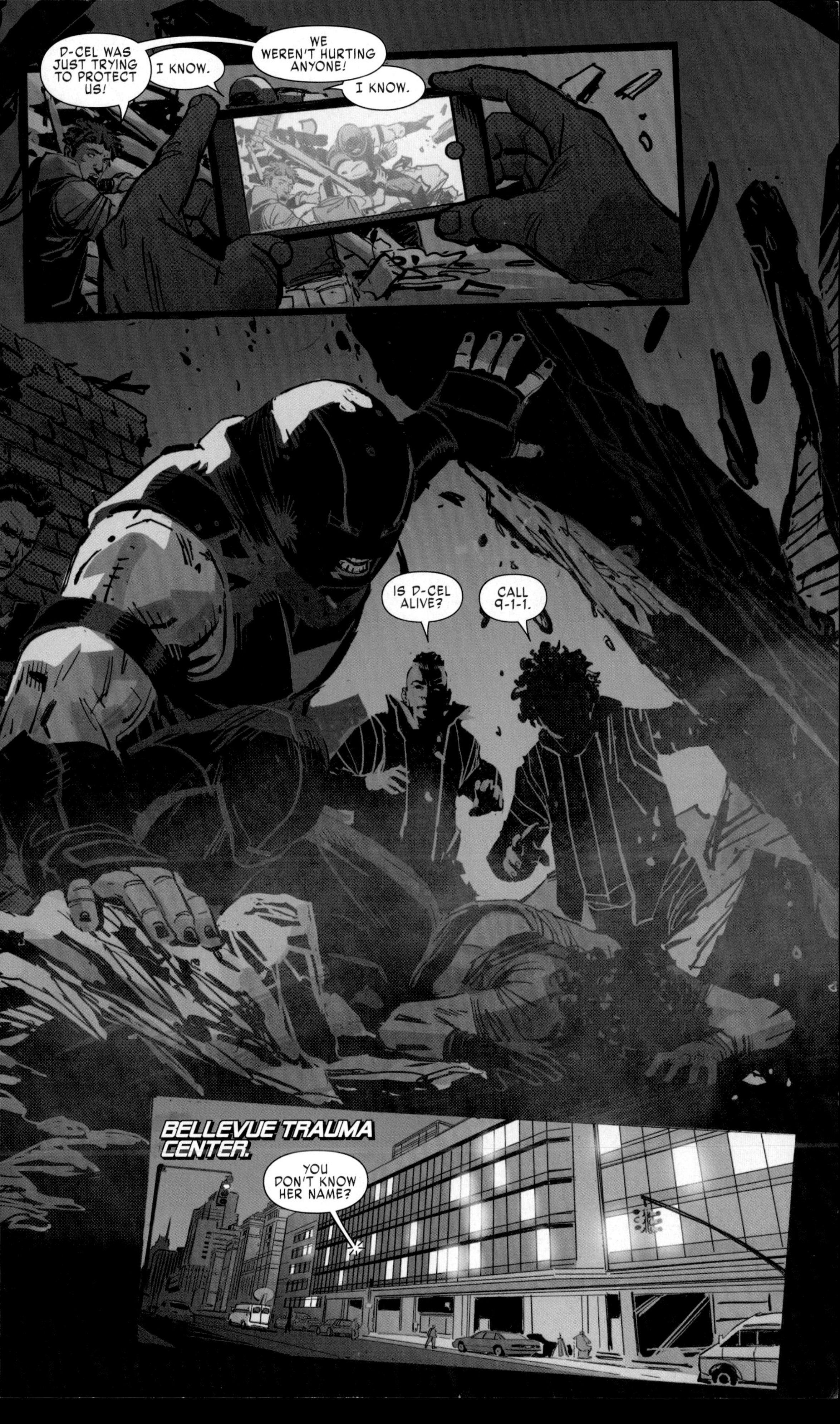
D-CEL WAS JUST TRYING TO PROTECT US!
I KNOW.
WE WEREN'T HURTING ANYONE!
I KNOW.
IS D-CEL ALIVE?
CALL 9-1-1.
BELLEVUE TRAUMA CENTER.
YOU DON'T KNOW HER NAME?

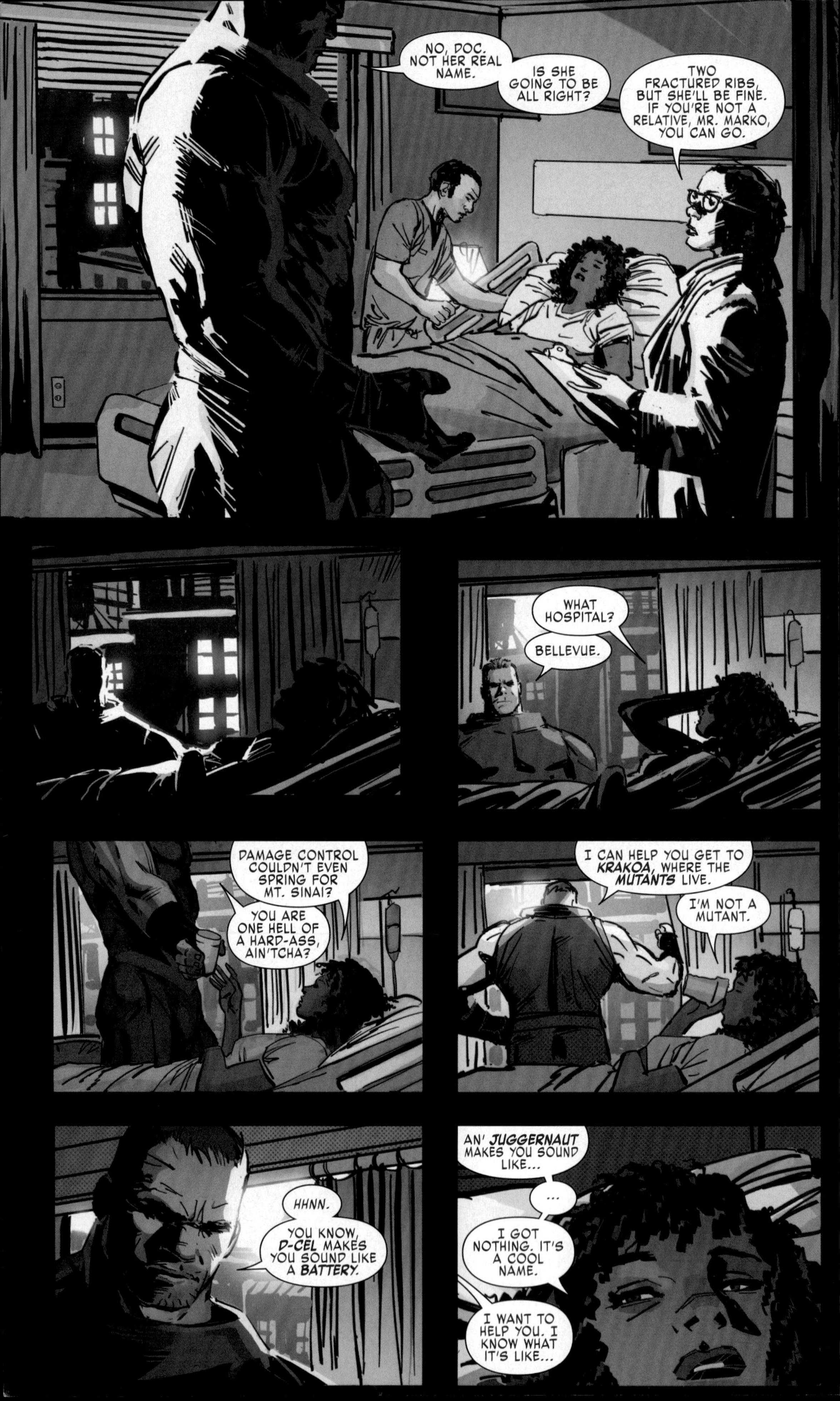
NO, DOC. NOT HER REAL NAME.
IS SHE GOING TO BE ALL RIGHT?
TWO FRACTURED RIBS, BUT SHE'LL BE FINE. IF YOU'RE NOT A RELATIVE, MR. MARKO, YOU CAN GO.
WHAT HOSPITAL?
BELLEVUE.
DAMAGE CONTROL COULDN'T EVEN SPRING FOR MT. SINAI?
YOU ARE ONE HELL OF A HARD-ASS, AIN'TCHA?
I CAN HELP YOU GET TO KRAKOA, WHERE THE MUTANTS LIVE.
I'M NOT A MUTANT.
HHNN.
YOU KNOW, D-CEL MAKES YOU SOUND LIKE A BATTERY.
AN' JUGGERNAUT MAKES YOU SOUND LIKE...
...
I GOT NOTHING. IT'S A COOL NAME.
I WANT TO HELP YOU. I KNOW WHAT IT'S LIKE...

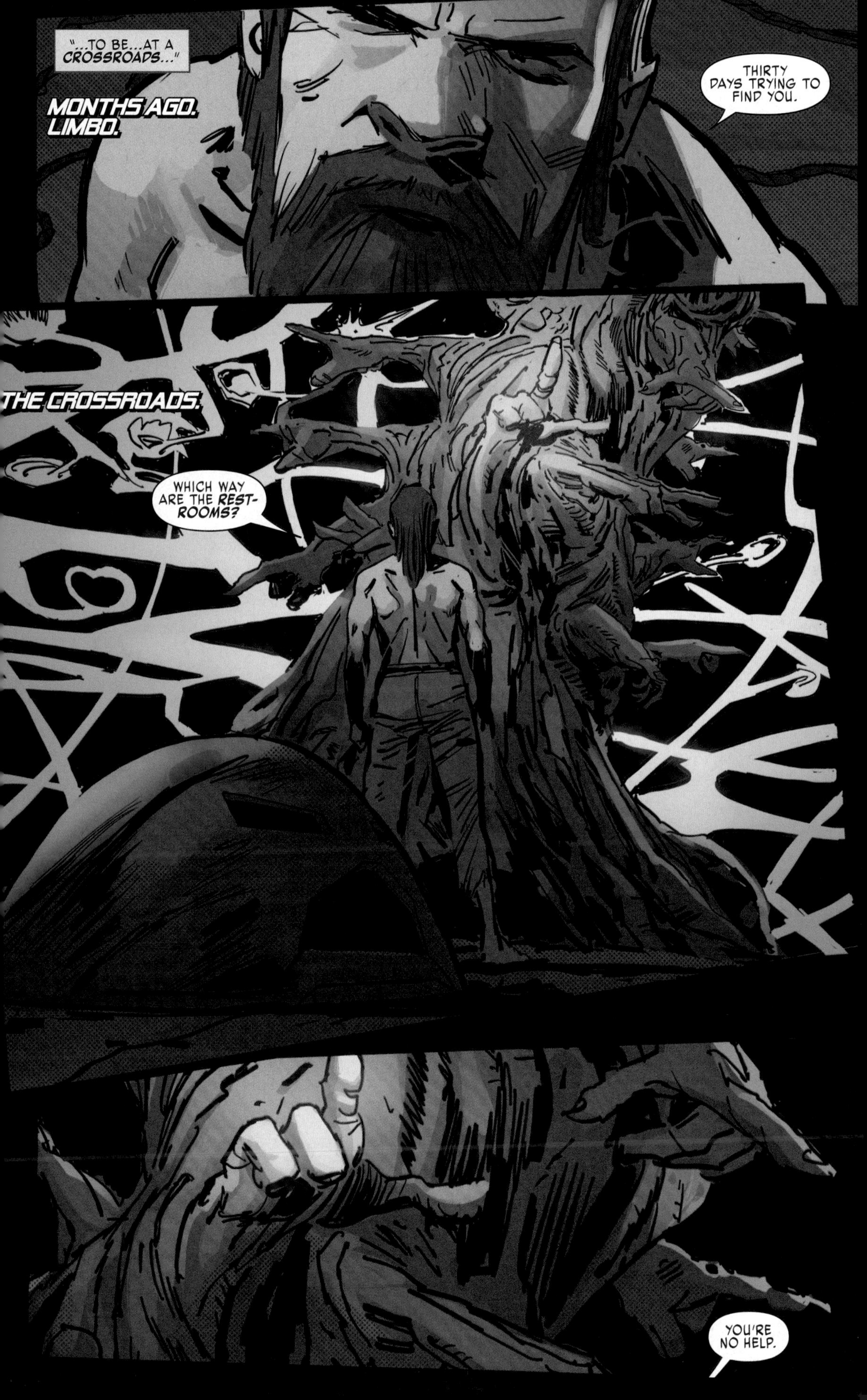
"...TO BE...AT A CROSSROADS..."
MONTHS AGO. LIMBO.
THIRTY DAYS TRYING TO FIND YOU.
THE CROSSROADS.
WHICH WAY ARE THE REST-ROOMS?
YOU'RE NO HELP.

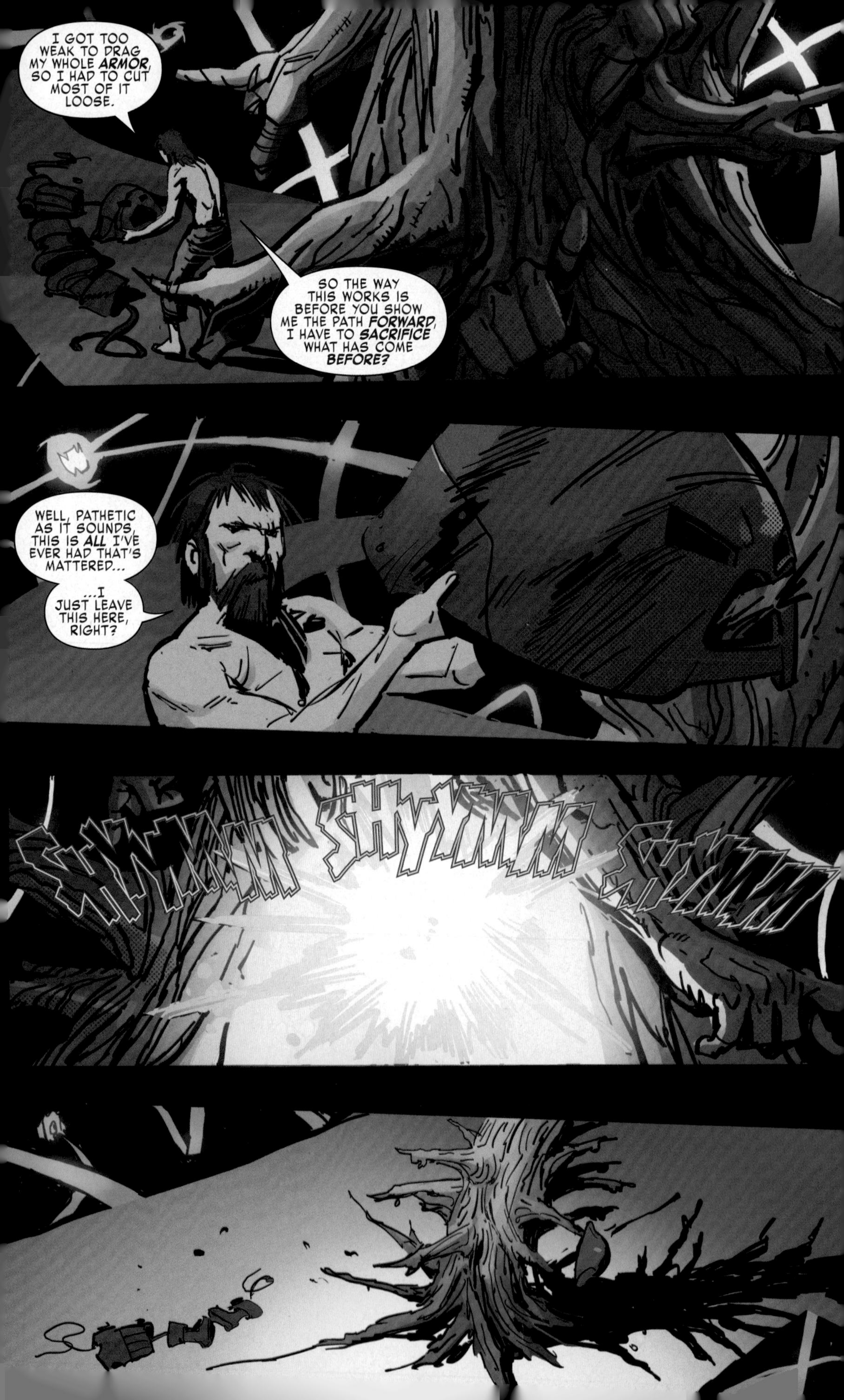
I GOT TOO WEAK TO DRAG MY WHOLE *ARMOR*, SO I HAD TO CUT MOST OF IT LOOSE.
SO THE WAY THIS WORKS IS BEFORE YOU SHOW ME THE PATH *FORWARD*, I HAVE TO *SACRIFICE* WHAT HAS COME *BEFORE?*
WELL, PATHETIC AS IT SOUNDS, THIS IS *ALL* I'VE EVER HAD THAT'S MATTERED...
...I JUST LEAVE THIS HERE, RIGHT?

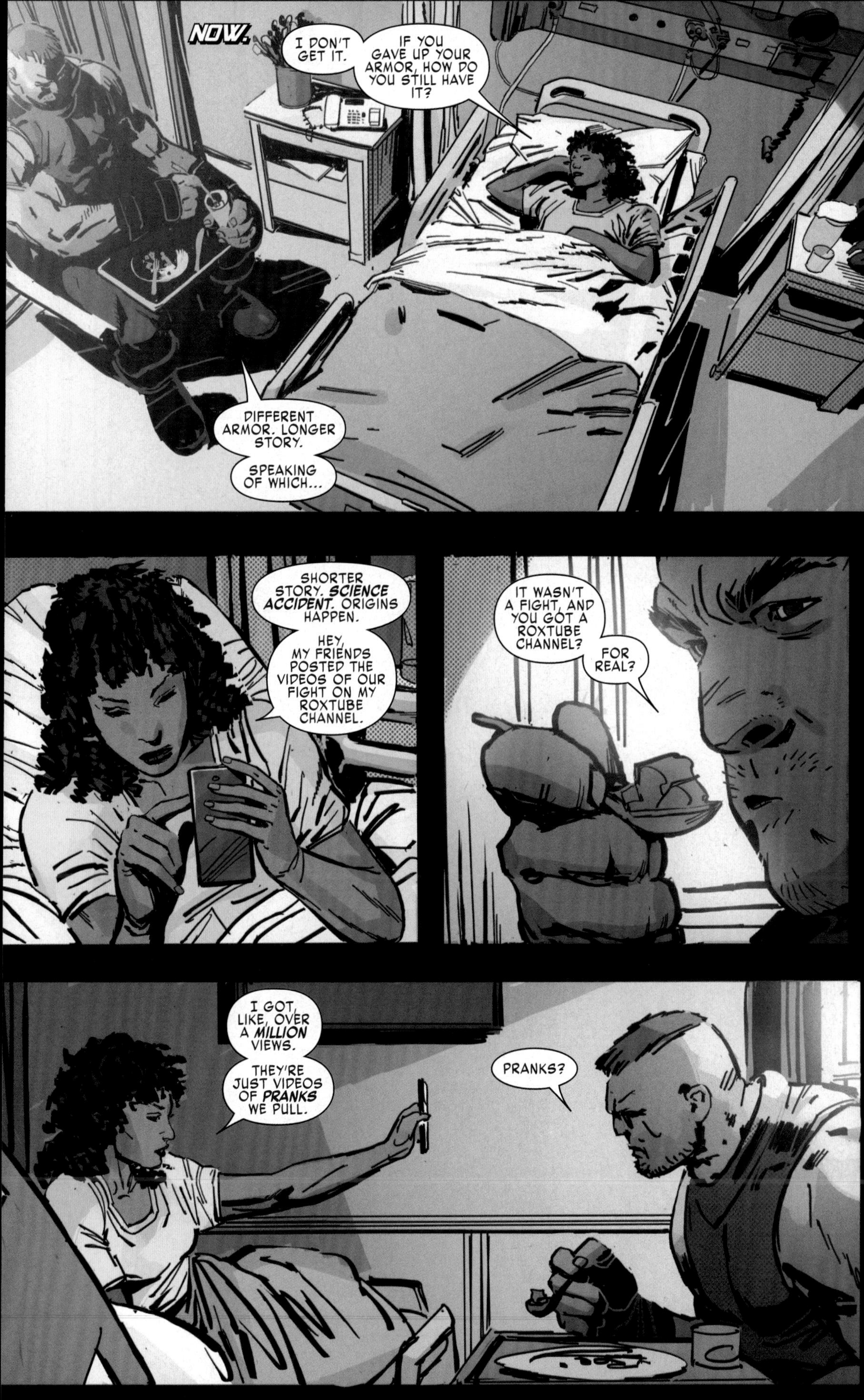
NOW.
I DON'T GET IT.
IF YOU GAVE UP YOUR ARMOR, HOW DO YOU STILL HAVE IT?
DIFFERENT ARMOR. LONGER STORY.
SPEAKING OF WHICH...
SHORTER STORY. SCIENCE ACCIDENT. ORIGINS HAPPEN.
HEY, MY FRIENDS POSTED THE VIDEOS OF OUR FIGHT ON MY ROXTUBE CHANNEL.
IT WASN'T A FIGHT, AND YOU GOT A ROXTUBE CHANNEL?
FOR REAL?
I GOT, LIKE, OVER A MILLION VIEWS.
THEY'RE JUST VIDEOS OF PRANKS WE PULL.
PRANKS?

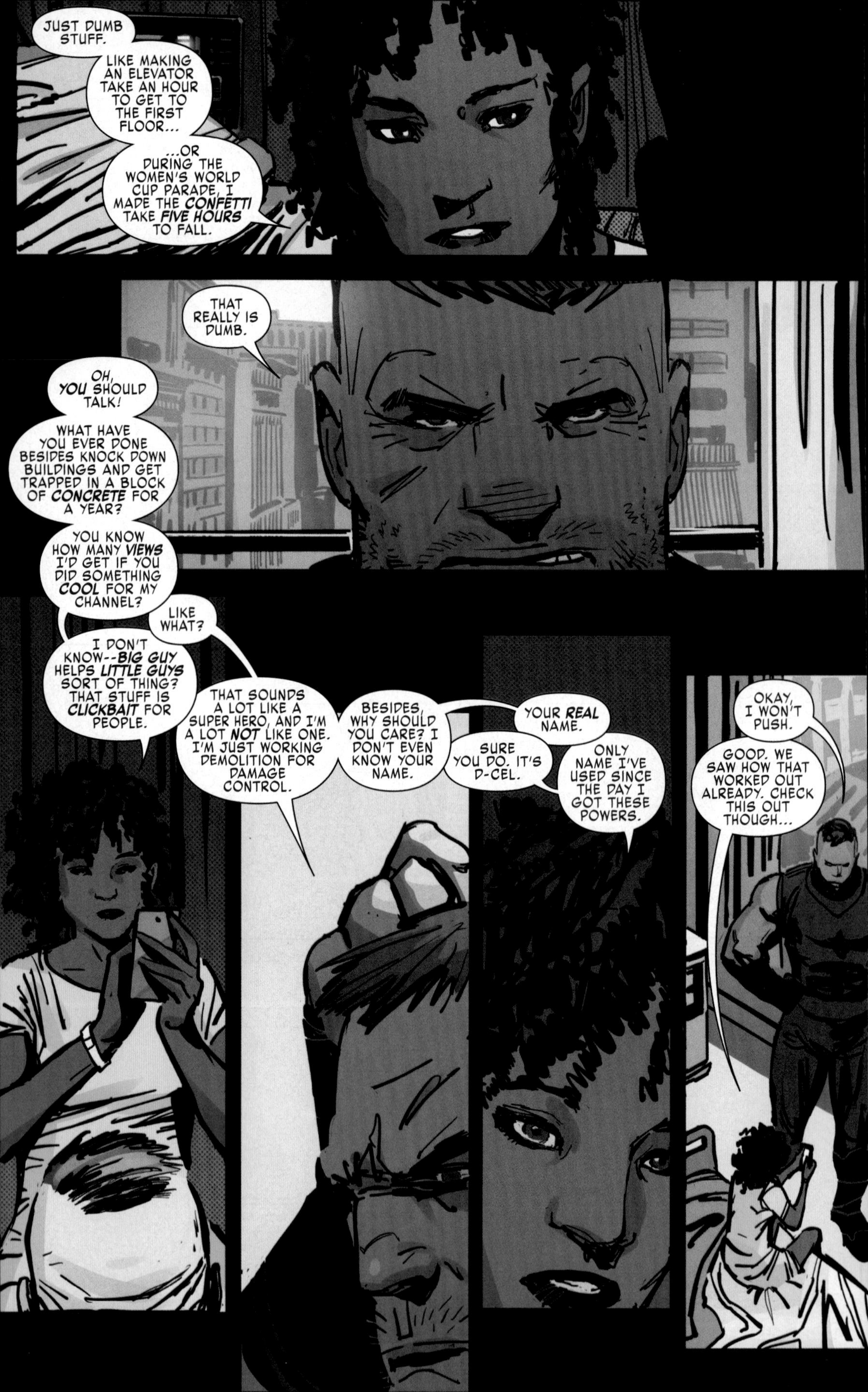
JUST DUMB STUFF.
LIKE MAKING AN ELEVATOR TAKE AN HOUR TO GET TO THE FIRST FLOOR...
...OR DURING THE WOMEN'S WORLD CUP PARADE, I MADE THE *CONFETTI* TAKE *FIVE HOURS* TO FALL.
THAT REALLY IS DUMB.
OH, *YOU* SHOULD TALK!
WHAT HAVE YOU EVER DONE BESIDES KNOCK DOWN BUILDINGS AND GET TRAPPED IN A BLOCK OF *CONCRETE* FOR A YEAR?
YOU KNOW HOW MANY *VIEWS* I'D GET IF YOU DID SOMETHING *COOL* FOR MY CHANNEL?
LIKE WHAT?
I DON'T KNOW--*BIG GUY* HELPS *LITTLE GUYS* SORT OF THING? THAT STUFF IS *CLICKBAIT* FOR PEOPLE.
THAT SOUNDS A LOT LIKE A SUPER HERO, AND I'M A LOT *NOT* LIKE ONE. I'M JUST WORKING DEMOLITION FOR DAMAGE CONTROL.
BESIDES, WHY SHOULD YOU CARE? I DON'T EVEN KNOW YOUR NAME.
SURE YOU DO. IT'S D-CEL.
YOUR *REAL* NAME.
ONLY NAME I'VE USED SINCE THE DAY I GOT THESE POWERS.
OKAY, I WON'T PUSH.
GOOD. WE SAW HOW THAT WORKED OUT ALREADY. CHECK THIS OUT THOUGH...

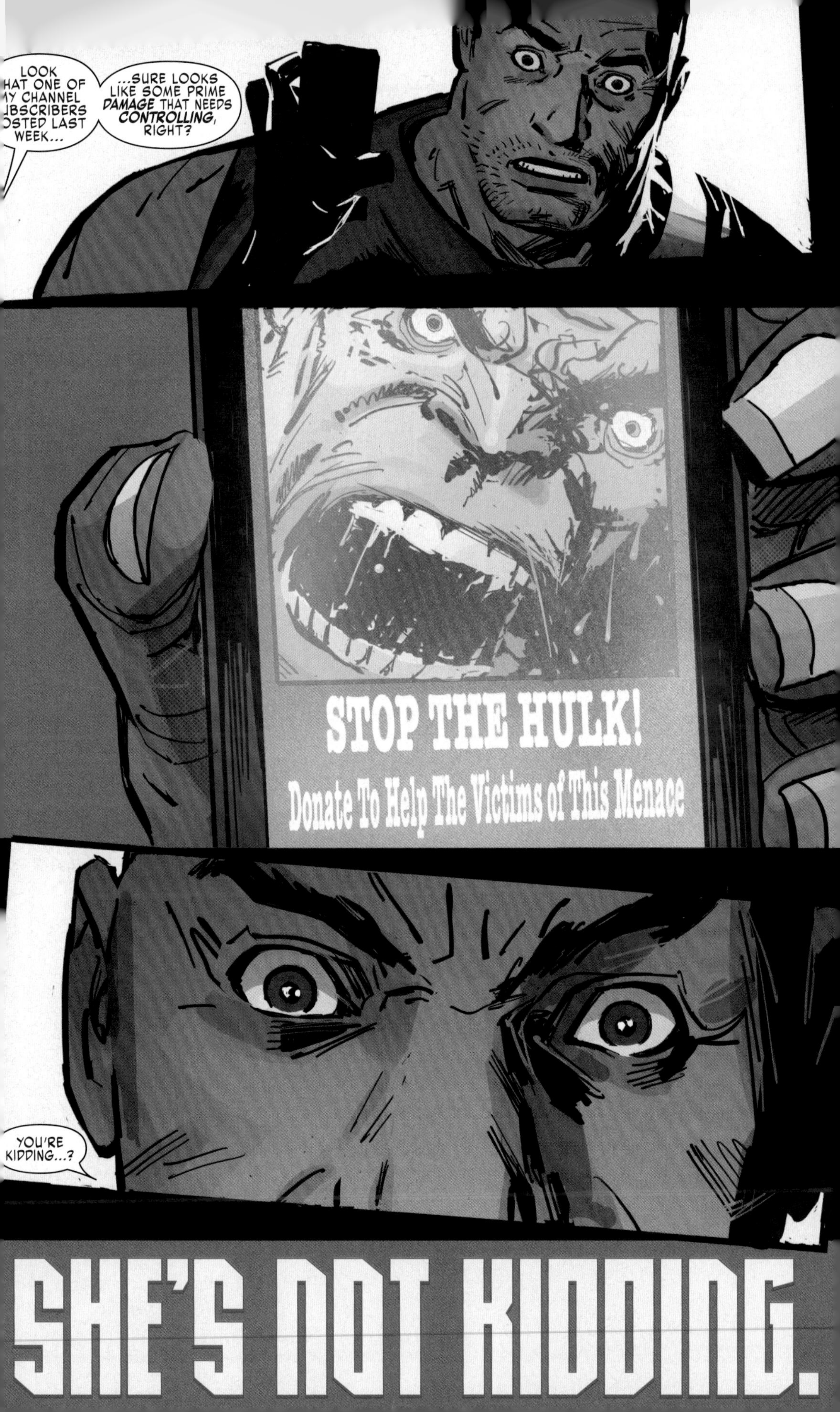
LOOK HAT ONE OF MY CHANNEL UBSCRIBERS OSTED LAST WEEK...
...SURE LOOKS LIKE SOME PRIME DAMAGE THAT NEEDS CONTROLLING, RIGHT?
STOP THE HULK!
Donate To Help The Victims of This Menace
YOU'RE KIDDING...?
SHE'S NOT KIDDING.

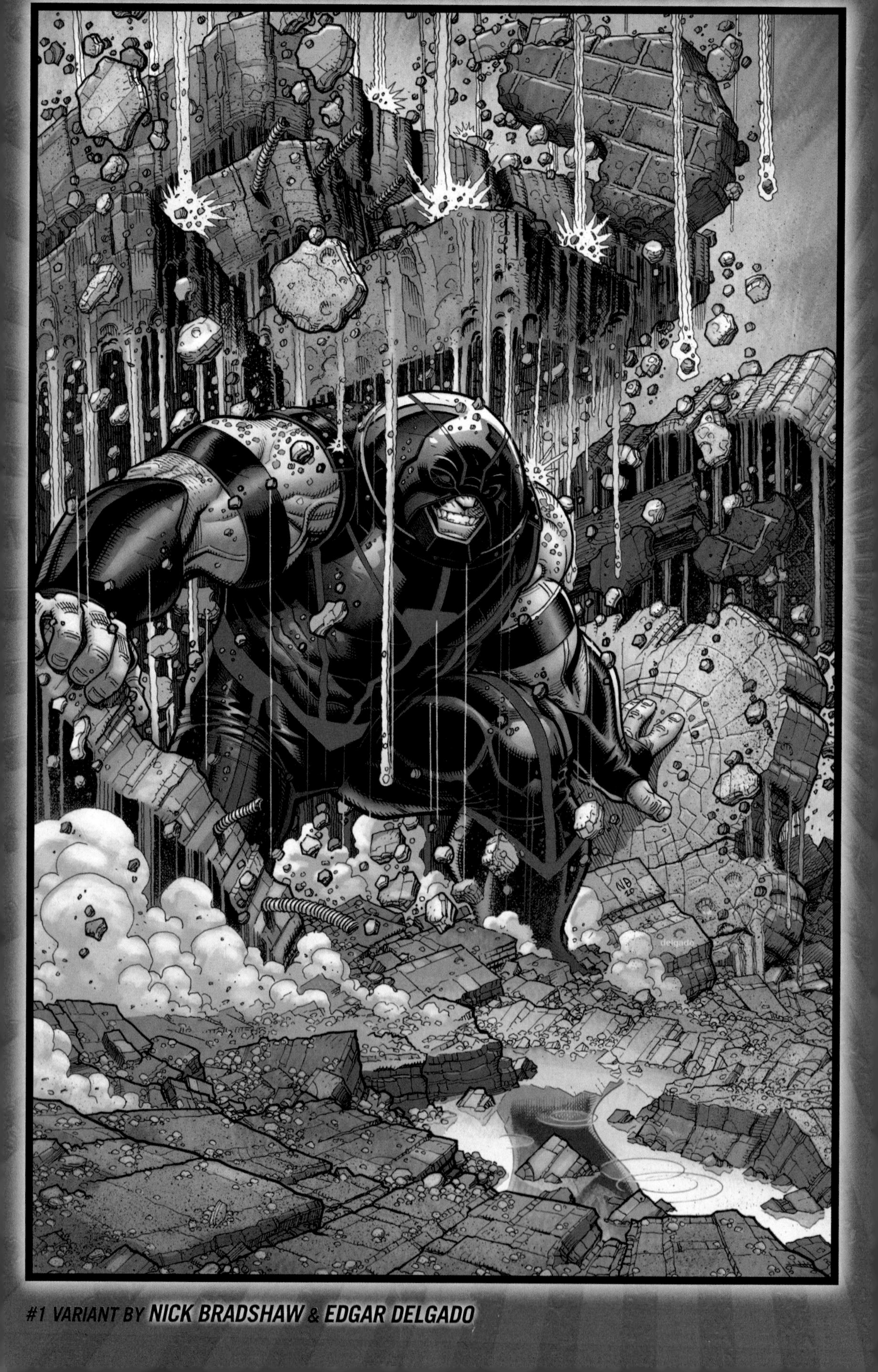

#1 VARIANT BY **NICK BRADSHAW & EDGAR DELGADO**

2

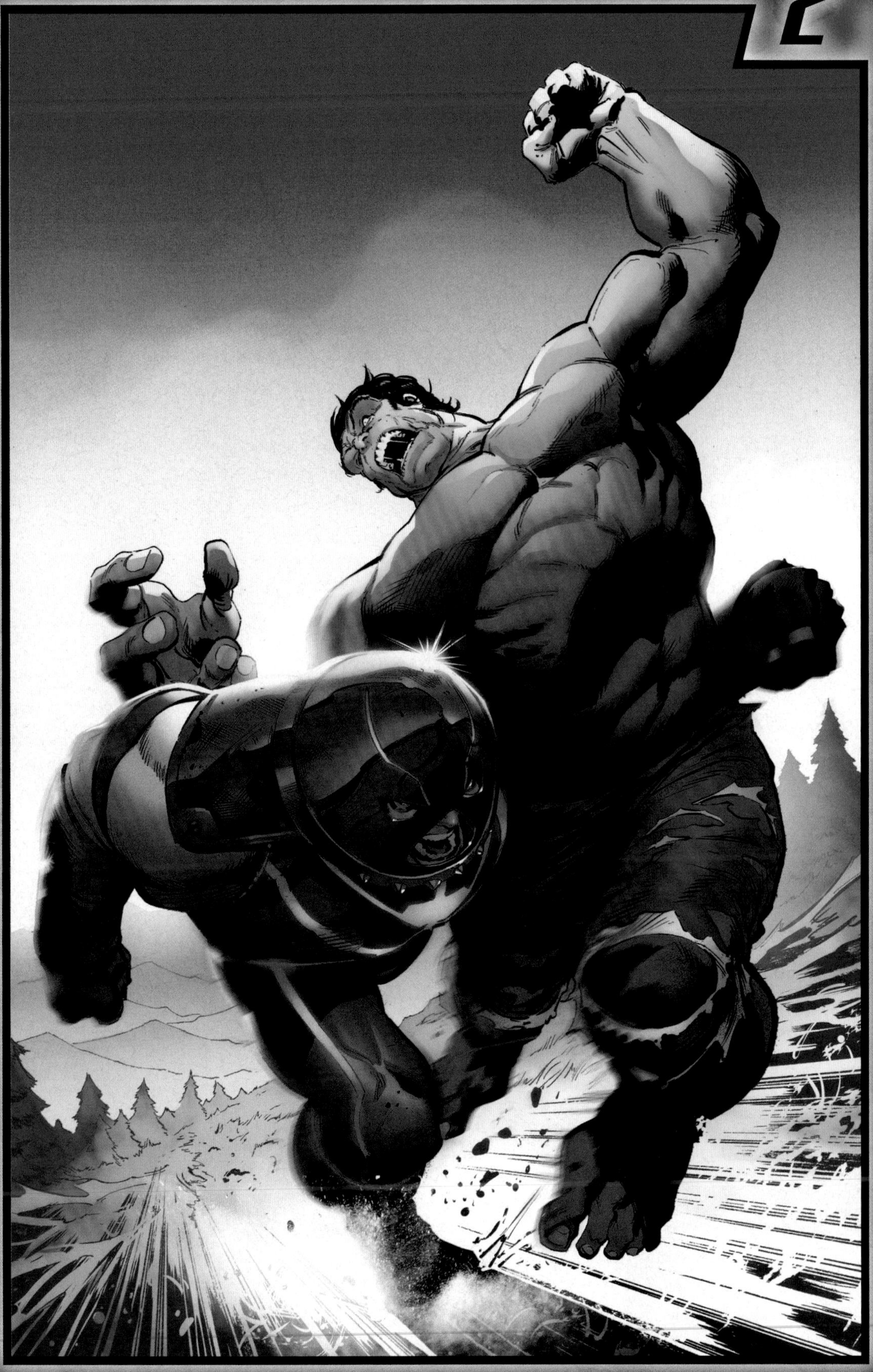

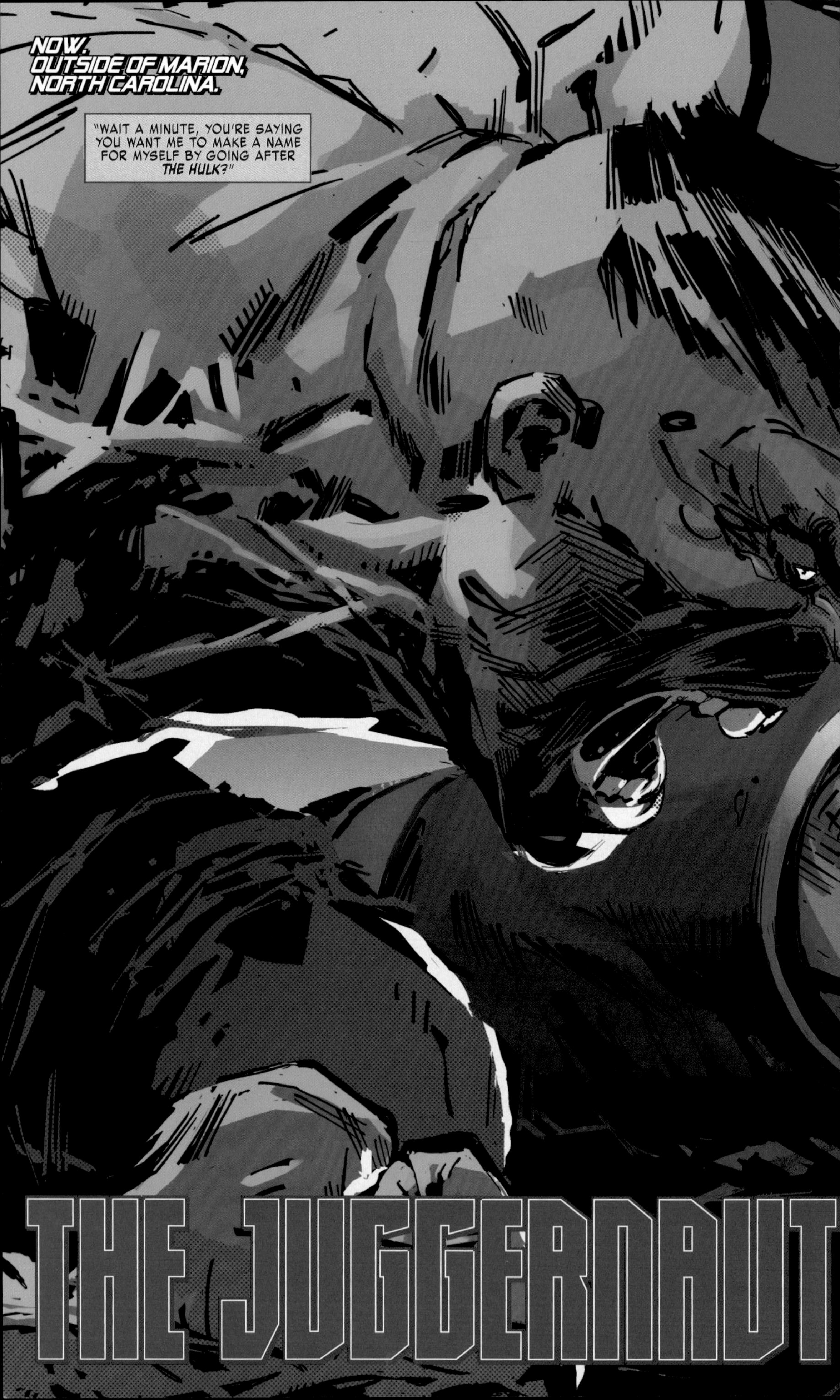
NOW. OUTSIDE OF MARION, NORTH CAROLINA.
"WAIT A MINUTE, YOU'RE SAYING YOU WANT ME TO MAKE A NAME FOR MYSELF BY GOING AFTER THE HULK?"
THE JUGGERNAUT

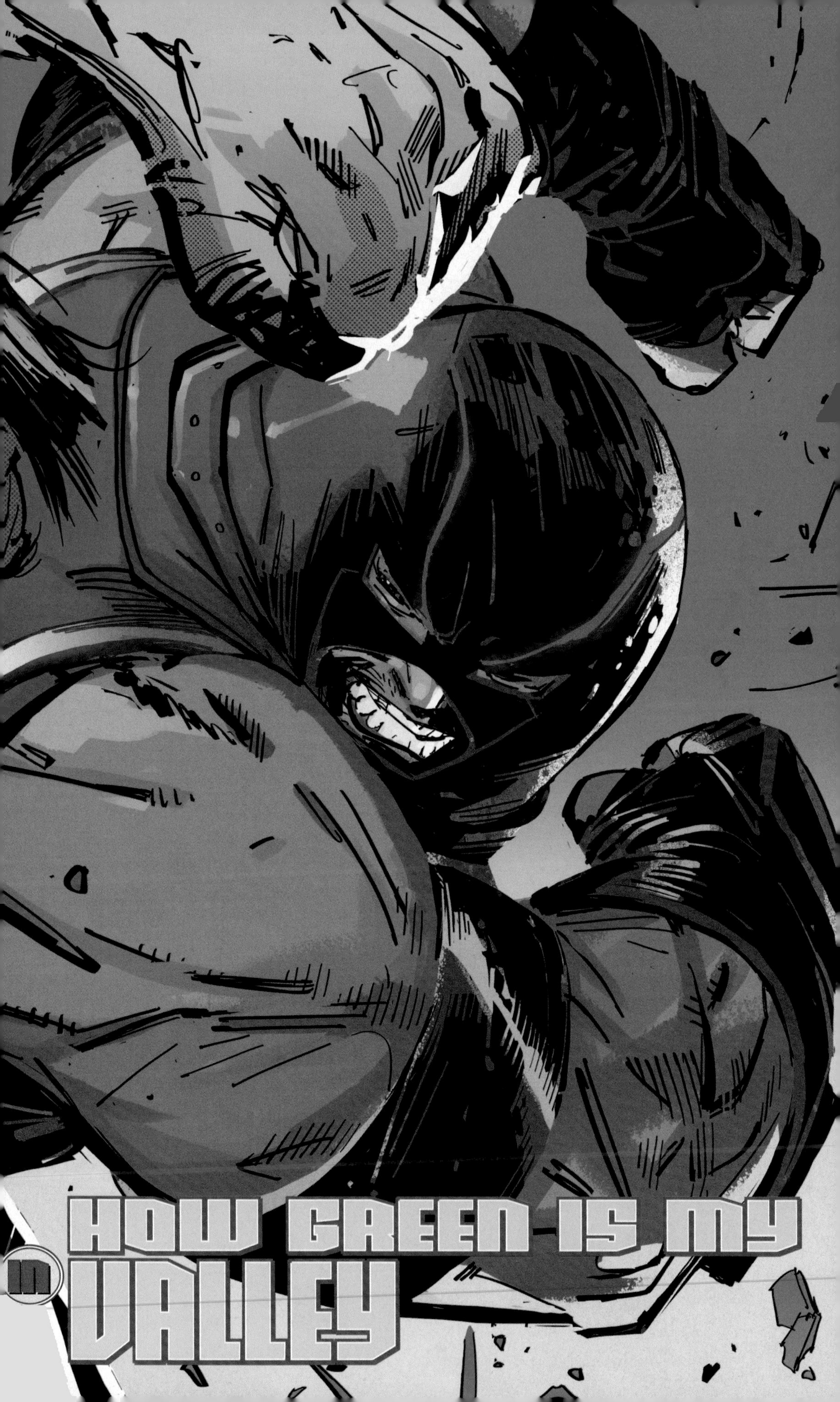

IN
HOW GREEN IS MY
VALLEY

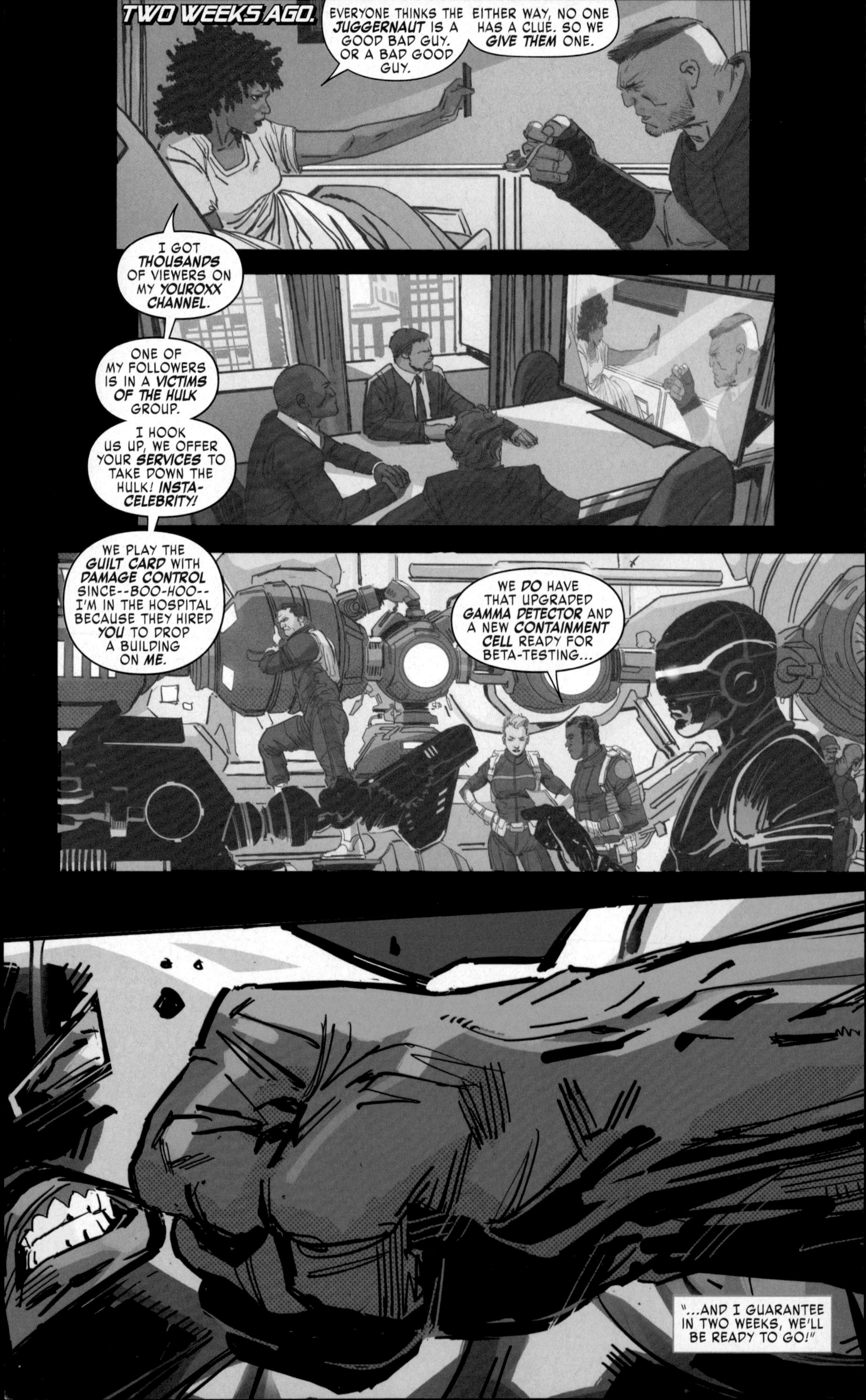

TWO WEEKS AGO.
EVERYONE THINKS THE JUGGERNAUT IS A GOOD BAD GUY. OR A BAD GOOD GUY.
EITHER WAY, NO ONE HAS A CLUE. SO WE GIVE THEM ONE.
I GOT THOUSANDS OF VIEWERS ON MY YOUROXX CHANNEL.
ONE OF MY FOLLOWERS IS IN A VICTIMS OF THE HULK GROUP.
I HOOK US UP, WE OFFER YOUR SERVICES TO TAKE DOWN THE HULK! INSTA-CELEBRITY!
WE PLAY THE GUILT CARD WITH DAMAGE CONTROL SINCE--BOO-HOO--I'M IN THE HOSPITAL BECAUSE THEY HIRED YOU TO DROP A BUILDING ON ME.
WE DO HAVE THAT UPGRADED GAMMA DETECTOR AND A NEW CONTAINMENT CELL READY FOR BETA-TESTING...
"...AND I GUARANTEE IN TWO WEEKS, WE'LL BE READY TO GO!"

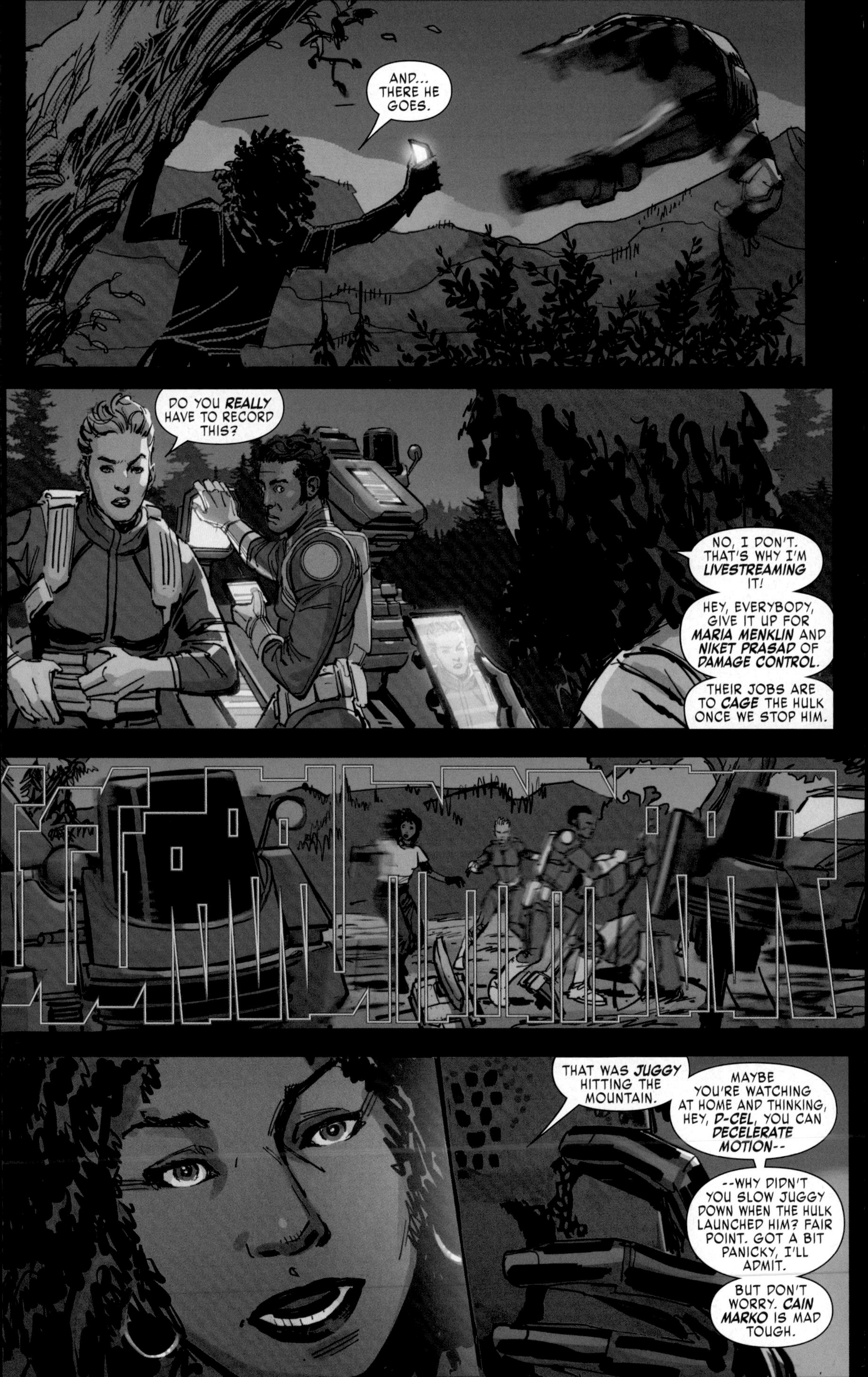
AND... THERE HE GOES.
DO YOU REALLY HAVE TO RECORD THIS?
NO, I DON'T. THAT'S WHY I'M LIVESTREAMING IT!
HEY, EVERYBODY, GIVE IT UP FOR MARIA MENKLIN AND NIKET PRASAD OF DAMAGE CONTROL.
THEIR JOBS ARE TO CAGE THE HULK ONCE WE STOP HIM.
THAT WAS JUGGY HITTING THE MOUNTAIN.
MAYBE YOU'RE WATCHING AT HOME AND THINKING, HEY, D-CEL, YOU CAN DECELERATE MOTION--
--WHY DIDN'T YOU SLOW JUGGY DOWN WHEN THE HULK LAUNCHED HIM? FAIR POINT. GOT A BIT PANICKY, I'LL ADMIT.
BUT DON'T WORRY. CAIN MARKO IS MAD TOUGH.

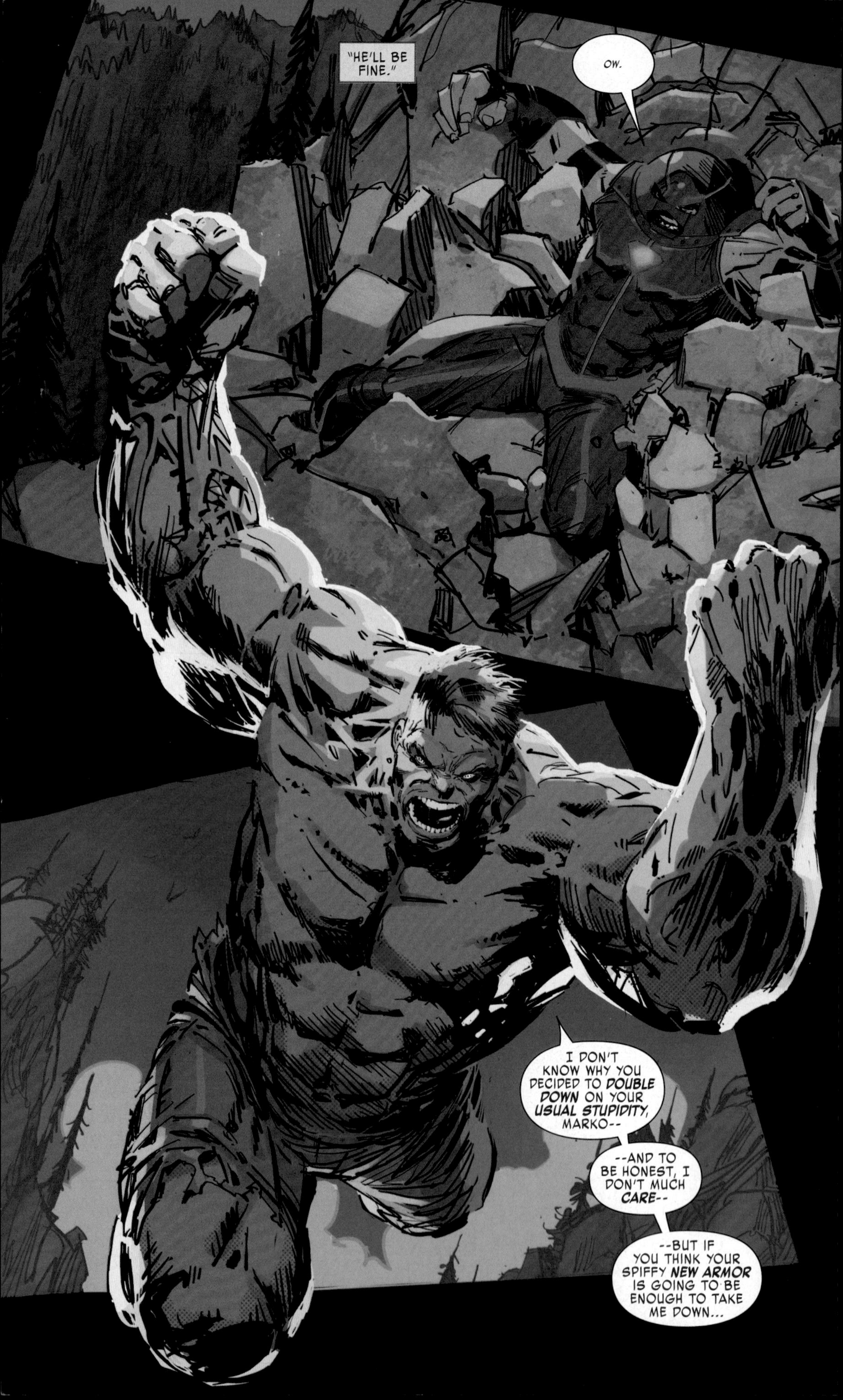
"HE'LL BE FINE."
OW.
I DON'T KNOW WHY YOU DECIDED TO DOUBLE DOWN ON YOUR USUAL STUPIDITY, MARKO--
--AND TO BE HONEST, I DON'T MUCH CARE--
--BUT IF YOU THINK YOUR SPIFFY NEW ARMOR IS GOING TO BE ENOUGH TO TAKE ME DOWN...

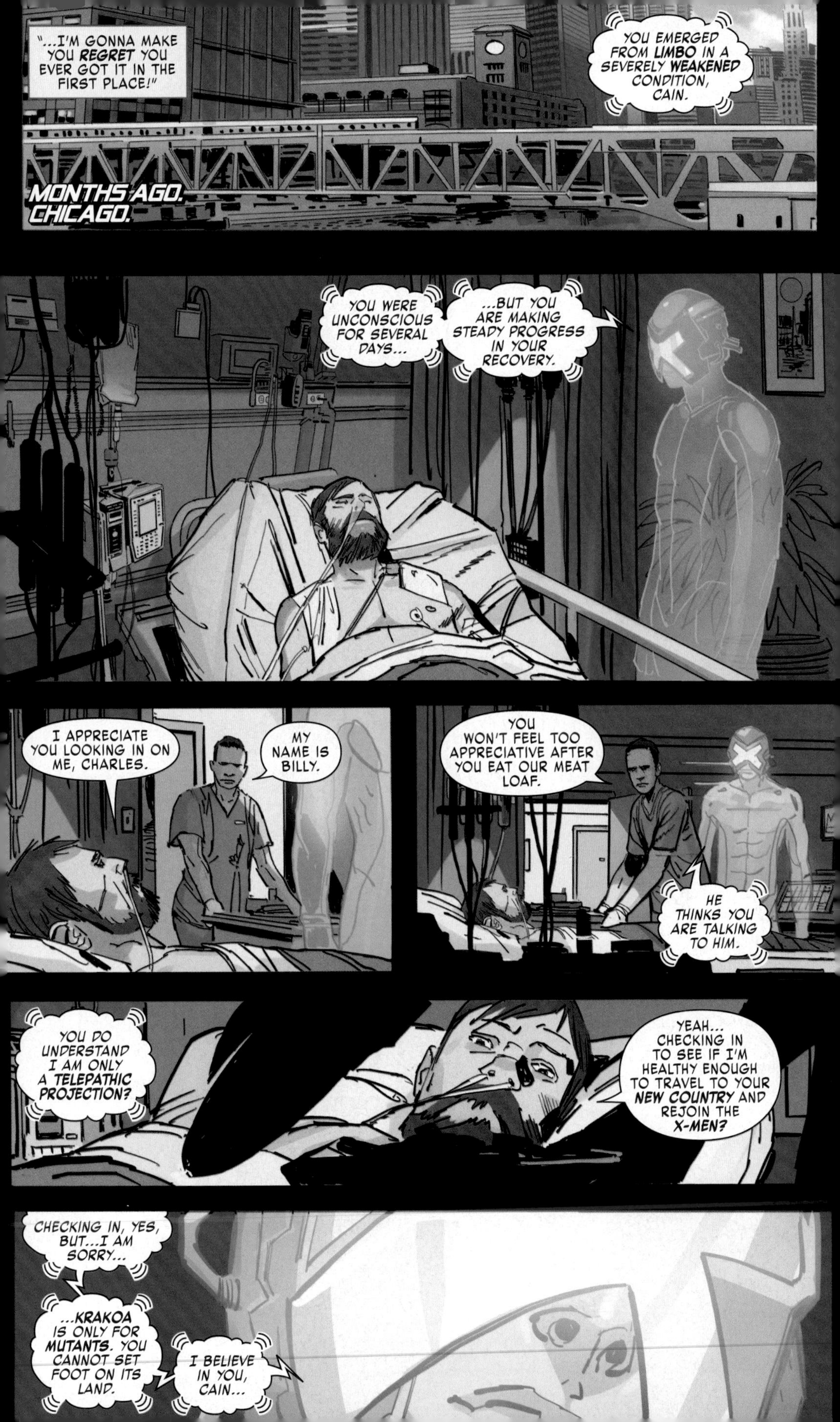
"...I'M GONNA MAKE YOU REGRET YOU EVER GOT IT IN THE FIRST PLACE!"
YOU EMERGED FROM LIMBO IN A SEVERELY WEAKENED CONDITION, CAIN.
MONTHS AGO. CHICAGO.
YOU WERE UNCONSCIOUS FOR SEVERAL DAYS...
...BUT YOU ARE MAKING STEADY PROGRESS IN YOUR RECOVERY.
I APPRECIATE YOU LOOKING IN ON ME, CHARLES.
MY NAME IS BILLY.
YOU WON'T FEEL TOO APPRECIATIVE AFTER YOU EAT OUR MEAT LOAF.
HE THINKS YOU ARE TALKING TO HIM.
YOU DO UNDERSTAND I AM ONLY A TELEPATHIC PROJECTION?
YEAH... CHECKING IN TO SEE IF I'M HEALTHY ENOUGH TO TRAVEL TO YOUR NEW COUNTRY AND REJOIN THE X-MEN?
CHECKING IN, YES, BUT...I AM SORRY...
...KRAKOA IS ONLY FOR MUTANTS. YOU CANNOT SET FOOT ON ITS LAND.
I BELIEVE IN YOU, CAIN...

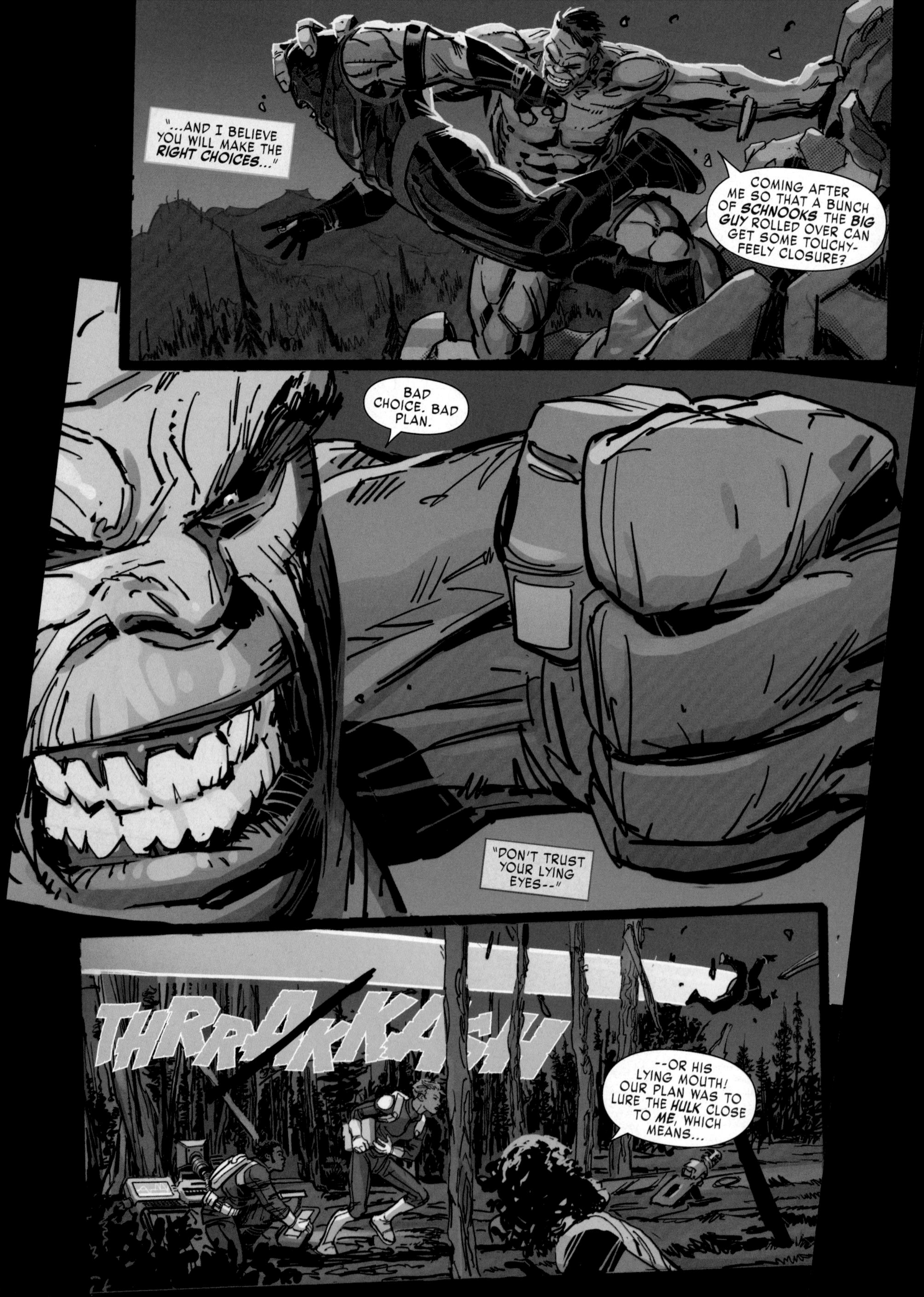
"...AND I BELIEVE YOU WILL MAKE THE RIGHT CHOICES..."
COMING AFTER ME SO THAT A BUNCH OF SCHNOOKS THE BIG GUY ROLLED OVER CAN GET SOME TOUCHY-FEELY CLOSURE?
BAD CHOICE. BAD PLAN.
"DON'T TRUST YOUR LYING EYES--"
THRRAKKASH
--OR HIS LYING MOUTH! OUR PLAN WAS TO LURE THE HULK CLOSE TO ME, WHICH MEANS...

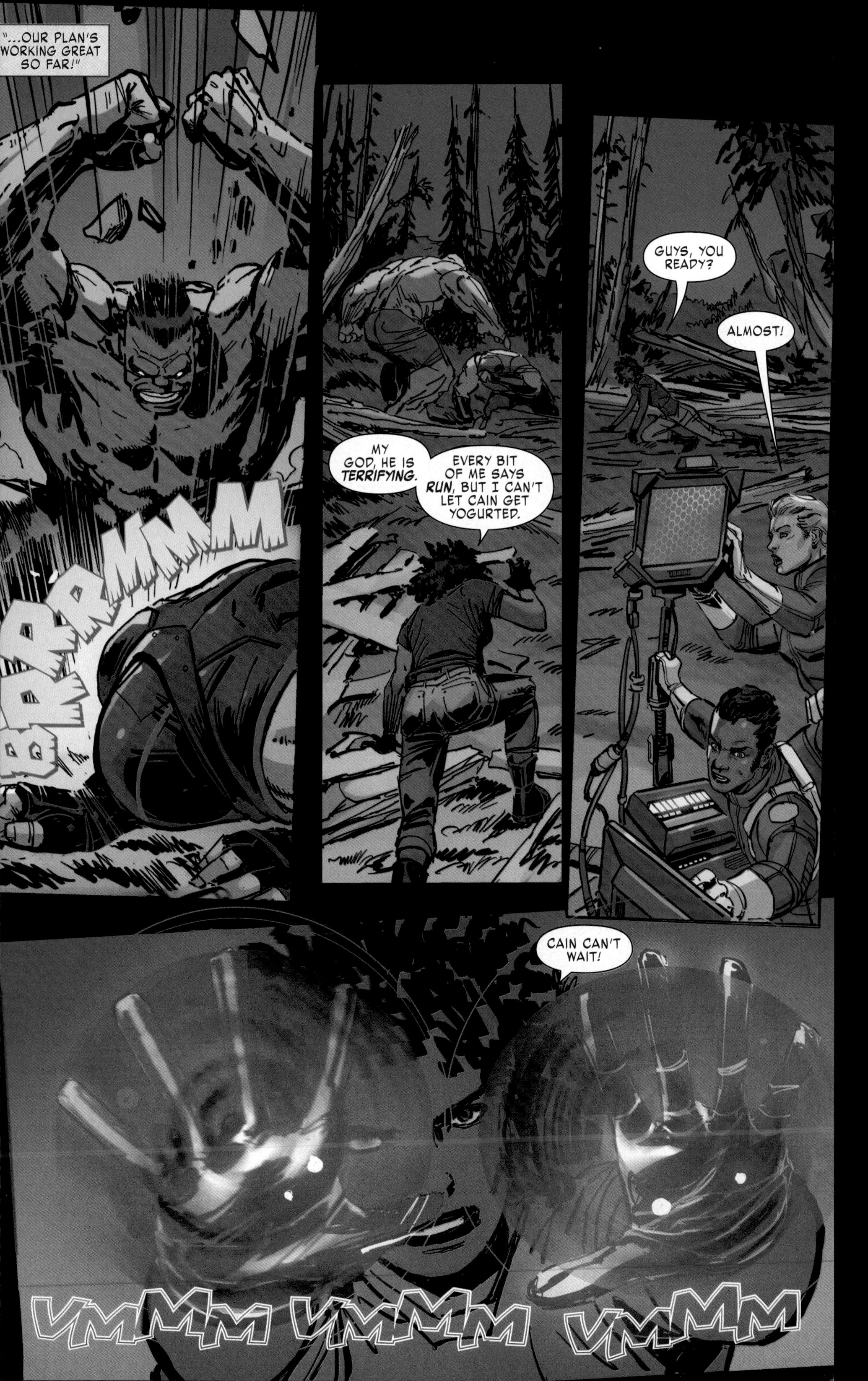
"...OUR PLAN'S WORKING GREAT SO FAR!"
BRRMMMM
MY GOD, HE IS TERRIFYING.
EVERY BIT OF ME SAYS RUN, BUT I CAN'T LET CAIN GET YOGURTED.
GUYS, YOU READY?
ALMOST!
CAIN CAN'T WAIT!
VMMM VMMM VMMM

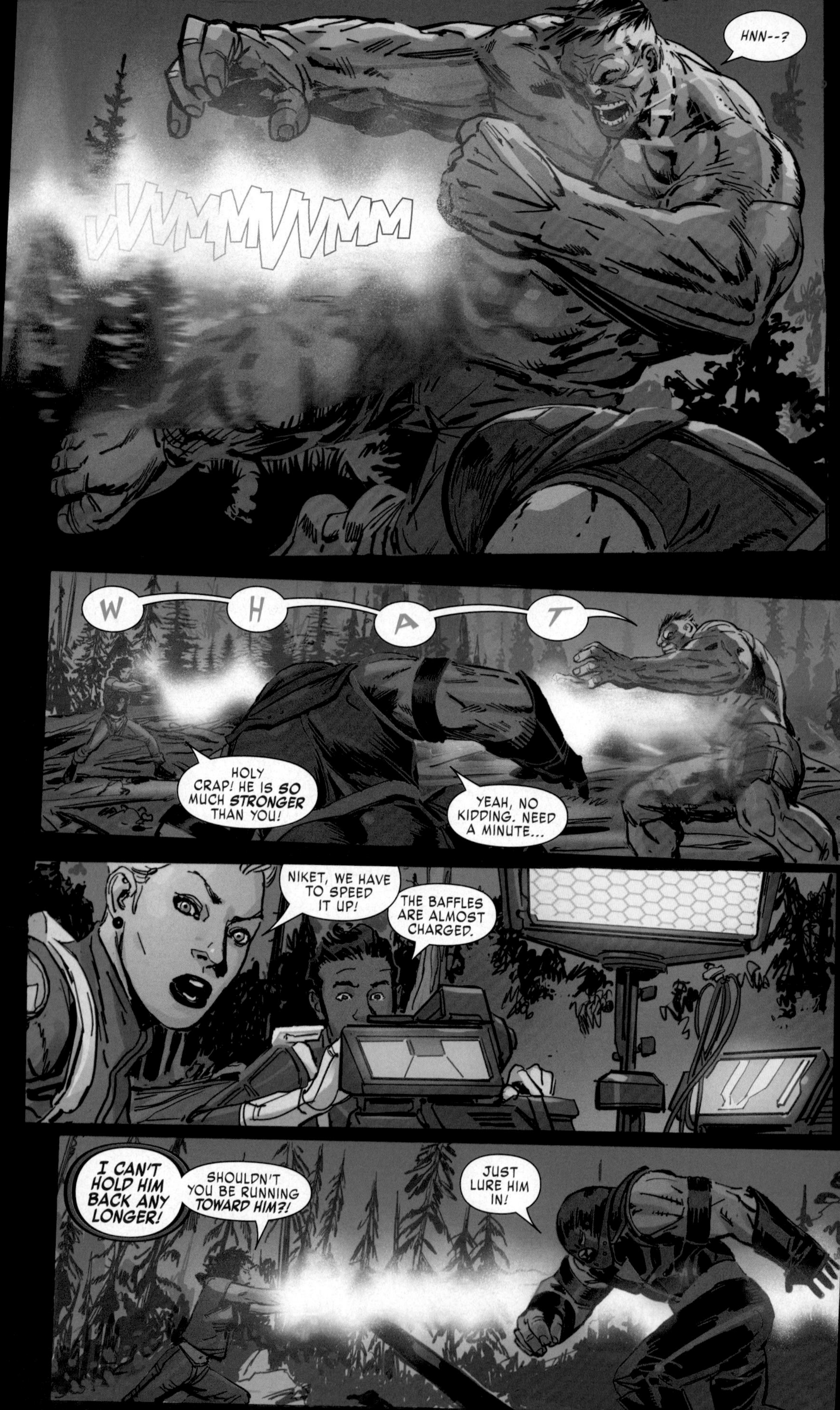
HNN--?
VVVMMMVVMM
W H A T
HOLY CRAP! HE IS SO MUCH STRONGER THAN YOU!
YEAH, NO KIDDING. NEED A MINUTE...
NIKET, WE HAVE TO SPEED IT UP!
THE BAFFLES ARE ALMOST CHARGED.
I CAN'T HOLD HIM BACK ANY LONGER!
SHOULDN'T YOU BE RUNNING TOWARD HIM?!
JUST LURE HIM IN!

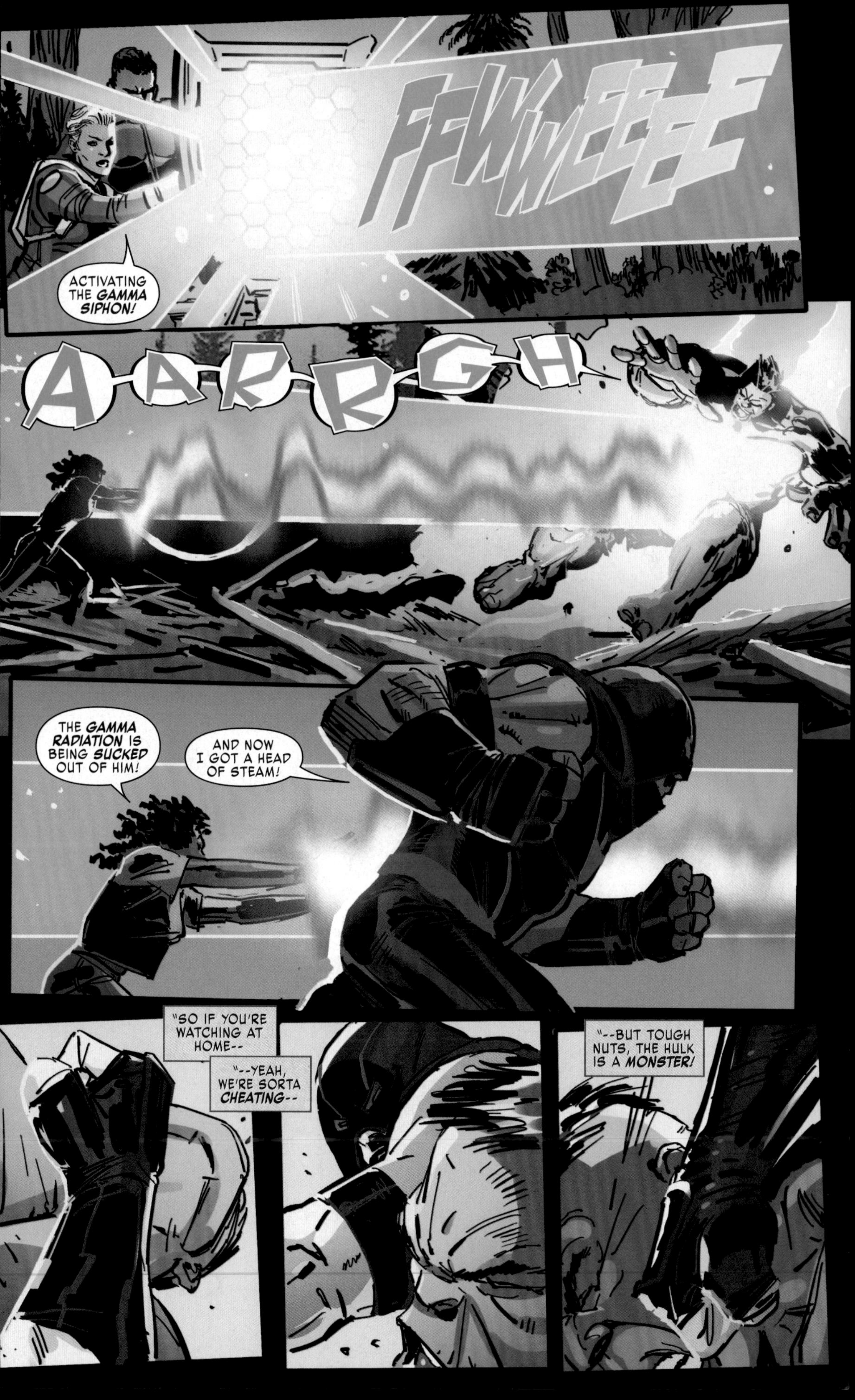
FFWWEEEE
ACTIVATING THE GAMMA SIPHON!
AARRGH
THE GAMMA RADIATION IS BEING SUCKED OUT OF HIM!
AND NOW I GOT A HEAD OF STEAM!
"SO IF YOU'RE WATCHING AT HOME--
"--YEAH, WE'RE SORTA CHEATING--
"--BUT TOUGH NUTS, THE HULK IS A MONSTER!

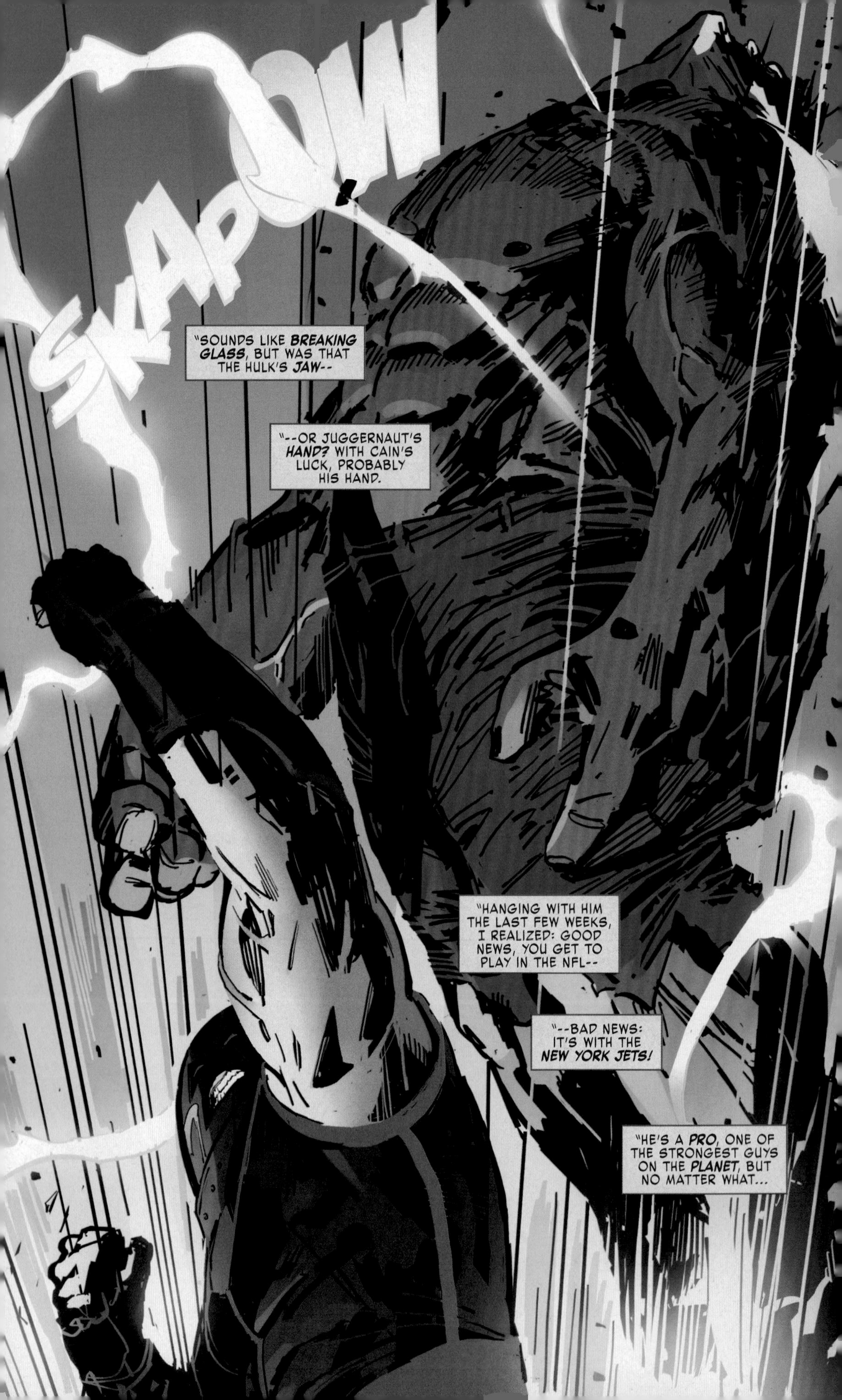
SKAPOW
"SOUNDS LIKE BREAKING GLASS, BUT WAS THAT THE HULK'S JAW--
"--OR JUGGERNAUT'S HAND? WITH CAIN'S LUCK, PROBABLY HIS HAND.
"HANGING WITH HIM THE LAST FEW WEEKS, I REALIZED: GOOD NEWS, YOU GET TO PLAY IN THE NFL--
"--BAD NEWS: IT'S WITH THE NEW YORK JETS!
"HE'S A PRO, ONE OF THE STRONGEST GUYS ON THE PLANET, BUT NO MATTER WHAT...

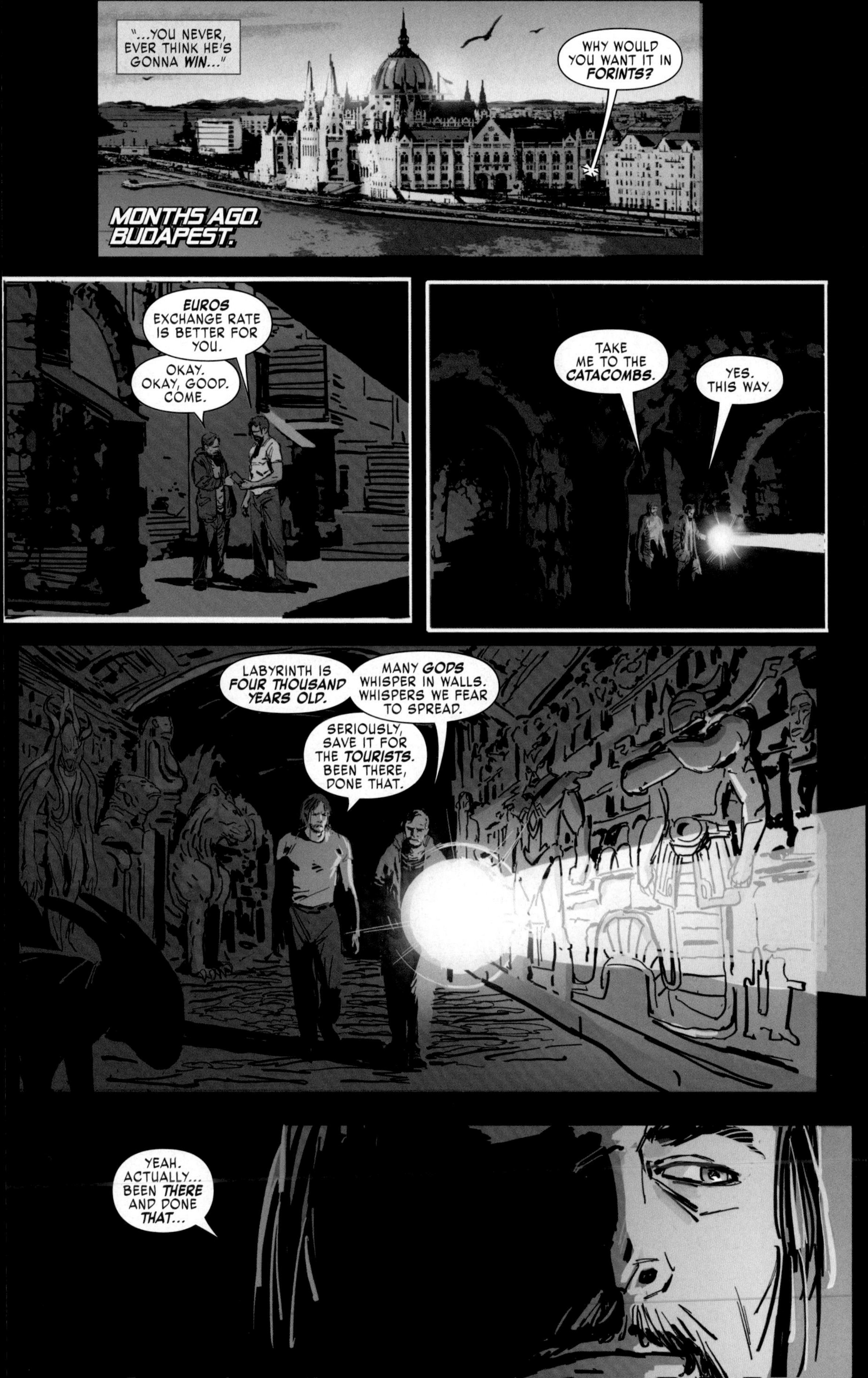
"...YOU NEVER, EVER THINK HE'S GONNA WIN..."
WHY WOULD YOU WANT IT IN FORINTS?
MONTHS AGO. BUDAPEST.
EUROS EXCHANGE RATE IS BETTER FOR YOU.
OKAY. OKAY, GOOD. COME.
TAKE ME TO THE CATACOMBS.
YES. THIS WAY.
LABYRINTH IS FOUR THOUSAND YEARS OLD.
MANY GODS WHISPER IN WALLS. WHISPERS WE FEAR TO SPREAD.
SERIOUSLY, SAVE IT FOR THE TOURISTS. BEEN THERE, DONE THAT.
YEAH. ACTUALLY... BEEN THERE AND DONE THAT...

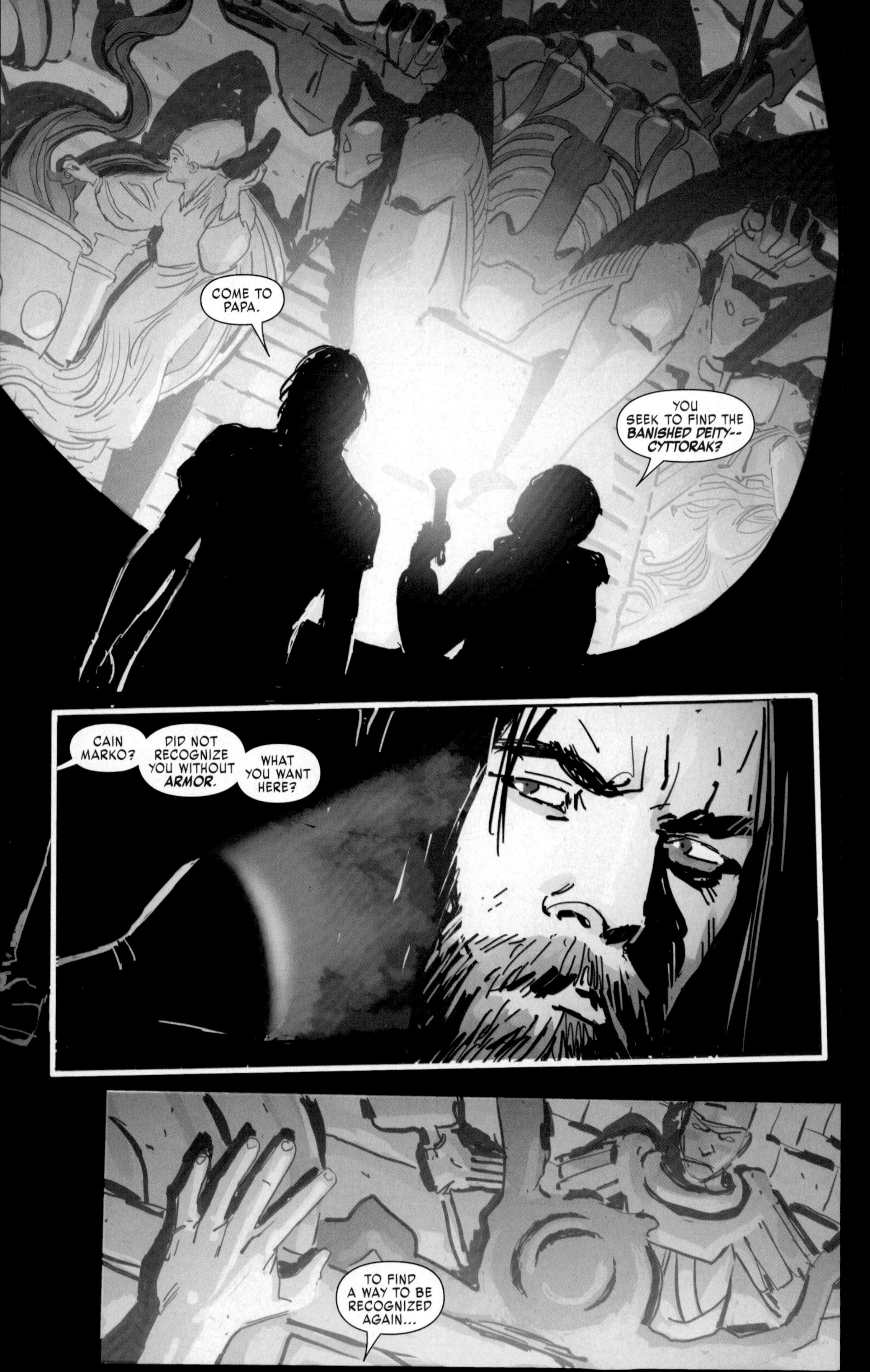
COME TO PAPA.
YOU SEEK TO FIND THE BANISHED DEITY--CYTTORAK?
CAIN MARKO?
DID NOT RECOGNIZE YOU WITHOUT ARMOR.
WHAT YOU WANT HERE?
TO FIND A WAY TO BE RECOGNIZED AGAIN...

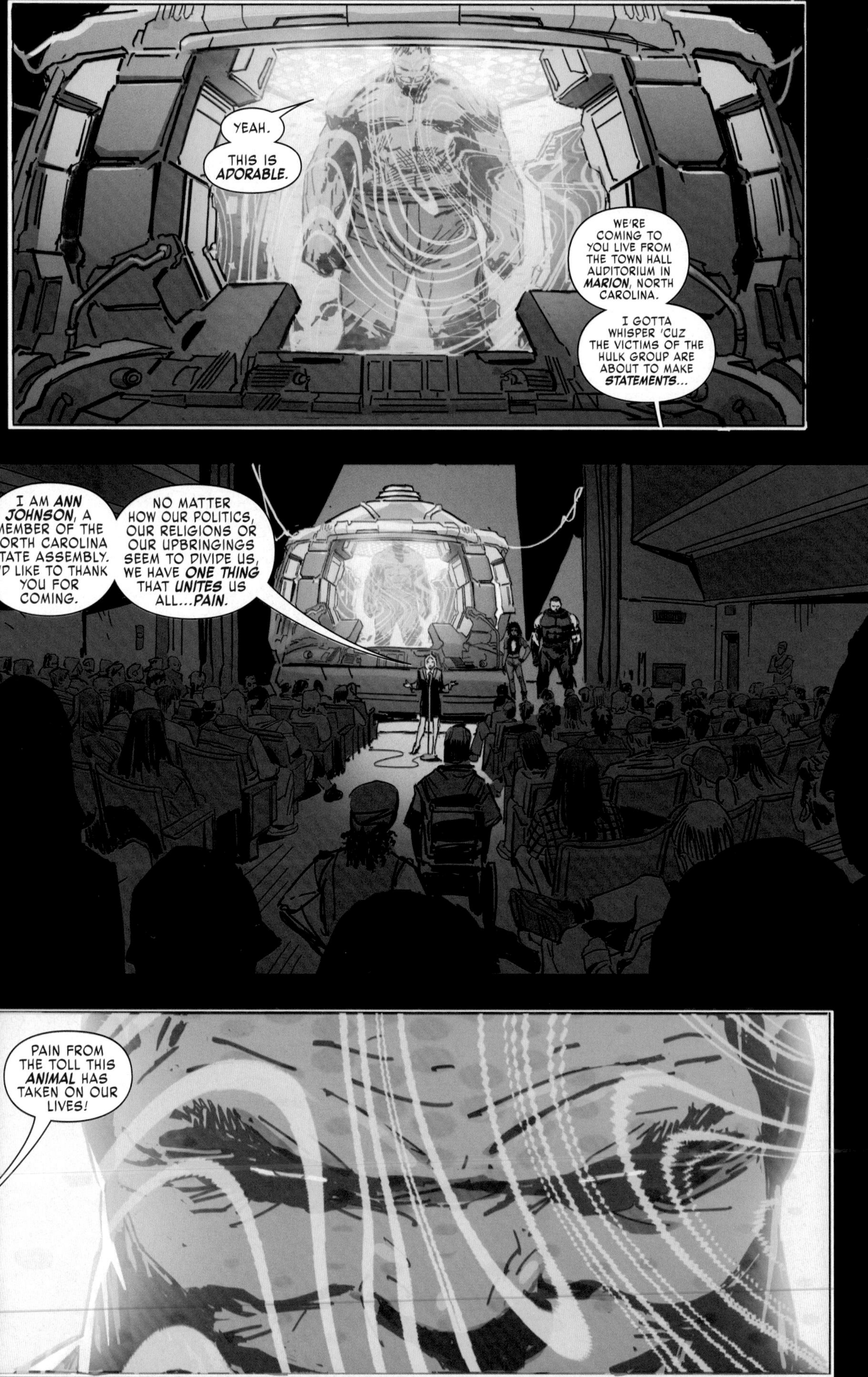
YEAH.
THIS IS ADORABLE.
WE'RE COMING TO YOU LIVE FROM THE TOWN HALL AUDITORIUM IN MARION, NORTH CAROLINA.
I GOTTA WHISPER 'CUZ THE VICTIMS OF THE HULK GROUP ARE ABOUT TO MAKE STATEMENTS...
I AM ANN JOHNSON, A MEMBER OF THE ORTH CAROLINA TATE ASSEMBLY. 'D LIKE TO THANK YOU FOR COMING.
NO MATTER HOW OUR POLITICS, OUR RELIGIONS OR OUR UPBRINGINGS SEEM TO DIVIDE US, WE HAVE ONE THING THAT UNITES US ALL...PAIN.
PAIN FROM THE TOLL THIS ANIMAL HAS TAKEN ON OUR LIVES!

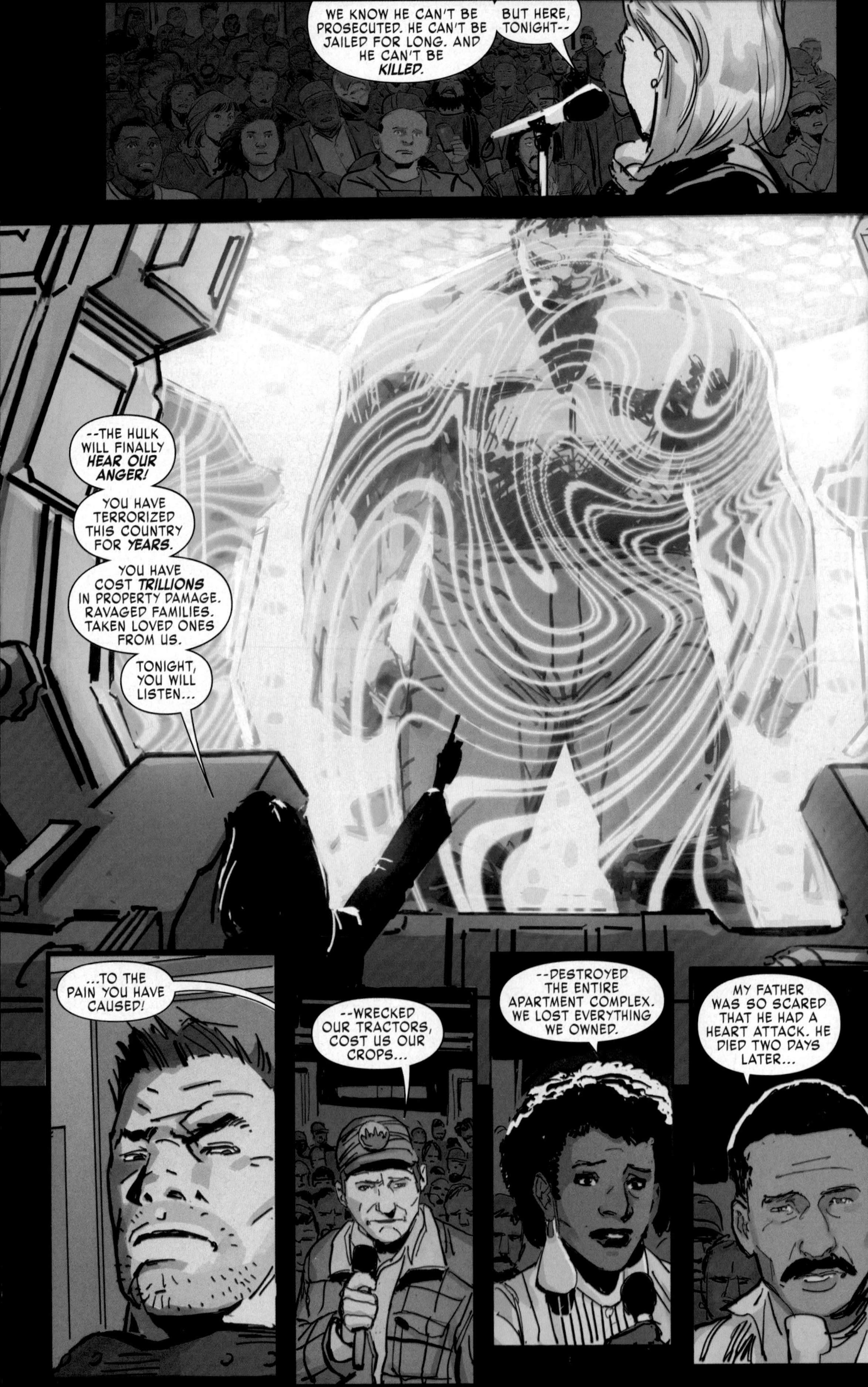
WE KNOW HE CAN'T BE PROSECUTED. HE CAN'T BE JAILED FOR LONG. AND HE CAN'T BE KILLED.
BUT HERE, TONIGHT--
--THE HULK WILL FINALLY HEAR OUR ANGER!
YOU HAVE TERRORIZED THIS COUNTRY FOR YEARS.
YOU HAVE COST TRILLIONS IN PROPERTY DAMAGE. RAVAGED FAMILIES. TAKEN LOVED ONES FROM US.
TONIGHT, YOU WILL LISTEN...
...TO THE PAIN YOU HAVE CAUSED!
--WRECKED OUR TRACTORS, COST US OUR CROPS...
--DESTROYED THE ENTIRE APARTMENT COMPLEX. WE LOST EVERYTHING WE OWNED.
MY FATHER WAS SO SCARED THAT HE HAD A HEART ATTACK. HE DIED TWO DAYS LATER...

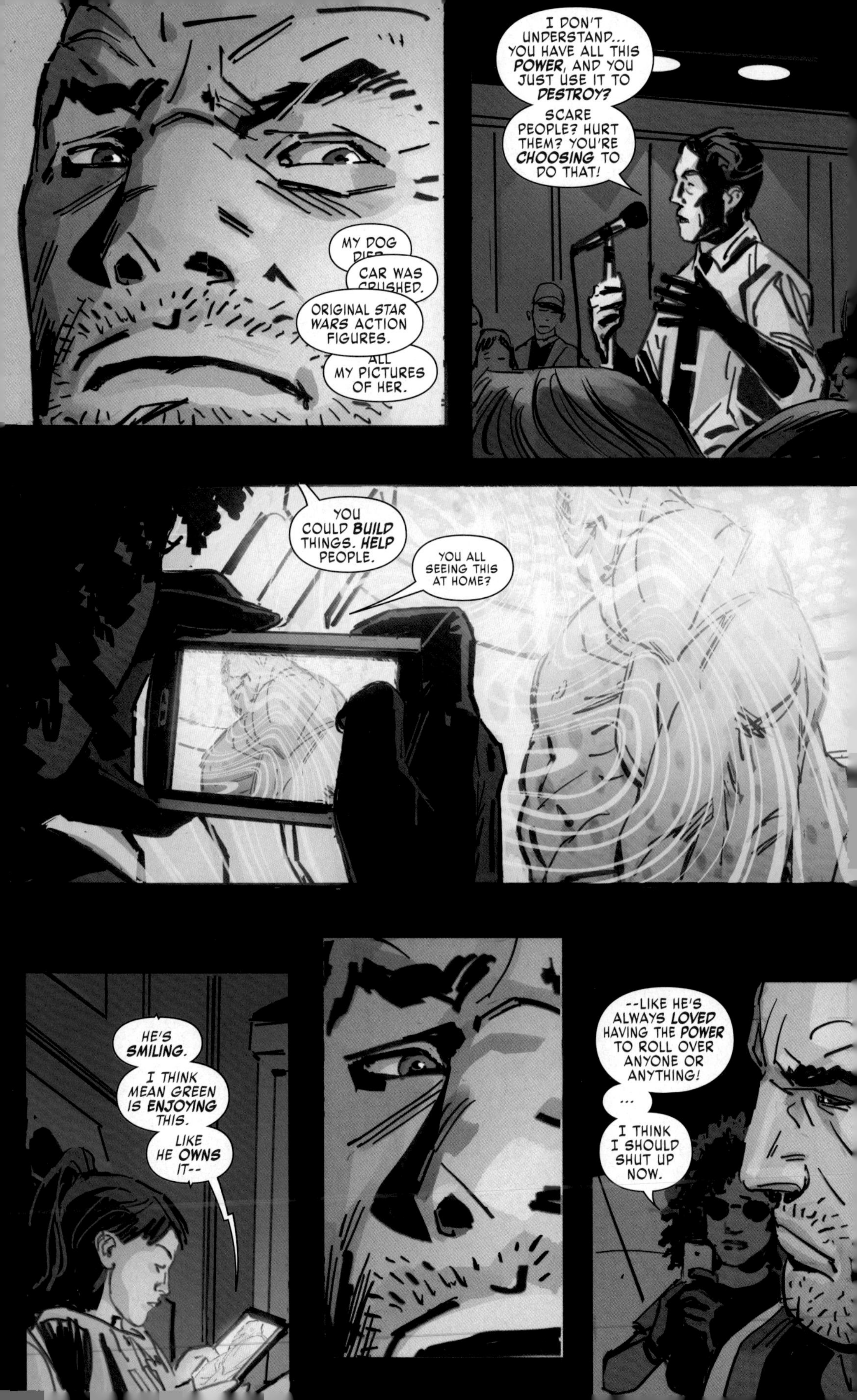
MY DOG DIED.
CAR WAS CRUSHED.
ORIGINAL STAR WARS ACTION FIGURES.
ALL MY PICTURES OF HER.
I DON'T UNDERSTAND... YOU HAVE ALL THIS POWER, AND YOU JUST USE IT TO DESTROY?
SCARE PEOPLE? HURT THEM? YOU'RE CHOOSING TO DO THAT!
YOU COULD BUILD THINGS. HELP PEOPLE.
YOU ALL SEEING THIS AT HOME?
HE'S SMILING.
I THINK MEAN GREEN IS ENJOYING THIS.
LIKE HE OWNS IT--
--LIKE HE'S ALWAYS LOVED HAVING THE POWER TO ROLL OVER ANYONE OR ANYTHING!
...
I THINK I SHOULD SHUT UP NOW.

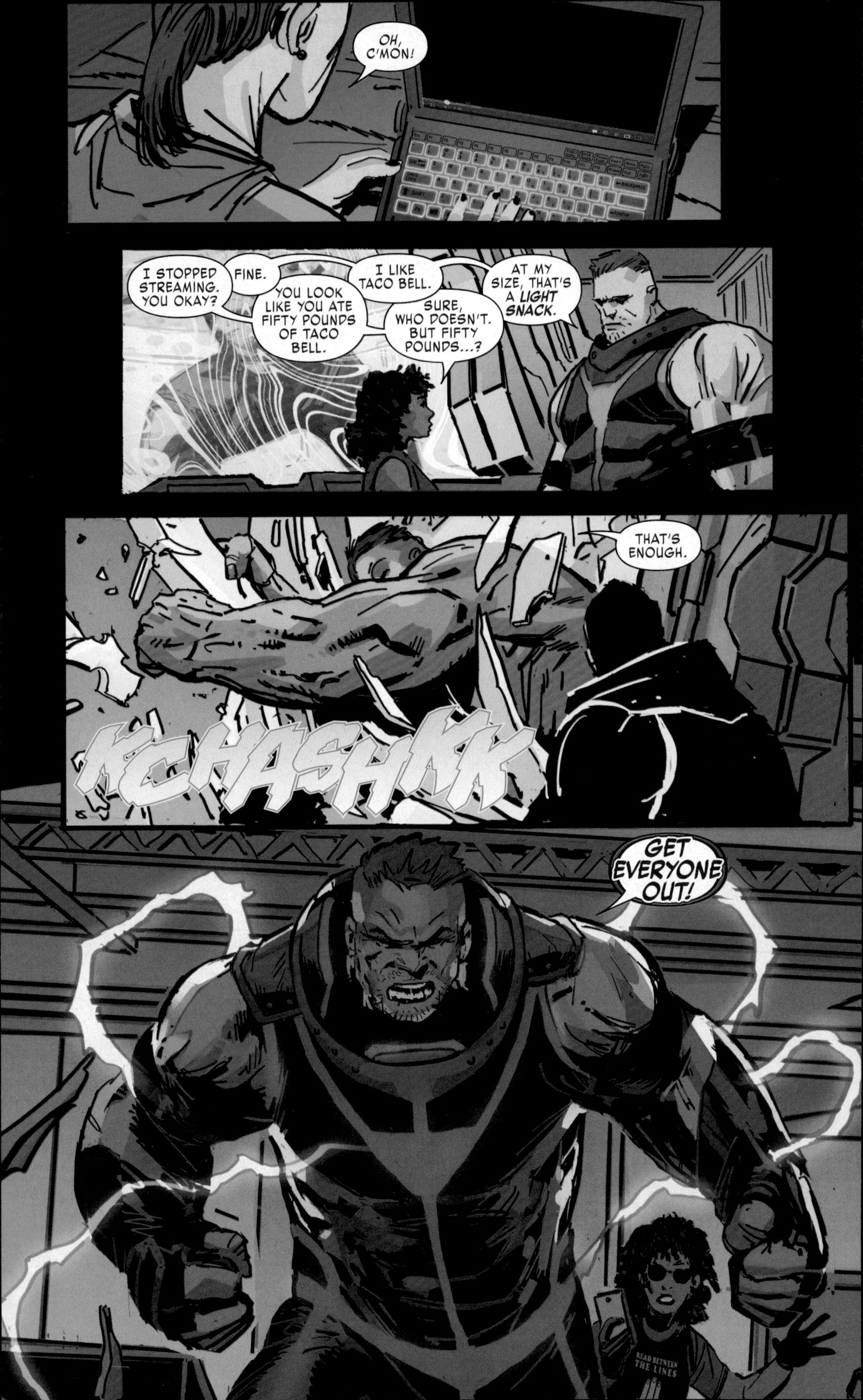
OH, C'MON!
I STOPPED STREAMING. YOU OKAY?
FINE.
YOU LOOK LIKE YOU ATE FIFTY POUNDS OF TACO BELL.
I LIKE TACO BELL.
SURE, WHO DOESN'T. BUT FIFTY POUNDS...?
AT MY SIZE, THAT'S A LIGHT SNACK.
THAT'S ENOUGH.
K'CHASHKK
GET EVERYONE OUT!
READ BETWEEN THE LINES

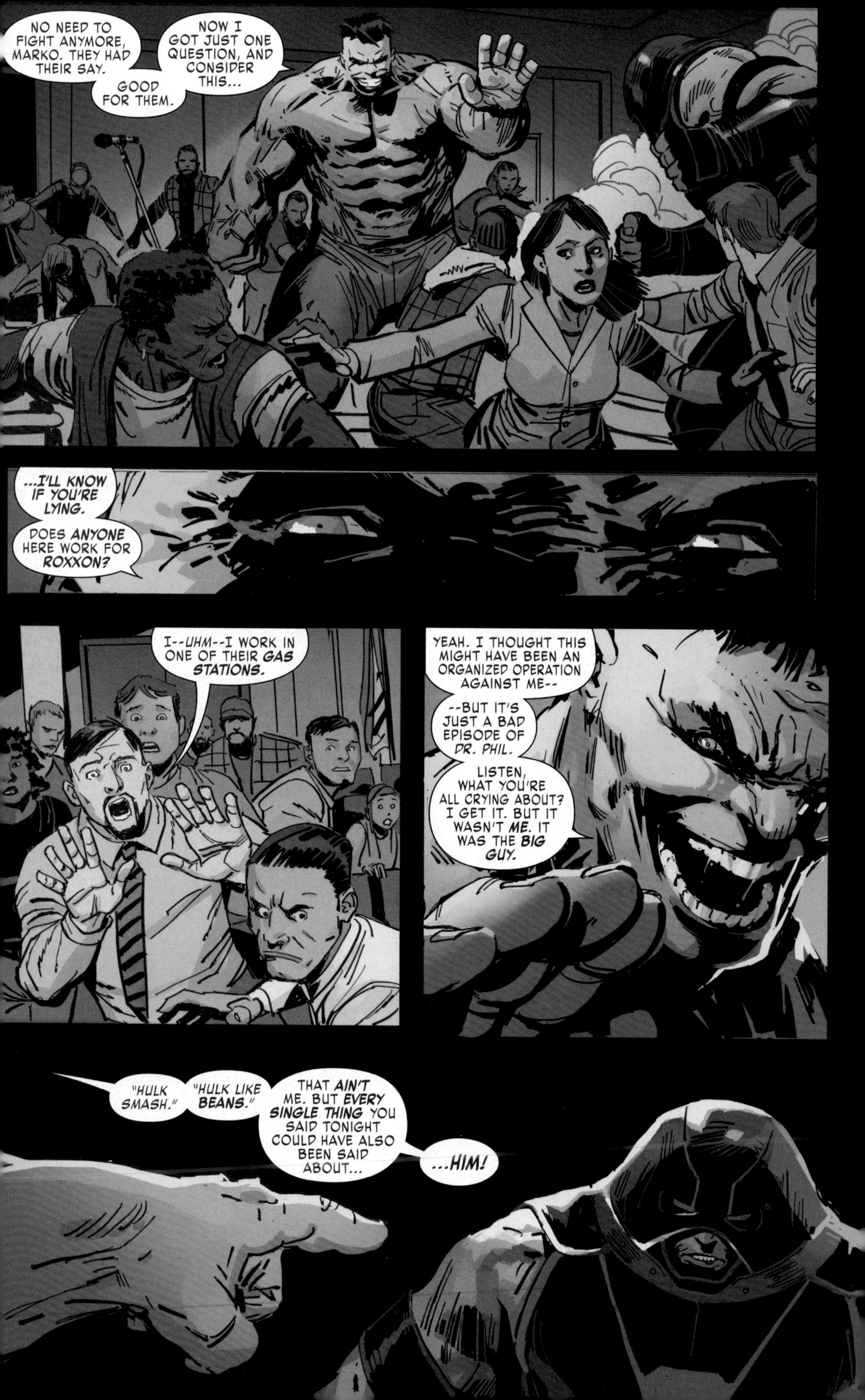

NO NEED TO FIGHT ANYMORE, MARKO. THEY HAD THEIR SAY.
GOOD FOR THEM.
NOW I GOT JUST ONE QUESTION, AND CONSIDER THIS...
...I'LL KNOW IF YOU'RE LYING.
DOES ANYONE HERE WORK FOR ROXXON?
I--UHM--I WORK IN ONE OF THEIR GAS STATIONS.
YEAH. I THOUGHT THIS MIGHT HAVE BEEN AN ORGANIZED OPERATION AGAINST ME--
--BUT IT'S JUST A BAD EPISODE OF DR. PHIL.
LISTEN, WHAT YOU'RE ALL CRYING ABOUT? I GET IT. BUT IT WASN'T ME. IT WAS THE BIG GUY.
"HULK SMASH."
"HULK LIKE BEANS."
THAT AIN'T ME. BUT EVERY SINGLE THING YOU SAID TONIGHT COULD HAVE ALSO BEEN SAID ABOUT...
...HIM!

SHADOW BASE, COPY.

COPY.

McGOWAN, GET ME OUT OF HERE.

HOPE THE *PAYCHECK* WAS WORTH THE *GUILT*, MARKO.

HE WAS RIGHT.

I'M GUILTY OF THE SAME THINGS THE HULK HAS CAUSED...

...BUT HE HAD AN *EXCUSE.* HE HAD THE MIND OF A *CHILD.*

I KNEW WHAT I WAS DOING EVERY TIME I DID IT.

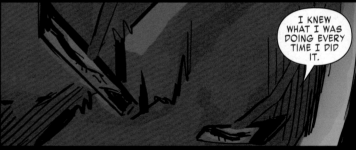

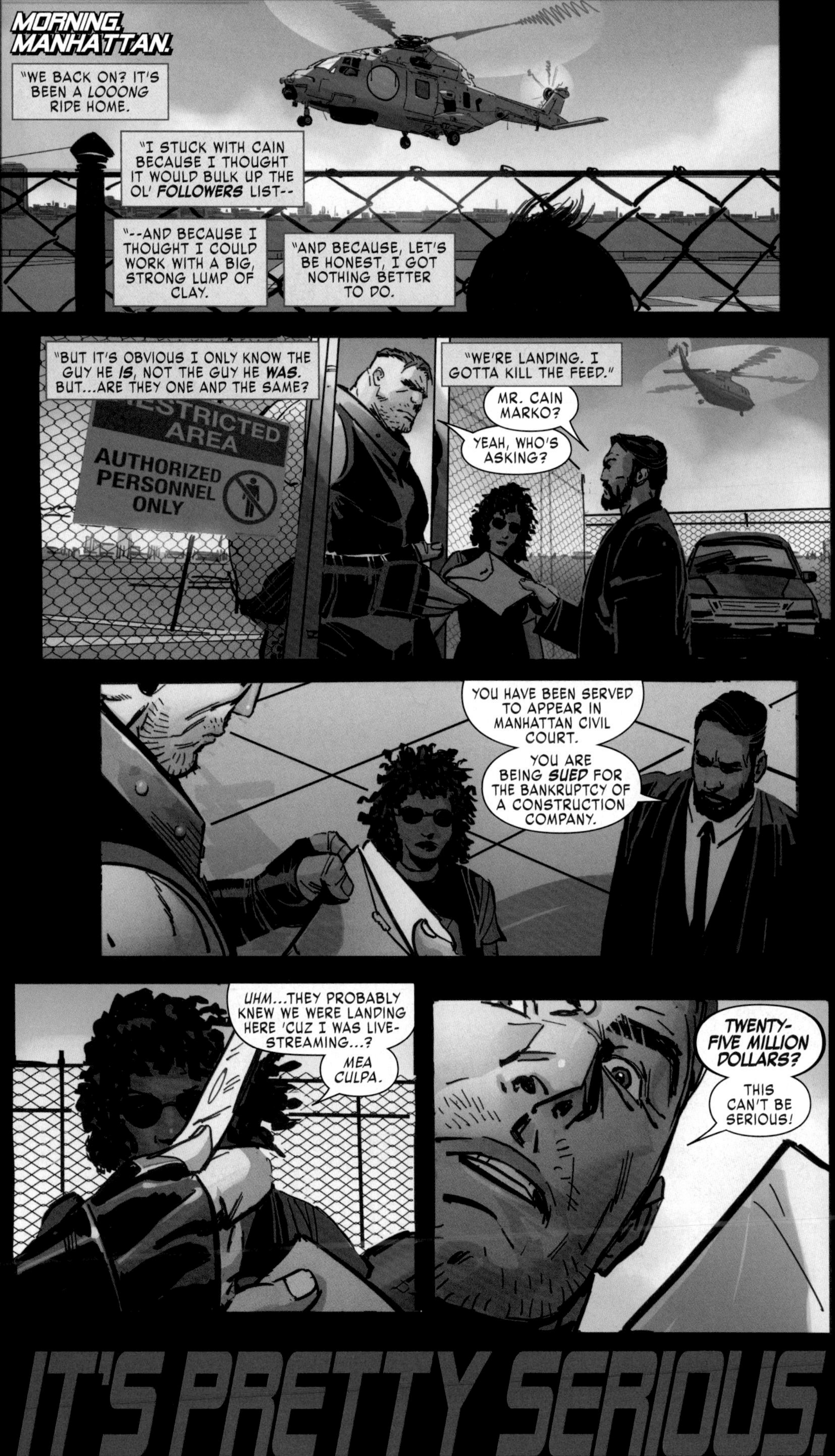
MORNING. MANHATTAN.
"WE BACK ON? IT'S BEEN A LOOONG RIDE HOME.
"I STUCK WITH CAIN BECAUSE I THOUGHT IT WOULD BULK UP THE OL' FOLLOWERS LIST--
"--AND BECAUSE I THOUGHT I COULD WORK WITH A BIG, STRONG LUMP OF CLAY.
"AND BECAUSE, LET'S BE HONEST, I GOT NOTHING BETTER TO DO.
"BUT IT'S OBVIOUS I ONLY KNOW THE GUY HE IS, NOT THE GUY HE WAS. BUT...ARE THEY ONE AND THE SAME?
RESTRICTED AREA
AUTHORIZED PERSONNEL ONLY
"WE'RE LANDING. I GOTTA KILL THE FEED."
MR. CAIN MARKO?
YEAH, WHO'S ASKING?
YOU HAVE BEEN SERVED TO APPEAR IN MANHATTAN CIVIL COURT.
YOU ARE BEING SUED FOR THE BANKRUPTCY OF A CONSTRUCTION COMPANY.
UHM...THEY PROBABLY KNEW WE WERE LANDING HERE 'CUZ I WAS LIVE-STREAMING...?
MEA CULPA.
TWENTY-FIVE MILLION DOLLARS?
THIS CAN'T BE SERIOUS!
IT'S PRETTY SERIOUS.

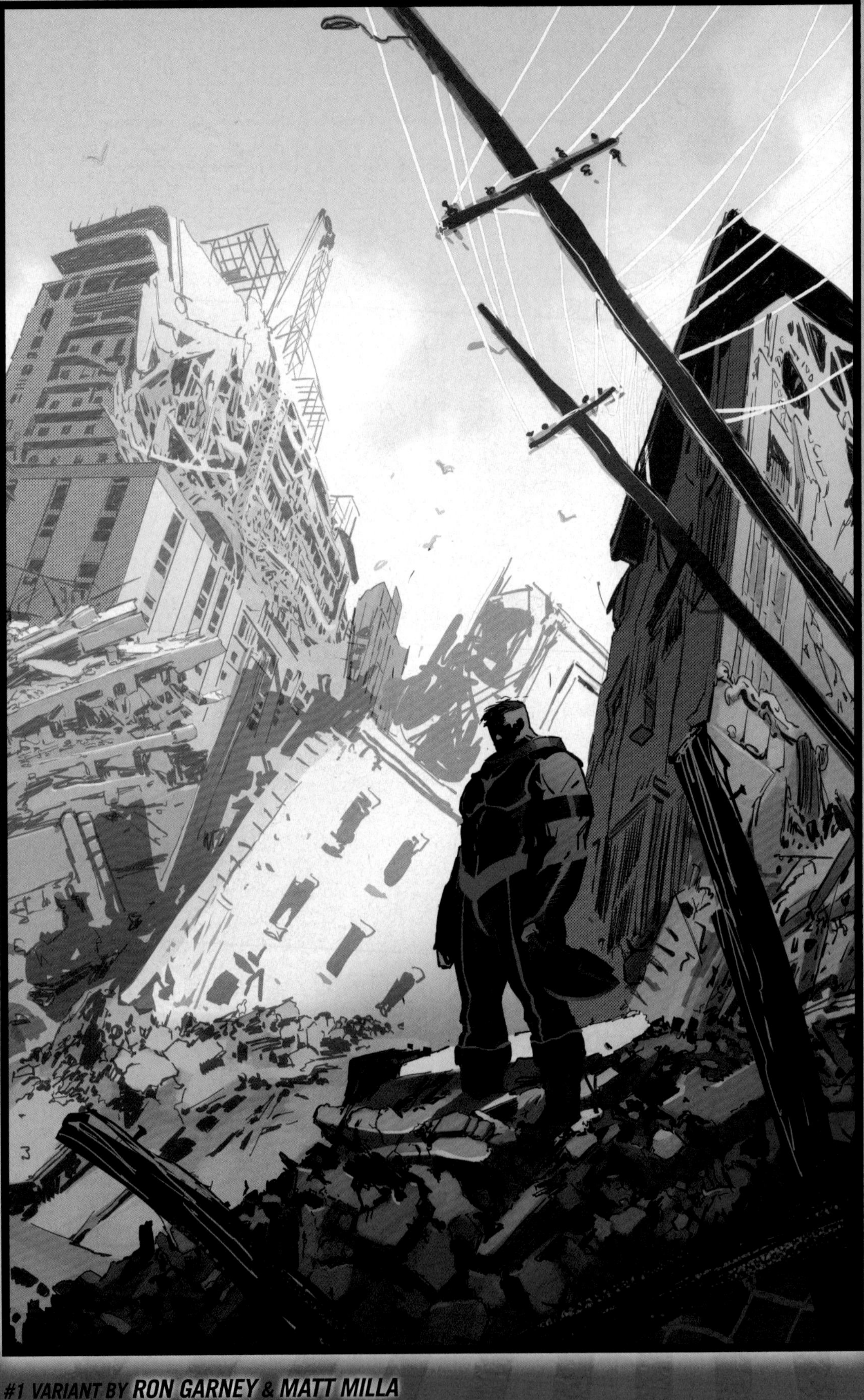

#1 VARIANT BY RON GARNEY & MATT MILLA

3

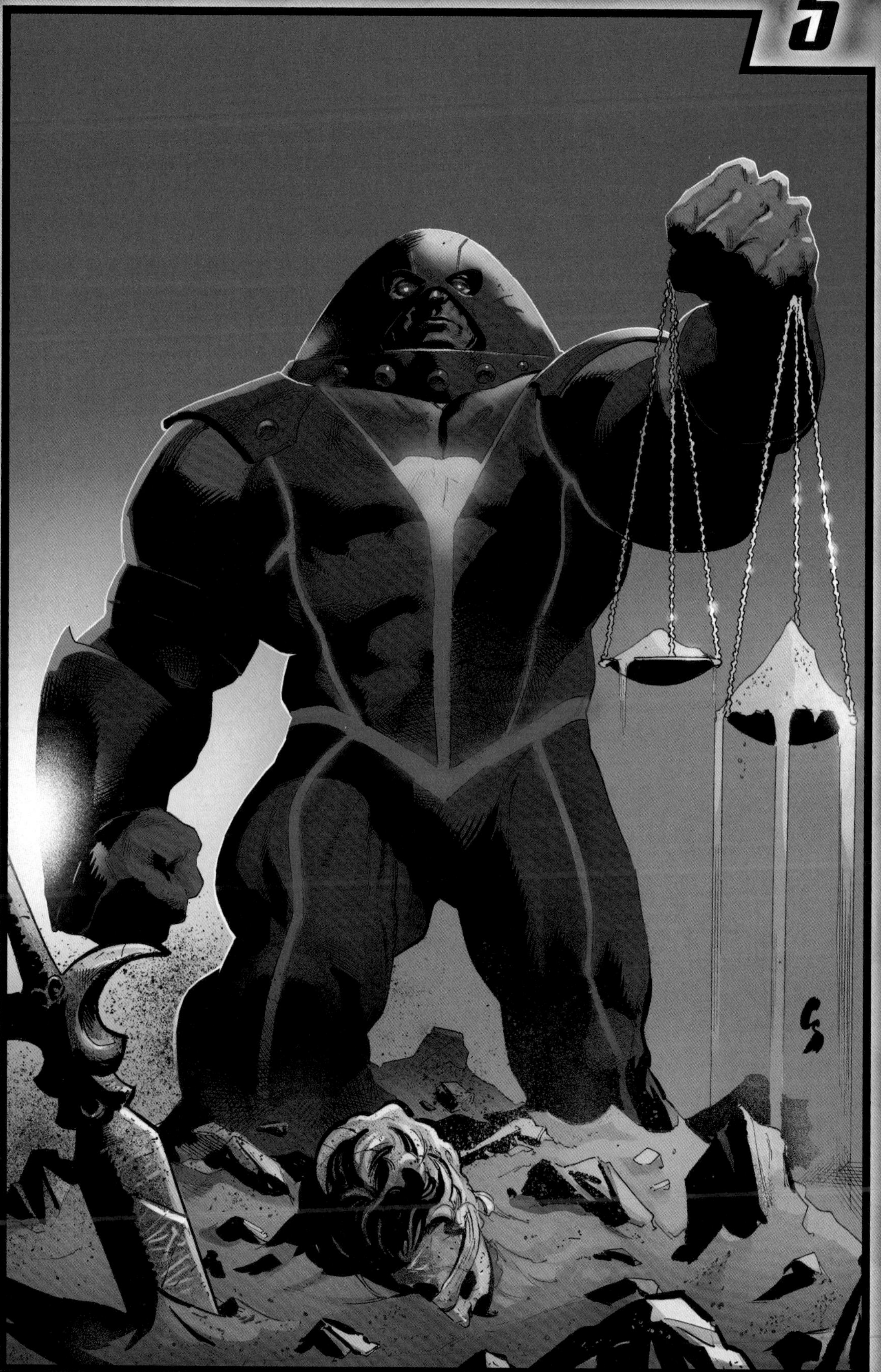

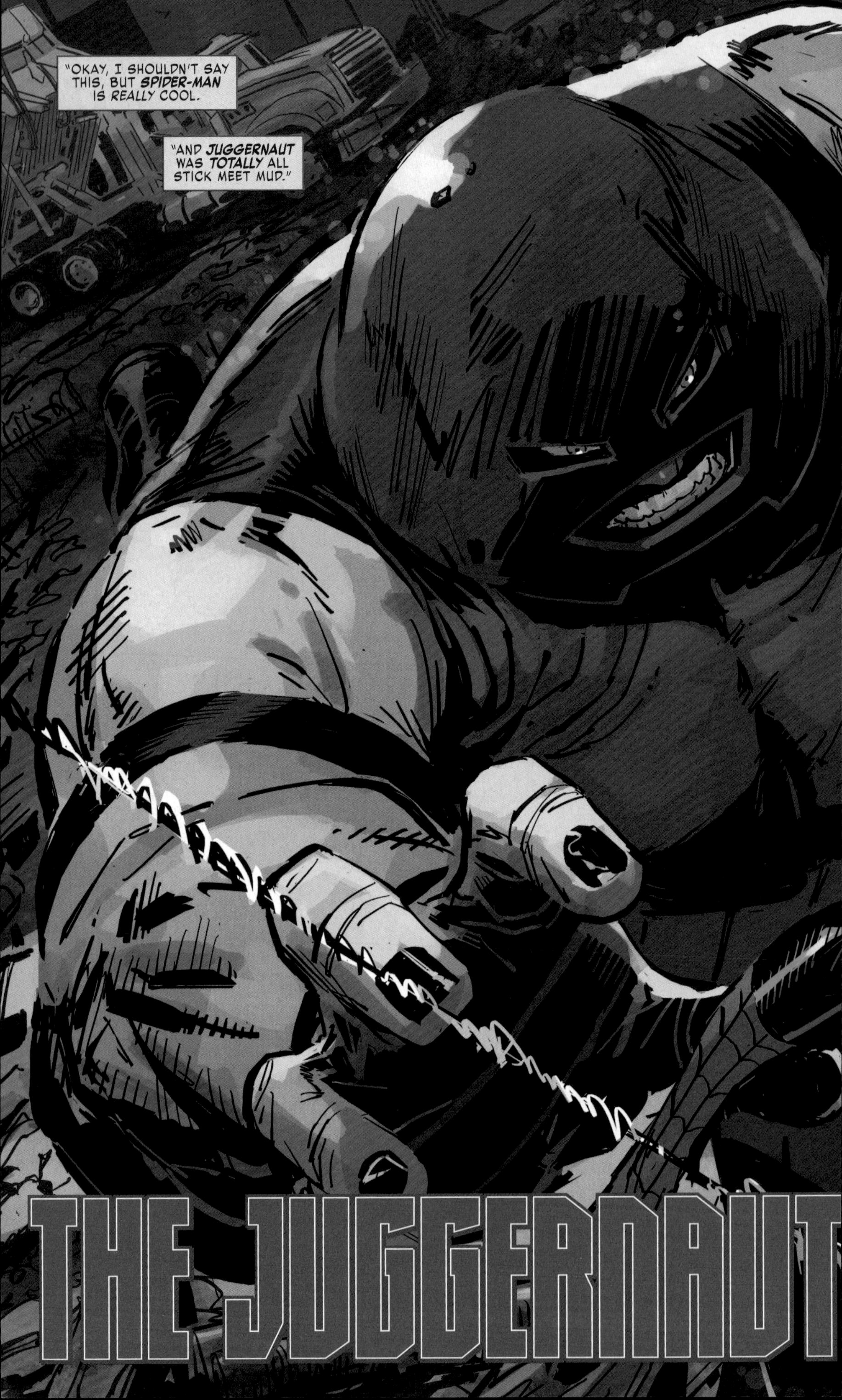
"OKAY, I SHOULDN'T SAY THIS, BUT SPIDER-MAN IS REALLY COOL.
"AND JUGGERNAUT WAS TOTALLY ALL STICK MEET MUD."
THE JUGGERNAUT

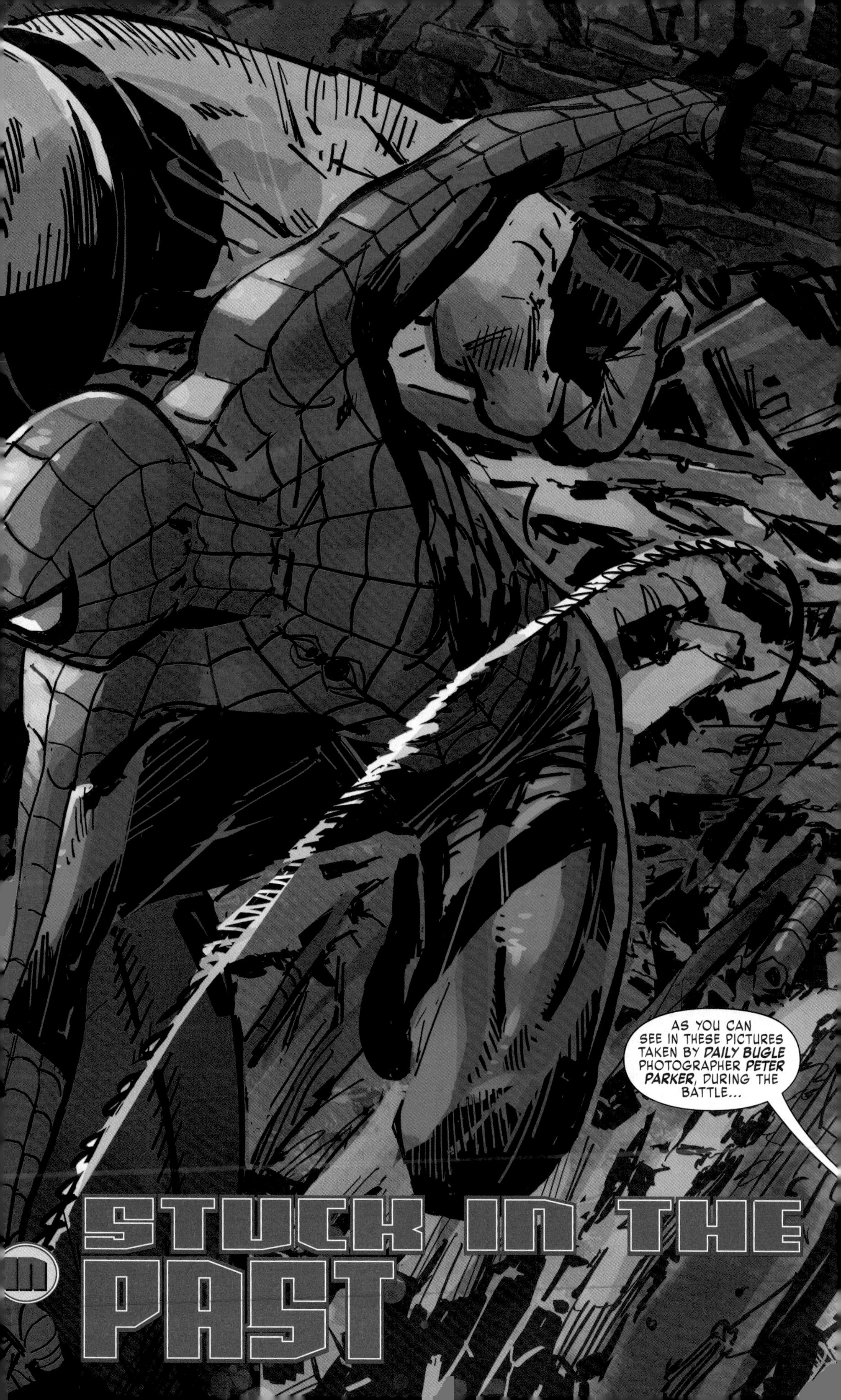

AS YOU CAN SEE IN THESE PICTURES TAKEN BY *DAILY BUGLE* PHOTOGRAPHER *PETER PARKER*, DURING THE BATTLE...
STUCK IN THE PAST

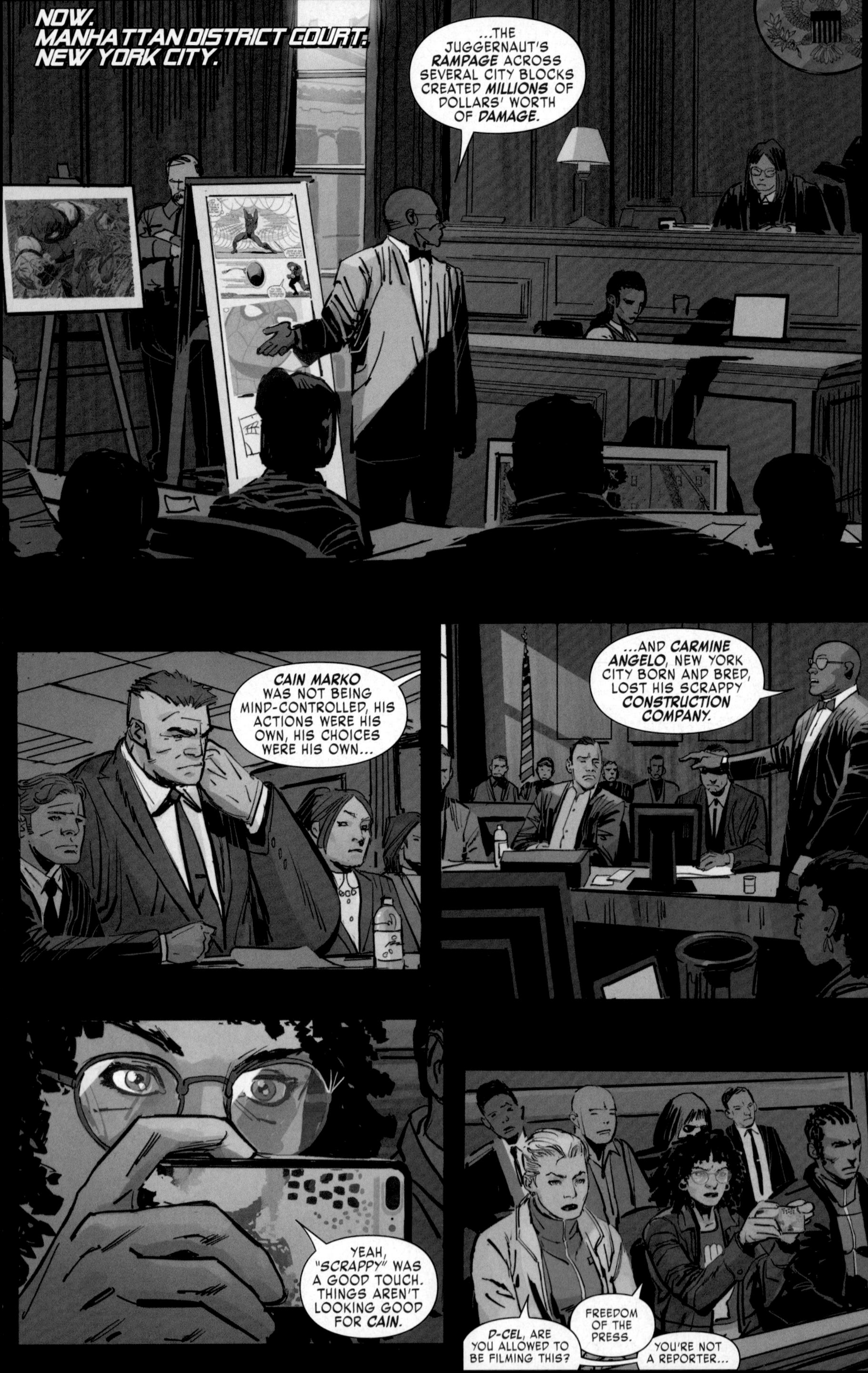
NOW. MANHATTAN DISTRICT COURT. NEW YORK CITY.
...THE JUGGERNAUT'S RAMPAGE ACROSS SEVERAL CITY BLOCKS CREATED MILLIONS OF DOLLARS' WORTH OF DAMAGE.
CAIN MARKO WAS NOT BEING MIND-CONTROLLED, HIS ACTIONS WERE HIS OWN, HIS CHOICES WERE HIS OWN...
...AND CARMINE ANGELO, NEW YORK CITY BORN AND BRED, LOST HIS SCRAPPY CONSTRUCTION COMPANY.
YEAH, "SCRAPPY" WAS A GOOD TOUCH. THINGS AREN'T LOOKING GOOD FOR CAIN.
D-CEL, ARE YOU ALLOWED TO BE FILMING THIS?
FREEDOM OF THE PRESS.
YOU'RE NOT A REPORTER...

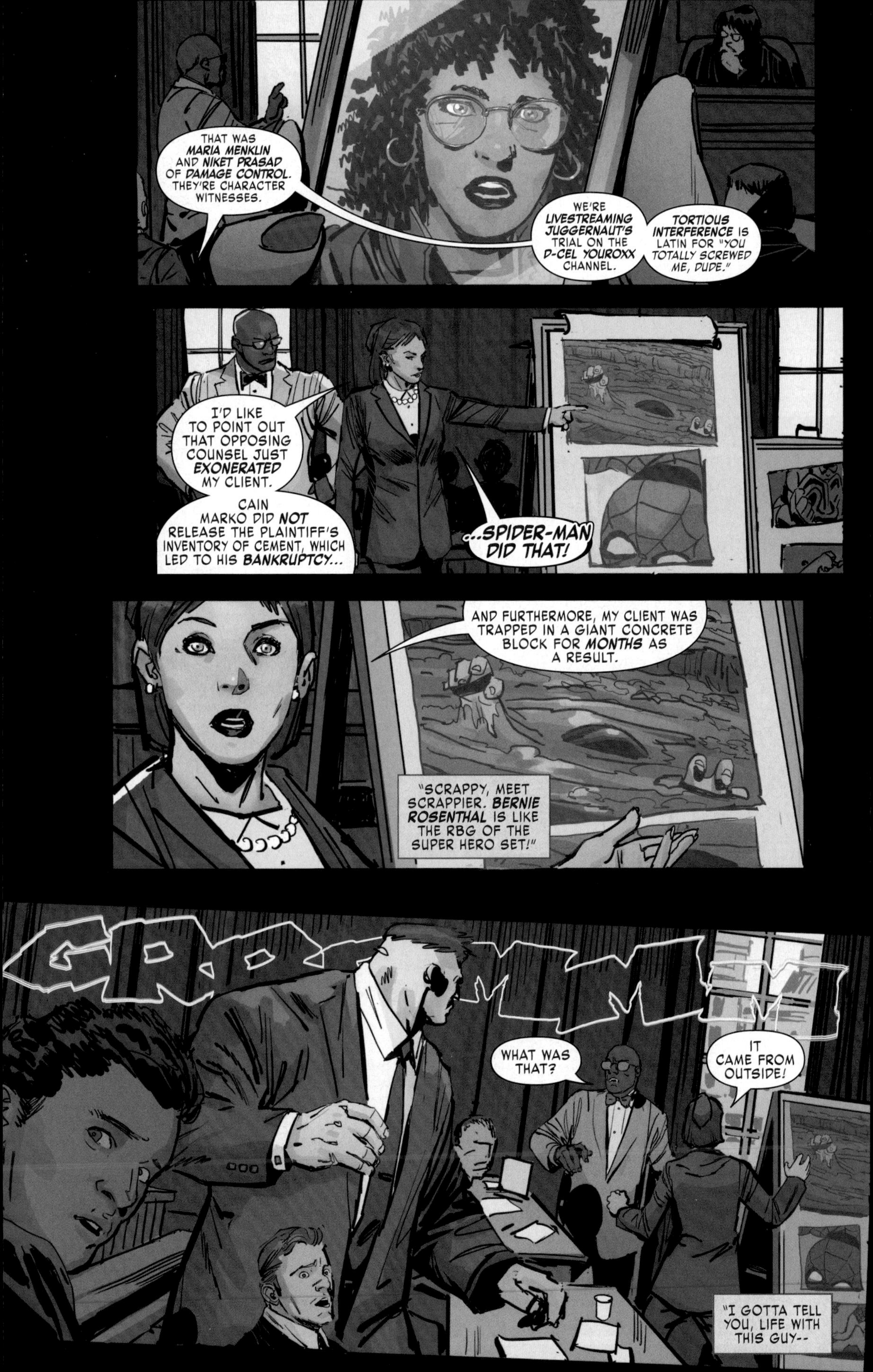
THAT WAS MARIA MENKLIN AND NIKET PRASAD OF DAMAGE CONTROL. THEY'RE CHARACTER WITNESSES.
WE'RE LIVESTREAMING JUGGERNAUT'S TRIAL ON THE D-CEL YOUROXX CHANNEL.
TORTIOUS INTERFERENCE IS LATIN FOR "YOU TOTALLY SCREWED ME, DUDE."
I'D LIKE TO POINT OUT THAT OPPOSING COUNSEL JUST EXONERATED MY CLIENT.
CAIN MARKO DID NOT RELEASE THE PLAINTIFF'S INVENTORY OF CEMENT, WHICH LED TO HIS BANKRUPTCY...
...SPIDER-MAN DID THAT!
AND FURTHERMORE, MY CLIENT WAS TRAPPED IN A GIANT CONCRETE BLOCK FOR MONTHS AS A RESULT.
"SCRAPPY, MEET SCRAPPIER. BERNIE ROSENTHAL IS LIKE THE RBG OF THE SUPER HERO SET!"
WHAT WAS THAT?
IT CAME FROM OUTSIDE!
"I GOTTA TELL YOU, LIFE WITH THIS GUY--

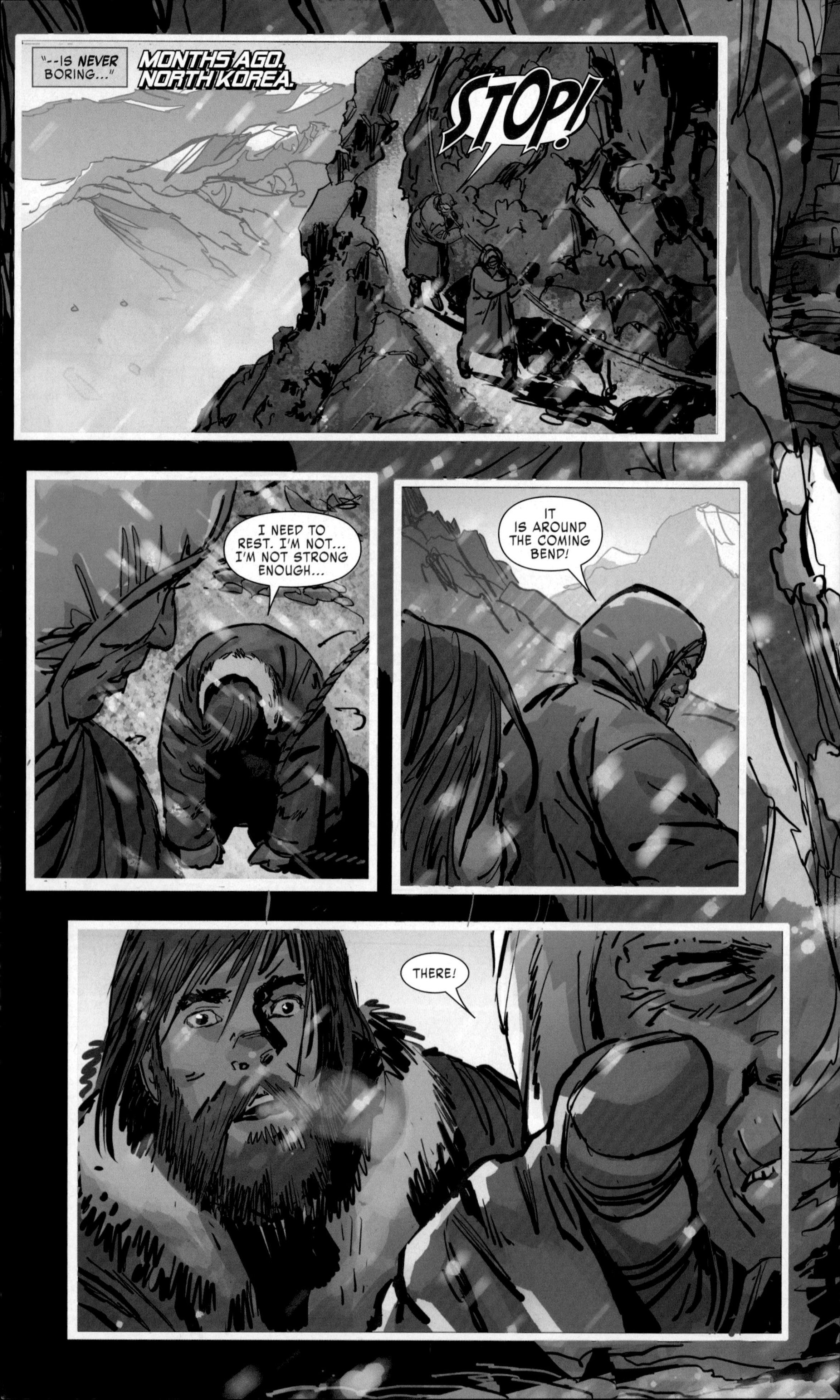
"--IS *NEVER* BORING..."
MONTHS AGO. NORTH KOREA.
STOP!
I NEED TO REST. I'M NOT... I'M NOT STRONG ENOUGH...
IT IS AROUND THE COMING BEND!
THERE!

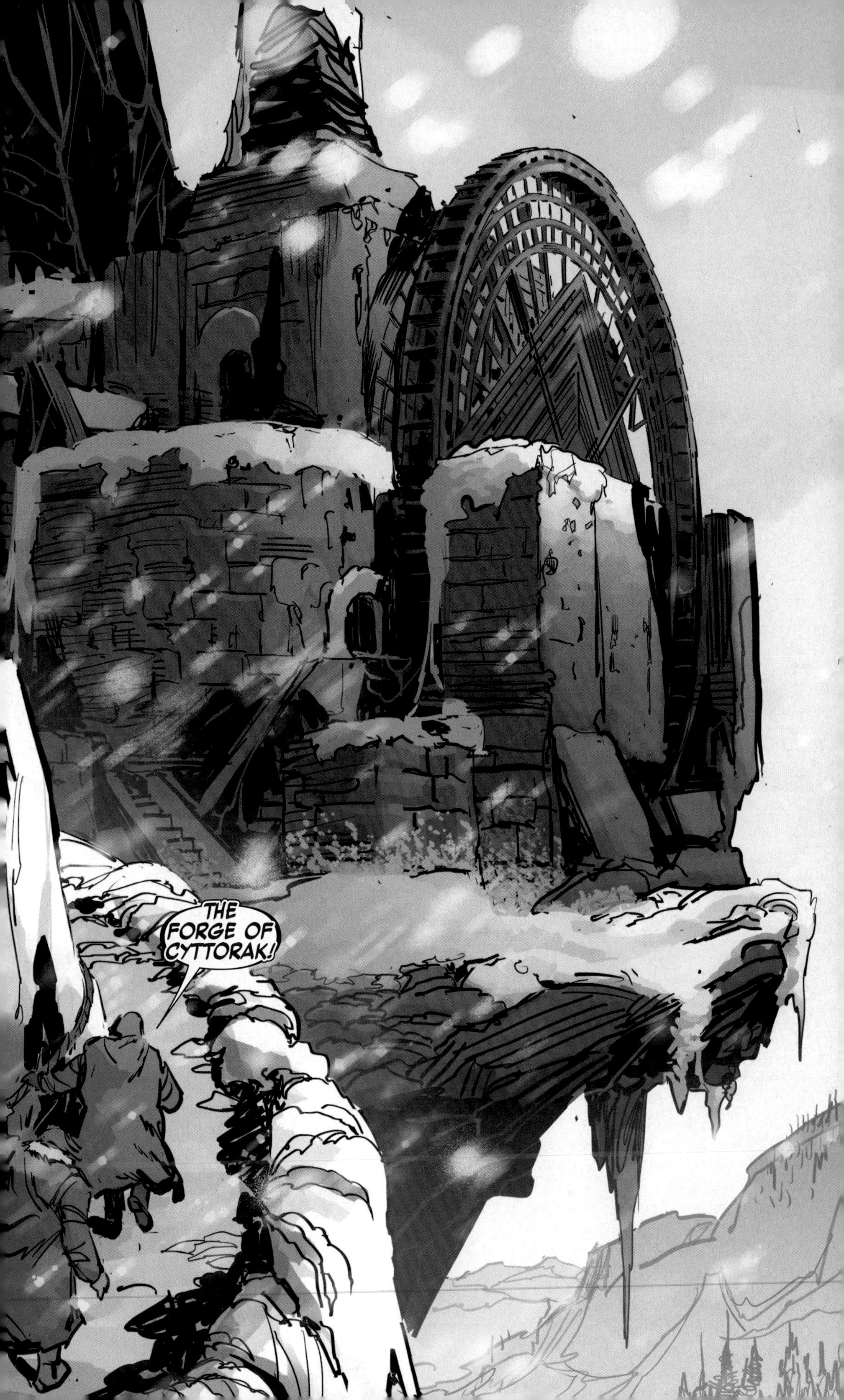
THE FORGE OF CYTTORAK!

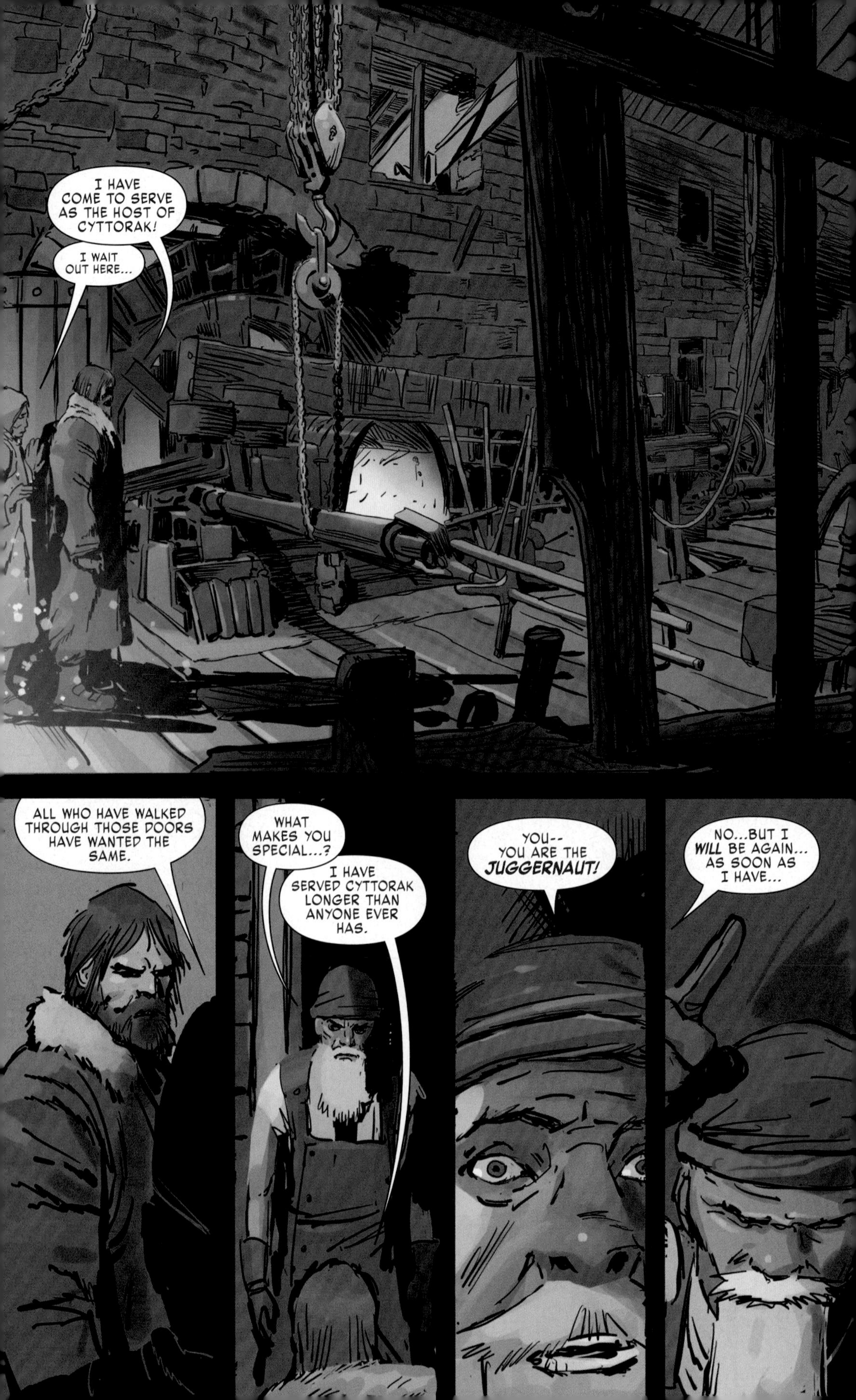
I HAVE COME TO SERVE AS THE HOST OF CYTTORAK!
I WAIT OUT HERE...
ALL WHO HAVE WALKED THROUGH THOSE DOORS HAVE WANTED THE SAME.
WHAT MAKES YOU SPECIAL...?
I HAVE SERVED CYTTORAK LONGER THAN ANYONE EVER HAS.
YOU-- YOU ARE THE JUGGERNAUT!
NO...BUT I WILL BE AGAIN... AS SOON AS I HAVE...

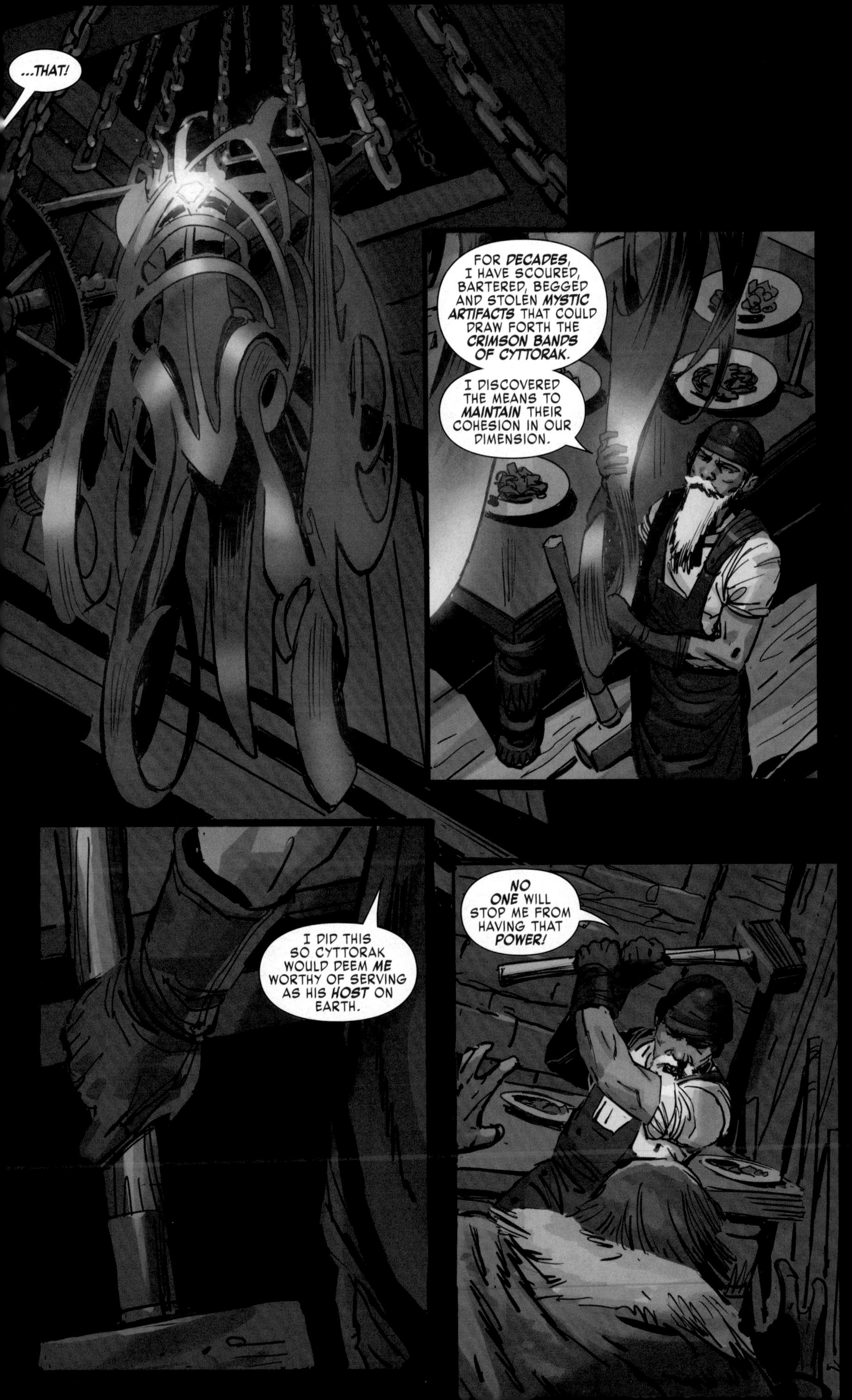
...THAT!
FOR DECADES, I HAVE SCOURED, BARTERED, BEGGED AND STOLEN MYSTIC ARTIFACTS THAT COULD DRAW FORTH THE CRIMSON BANDS OF CYTTORAK.
I DISCOVERED THE MEANS TO MAINTAIN THEIR COHESION IN OUR DIMENSION.
I DID THIS SO CYTTORAK WOULD DEEM ME WORTHY OF SERVING AS HIS HOST ON EARTH.
NO ONE WILL STOP ME FROM HAVING THAT POWER!

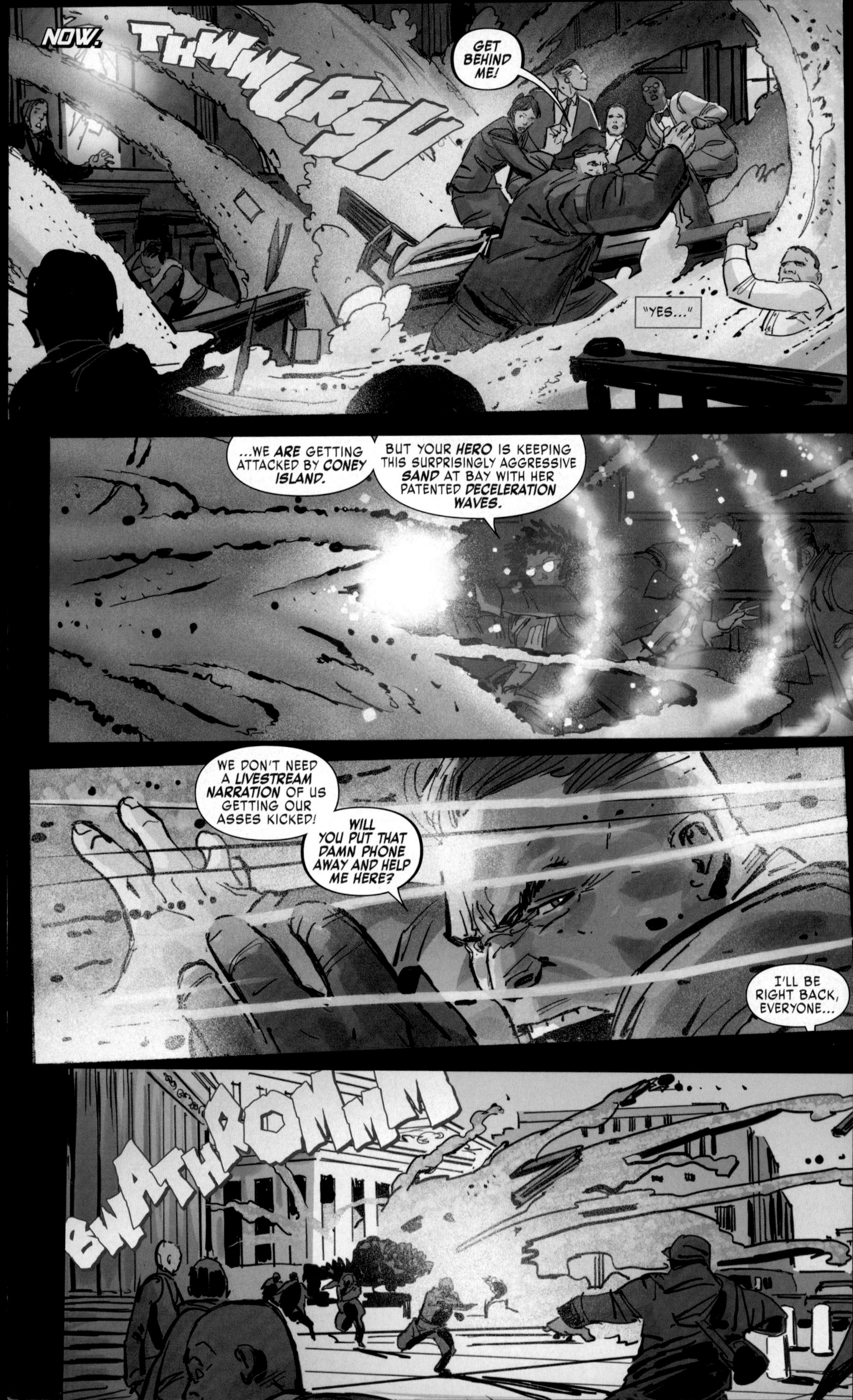
NOW.
THWWURSH
GET BEHIND ME!
"YES..."
...WE ARE GETTING ATTACKED BY CONEY ISLAND.
BUT YOUR HERO IS KEEPING THIS SURPRISINGLY AGGRESSIVE SAND AT BAY WITH HER PATENTED DECELERATION WAVES.
WE DON'T NEED A LIVESTREAM NARRATION OF US GETTING OUR ASSES KICKED!
WILL YOU PUT THAT DAMN PHONE AWAY AND HELP ME HERE?
I'LL BE RIGHT BACK, EVERYONE...
BWATHROMMM

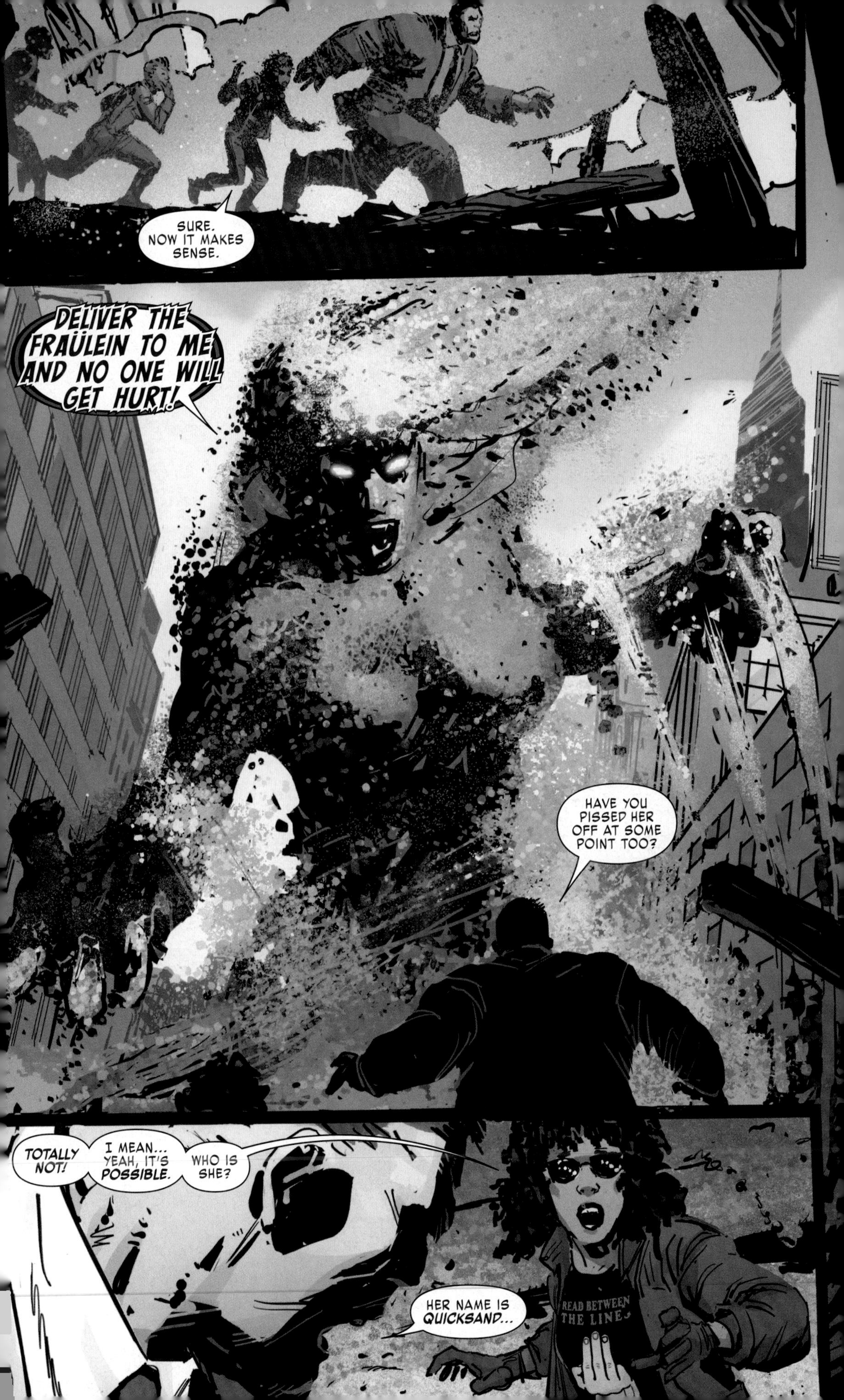
SURE. NOW IT MAKES SENSE.
DELIVER THE FRAÜLEIN TO ME AND NO ONE WILL GET HURT!
HAVE YOU PISSED HER OFF AT SOME POINT TOO?
TOTALLY NOT!
I MEAN... YEAH, IT'S POSSIBLE.
WHO IS SHE?
HER NAME IS QUICKSAND...
READ BETWEEN THE LINES

...BUT SOMETHING'S NOT RIGHT.

SAID THE GUY DIALING UP HIS *ARMOR* FROM ANOTHER DIMENSION AS HE GOES TO FIGHT A *TOWER* OF *SAND?*

THAT DIDN'T SOUND LIKE THE WAY NGUYET TALKS...

OF COURSE HE KNOWS HER. *PRISON* IS LIKE A *SUPER VILLAIN BREAKFAST CLUB* FOR THESE GUYS.

WHY IS SHE AFTER *D-CEL?*

I'M SURE MY *VIEWERS* WOULD LOVE TO KNOW. HEY EVERYONE, I'M BACK!

CAIN WON'T TALK ABOUT HOW HE GOT THIS *NEW ARMOR...*

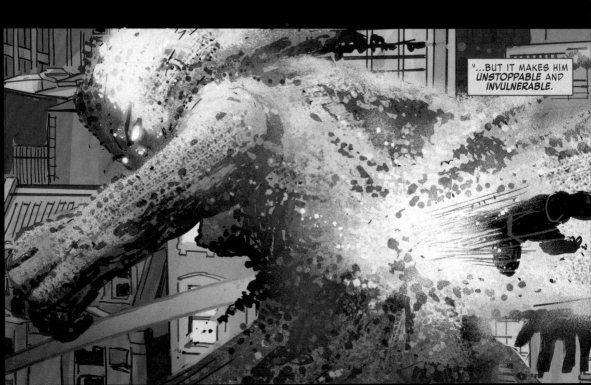

"...BUT IT MAKES HIM *UNSTOPPABLE* AND *INVULNERABLE.*

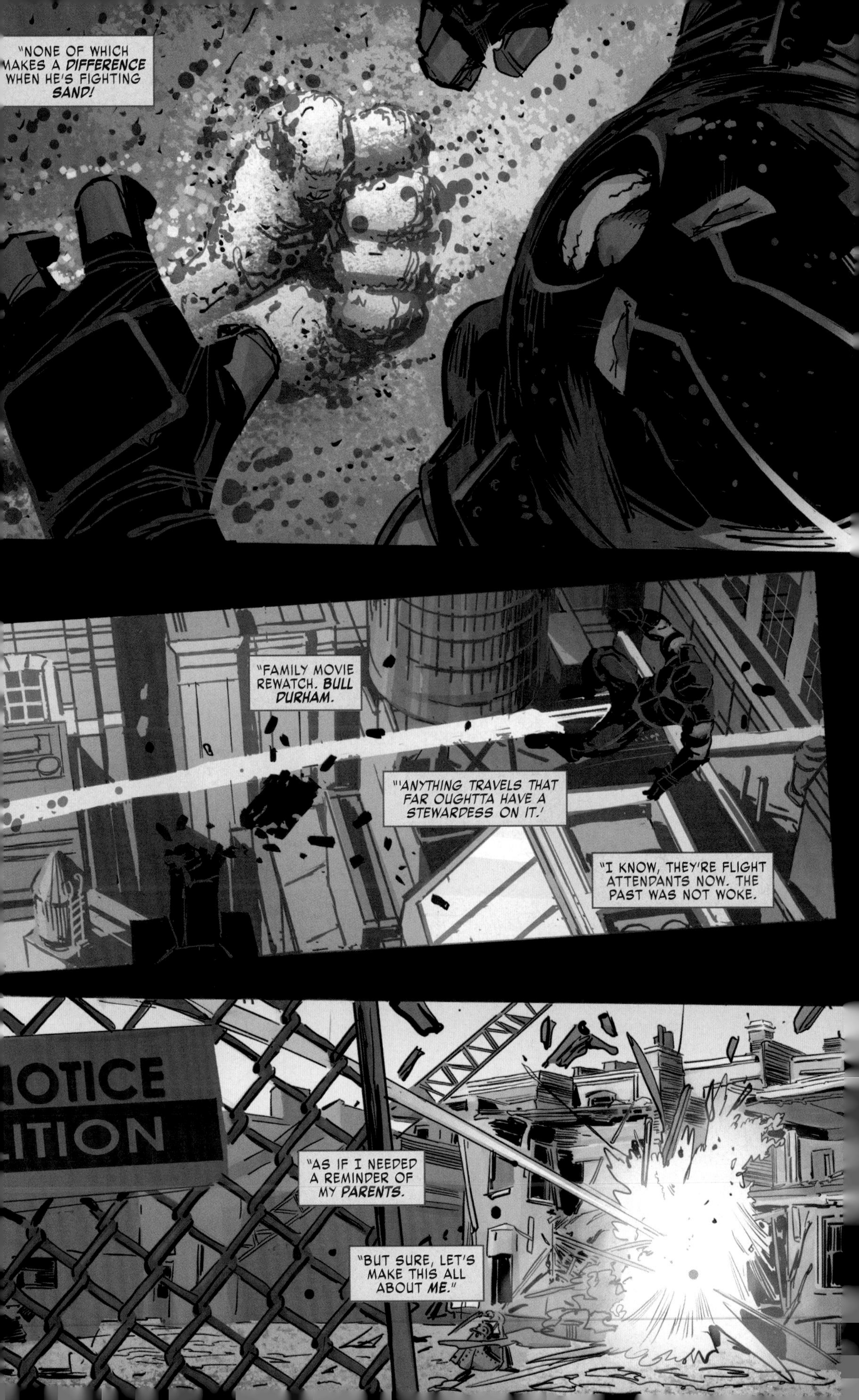
"NONE OF WHICH MAKES A *DIFFERENCE* WHEN HE'S FIGHTING *SAND!*
"FAMILY MOVIE REWATCH. *BULL DURHAM*.
"'ANYTHING TRAVELS THAT FAR OUGHTTA HAVE A STEWARDESS ON IT.'
"I KNOW, THEY'RE FLIGHT ATTENDANTS NOW. THE PAST WAS NOT WOKE.
"AS IF I NEEDED A REMINDER OF MY *PARENTS*.
"BUT SURE, LET'S MAKE THIS ALL ABOUT *ME*."
NOTICE
ITION

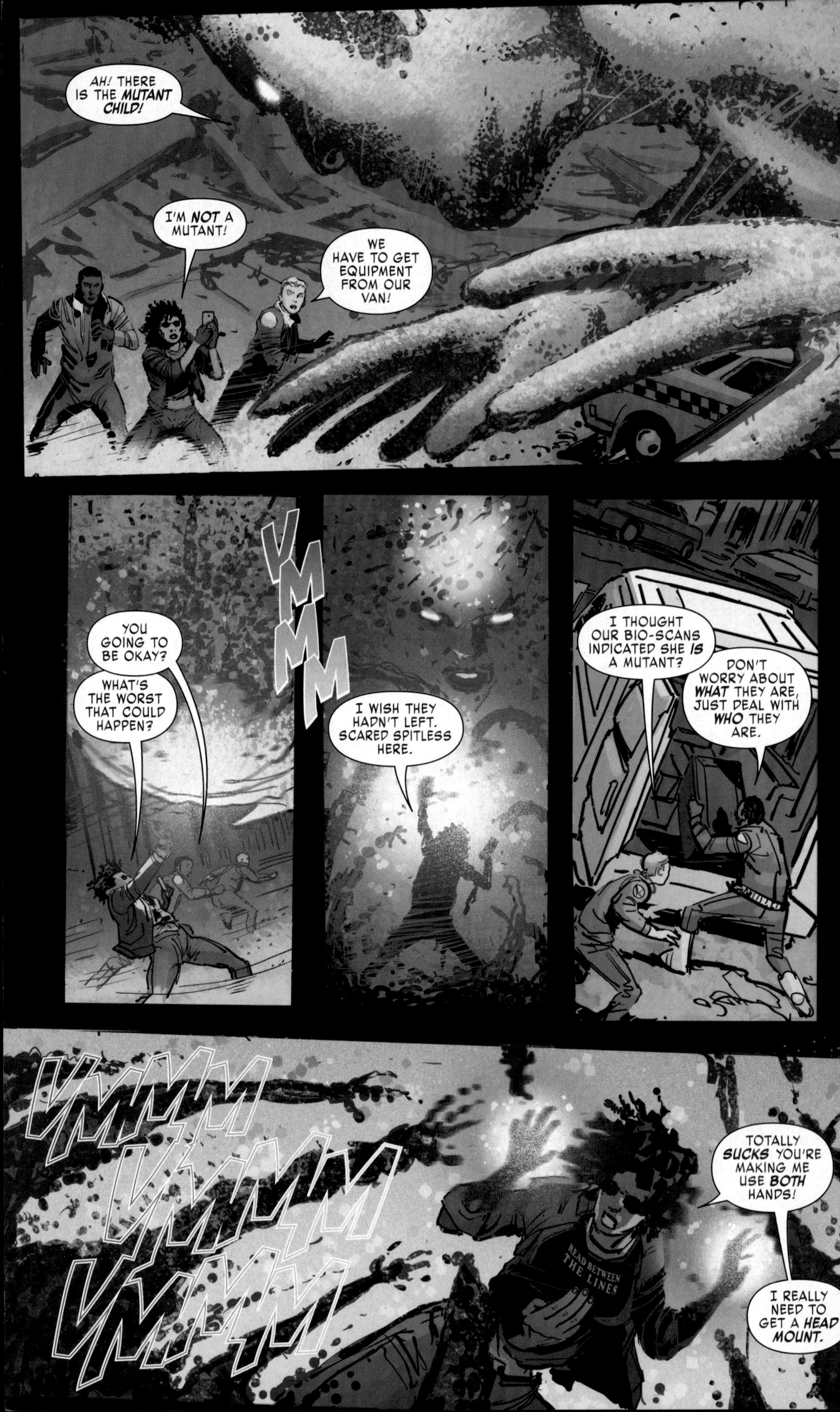
AH! THERE IS THE MUTANT CHILD!
I'M NOT A MUTANT!
WE HAVE TO GET EQUIPMENT FROM OUR VAN!
VMMM
YOU GOING TO BE OKAY?
WHAT'S THE WORST THAT COULD HAPPEN?
I WISH THEY HADN'T LEFT. SCARED SPITLESS HERE.
I THOUGHT OUR BIO-SCANS INDICATED SHE IS A MUTANT?
DON'T WORRY ABOUT WHAT THEY ARE, JUST DEAL WITH WHO THEY ARE.
VMMM
VMMM
VMMM
TOTALLY SUCKS YOU'RE MAKING ME USE BOTH HANDS!
I REALLY NEED TO GET A HEAD MOUNT.
READ BETWEEN THE LINES

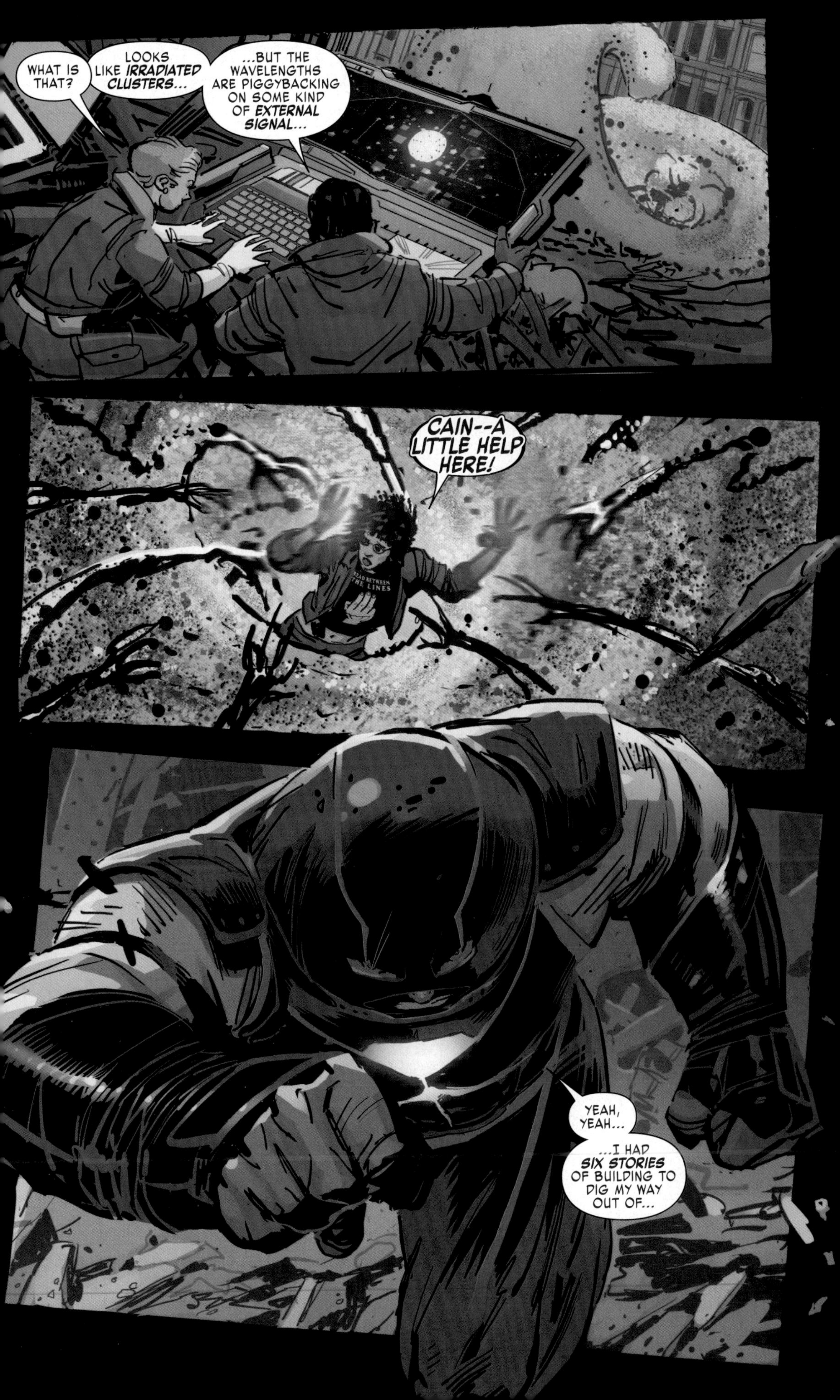
WHAT IS THAT?
LOOKS LIKE IRRADIATED CLUSTERS...
...BUT THE WAVELENGTHS ARE PIGGYBACKING ON SOME KIND OF EXTERNAL SIGNAL...
CAIN--A LITTLE HELP HERE!
READ BETWEEN THE LINES
YEAH, YEAH...
...I HAD SIX STORIES OF BUILDING TO DIG MY WAY OUT OF...

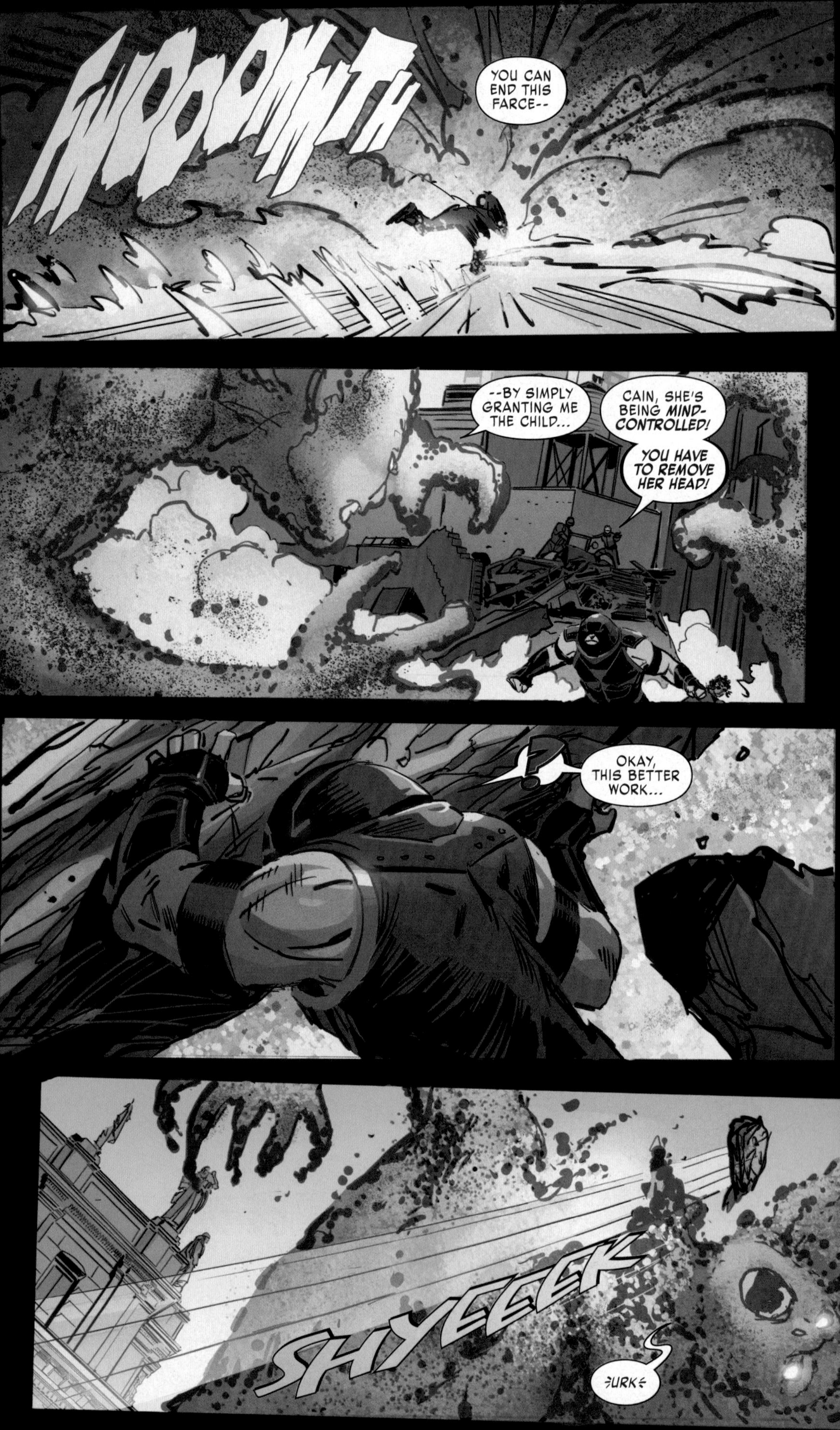
FWOOOMMTH
YOU CAN END THIS FARCE--
--BY SIMPLY GRANTING ME THE CHILD...
CAIN, SHE'S BEING MIND-CONTROLLED!
YOU HAVE TO REMOVE HER HEAD!
?
OKAY, THIS BETTER WORK...
SHYEEEK
URK

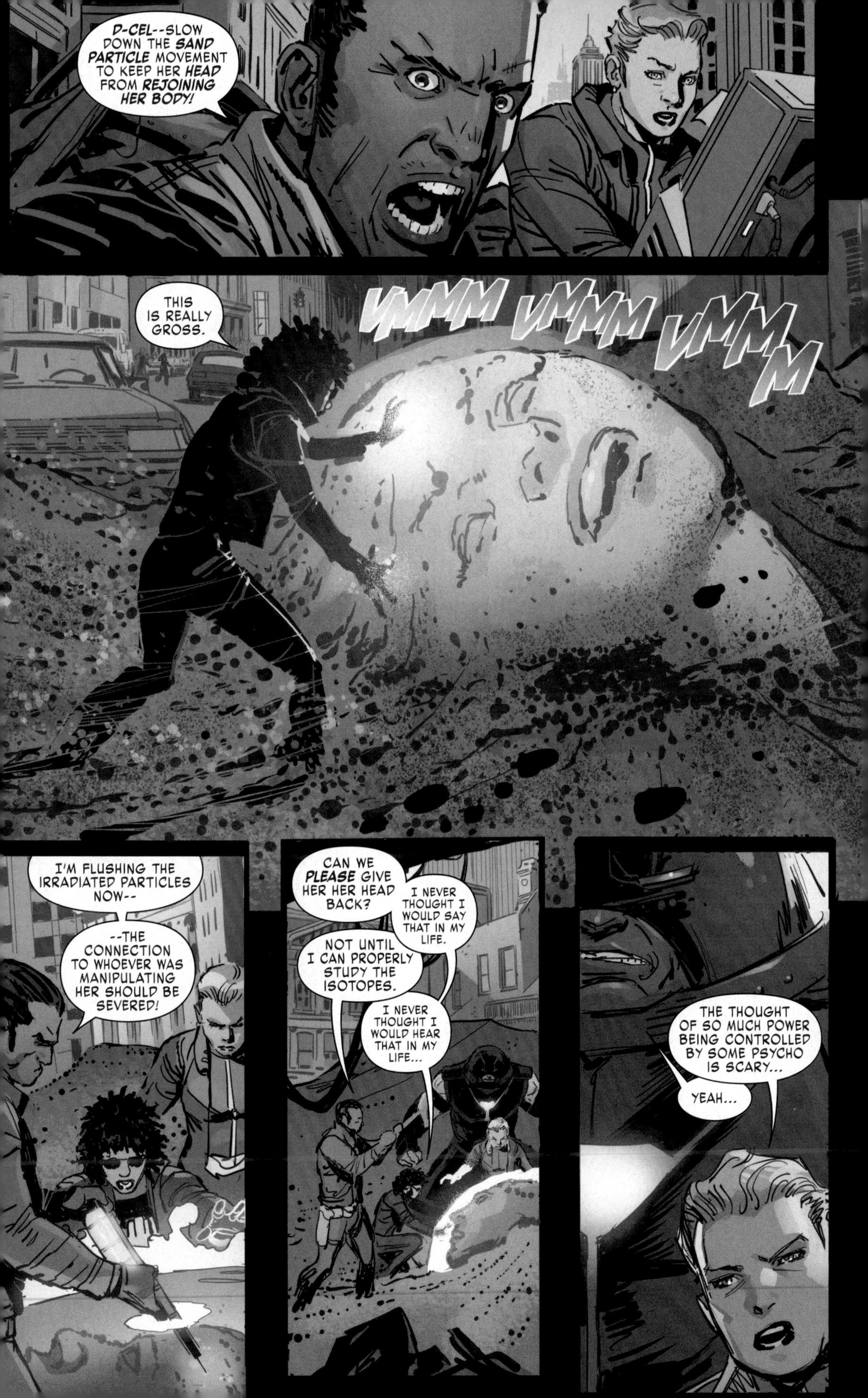
D-CEL--SLOW DOWN THE SAND PARTICLE MOVEMENT TO KEEP HER HEAD FROM REJOINING HER BODY!
THIS IS REALLY GROSS.
VMMM VMMM VMMM
I'M FLUSHING THE IRRADIATED PARTICLES NOW--
--THE CONNECTION TO WHOEVER WAS MANIPULATING HER SHOULD BE SEVERED!
CAN WE PLEASE GIVE HER HER HEAD BACK?
I NEVER THOUGHT I WOULD SAY THAT IN MY LIFE.
NOT UNTIL I CAN PROPERLY STUDY THE ISOTOPES.
I NEVER THOUGHT I WOULD HEAR THAT IN MY LIFE...
THE THOUGHT OF SO MUCH POWER BEING CONTROLLED BY SOME PSYCHO IS SCARY...
YEAH...

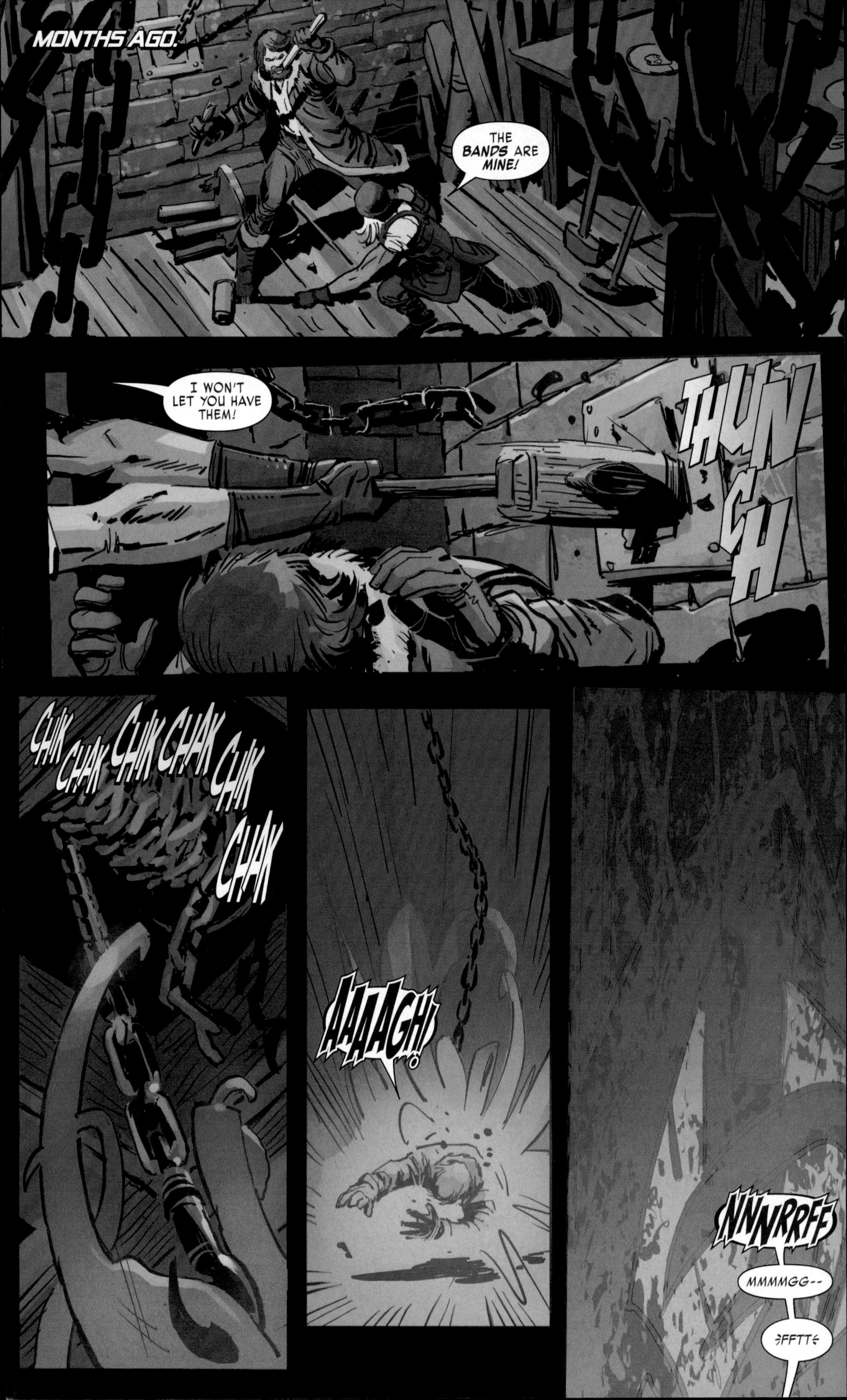
MONTHS AGO.
THE BANDS ARE MINE!
I WON'T LET YOU HAVE THEM!
THUNCH
CHIK CHAK CHIK CHAK CHIK CHAK
AAAAGH!
NNNRRFF
MMMMGG--
FFTT

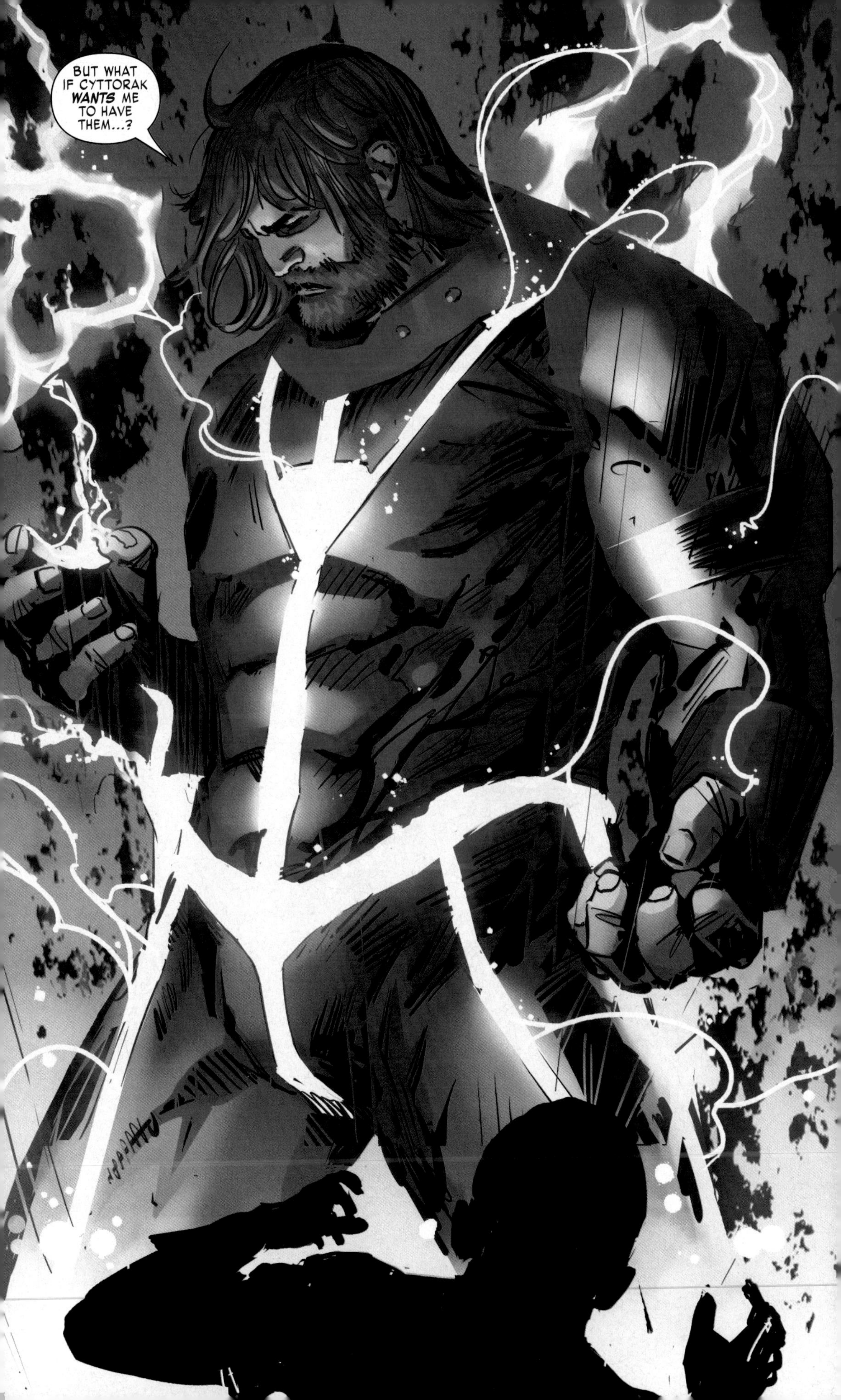
BUT WHAT IF CYTTORAK **WANTS** ME TO HAVE THEM...?

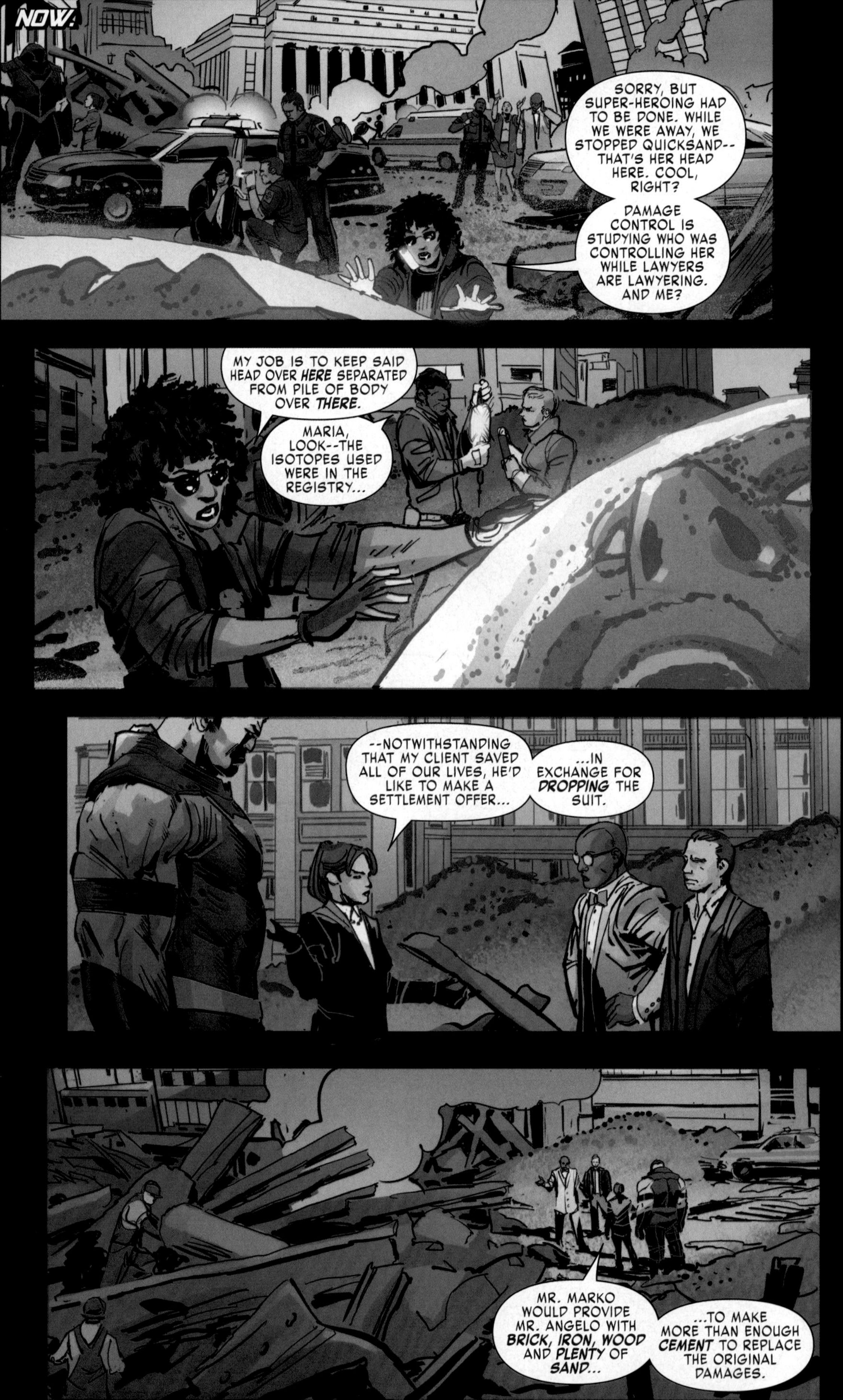
NOW:
SORRY, BUT SUPER-HEROING HAD TO BE DONE. WHILE WE WERE AWAY, WE STOPPED QUICKSAND--THAT'S HER HEAD HERE. COOL, RIGHT?
DAMAGE CONTROL IS STUDYING WHO WAS CONTROLLING HER WHILE LAWYERS ARE LAWYERING. AND ME?
MY JOB IS TO KEEP SAID HEAD OVER *HERE* SEPARATED FROM PILE OF BODY OVER *THERE.*
MARIA, LOOK--THE ISOTOPES USED WERE IN THE REGISTRY...
--NOTWITHSTANDING THAT MY CLIENT SAVED ALL OF OUR LIVES, HE'D LIKE TO MAKE A SETTLEMENT OFFER...
...IN EXCHANGE FOR *DROPPING* THE SUIT.
MR. MARKO WOULD PROVIDE MR. ANGELO WITH *BRICK, IRON, WOOD* AND *PLENTY* OF *SAND...*
...TO MAKE MORE THAN ENOUGH *CEMENT* TO REPLACE THE ORIGINAL DAMAGES.

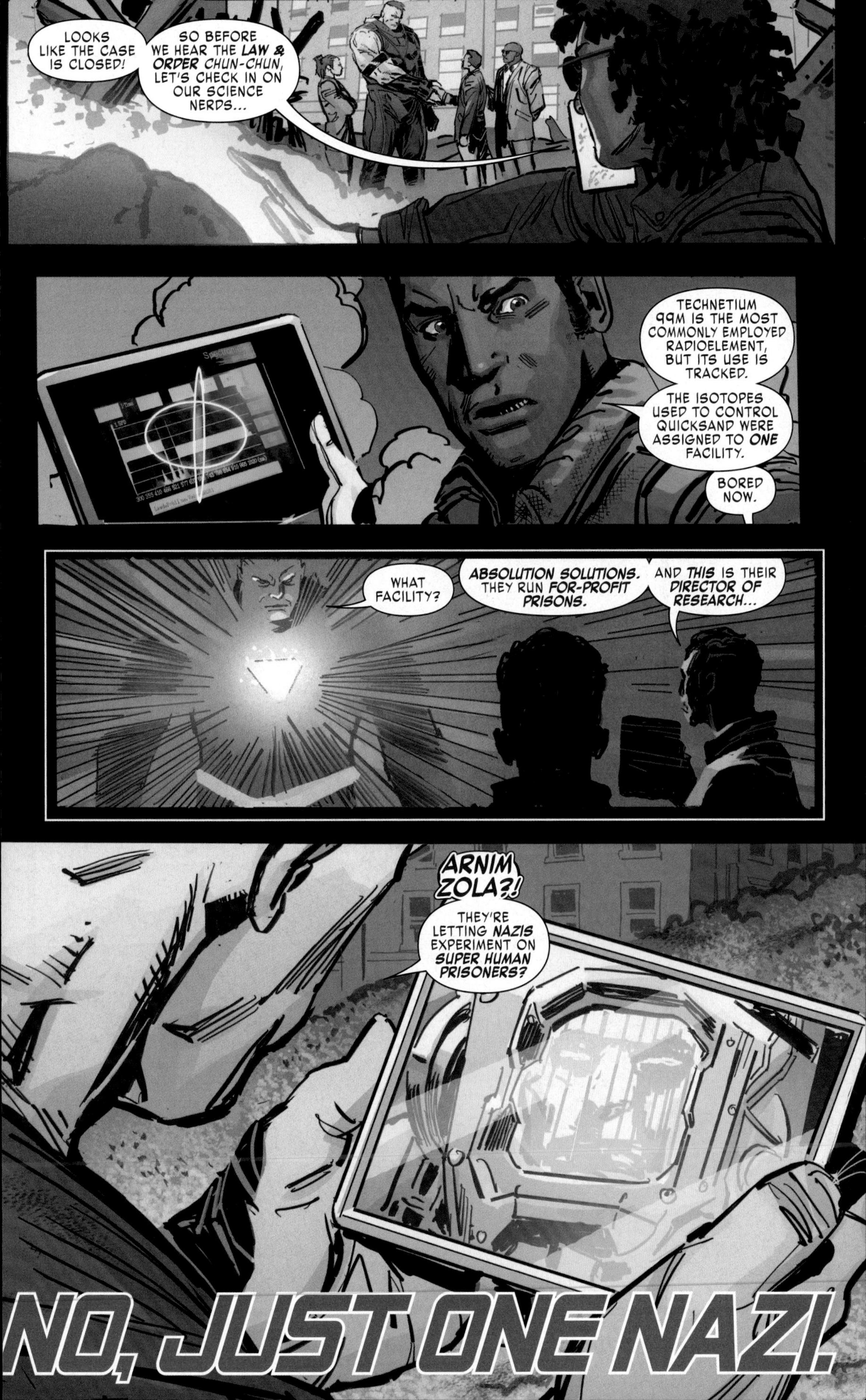
LOOKS LIKE THE CASE IS CLOSED!
SO BEFORE WE HEAR THE LAW & ORDER CHUN-CHUN, LET'S CHECK IN ON OUR SCIENCE NERDS...
TECHNETIUM 99M IS THE MOST COMMONLY EMPLOYED RADIOELEMENT, BUT ITS USE IS TRACKED.
THE ISOTOPES USED TO CONTROL QUICKSAND WERE ASSIGNED TO ONE FACILITY.
BORED NOW.
WHAT FACILITY?
ABSOLUTION SOLUTIONS. THEY RUN FOR-PROFIT PRISONS.
AND THIS IS THEIR DIRECTOR OF RESEARCH...
ARNIM ZOLA?!
THEY'RE LETTING NAZIS EXPERIMENT ON SUPER HUMAN PRISONERS?
NO, JUST ONE NAZI.

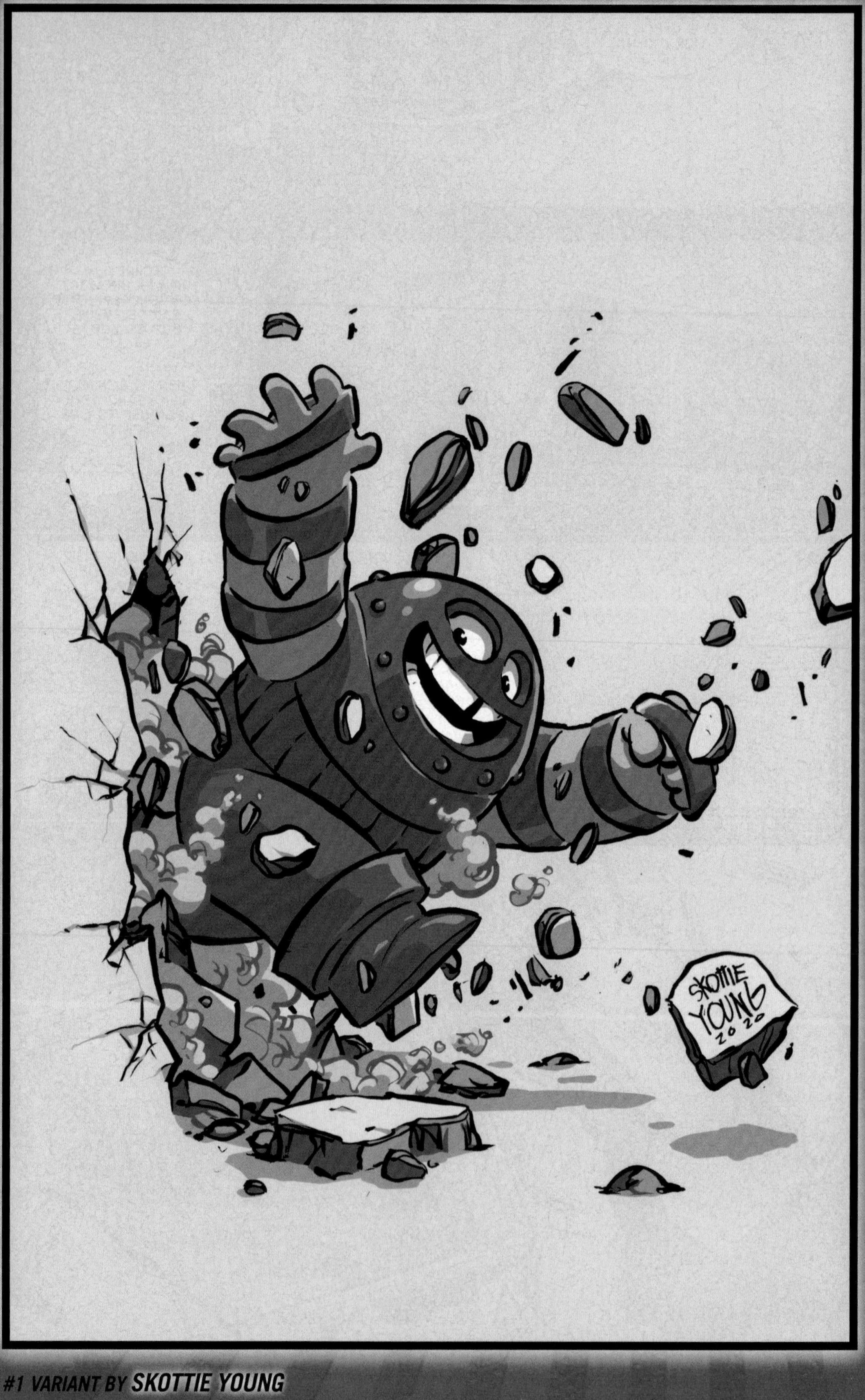
SKOTTIE YOUNG 2020
#1 VARIANT BY **SKOTTIE YOUNG**

4

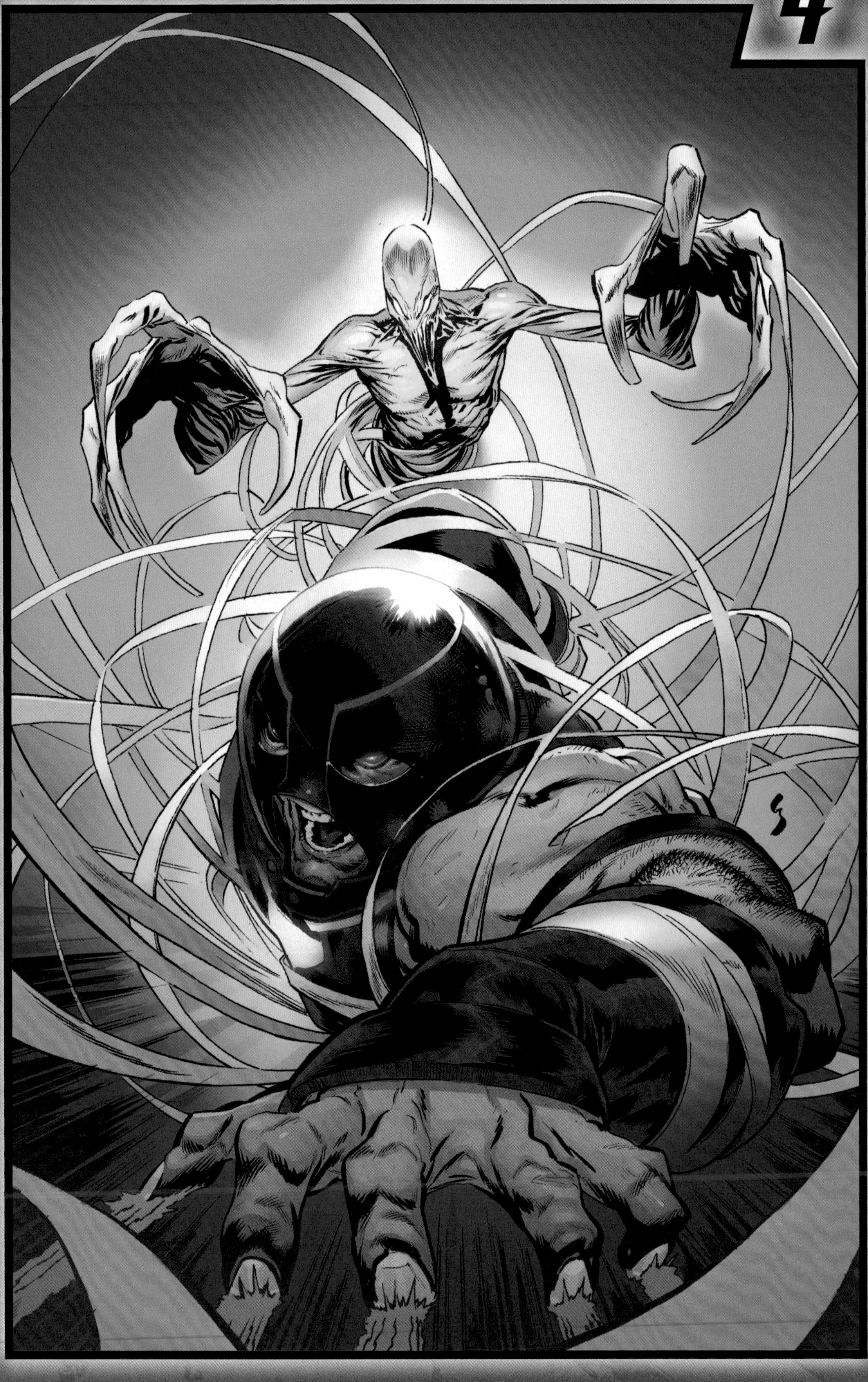

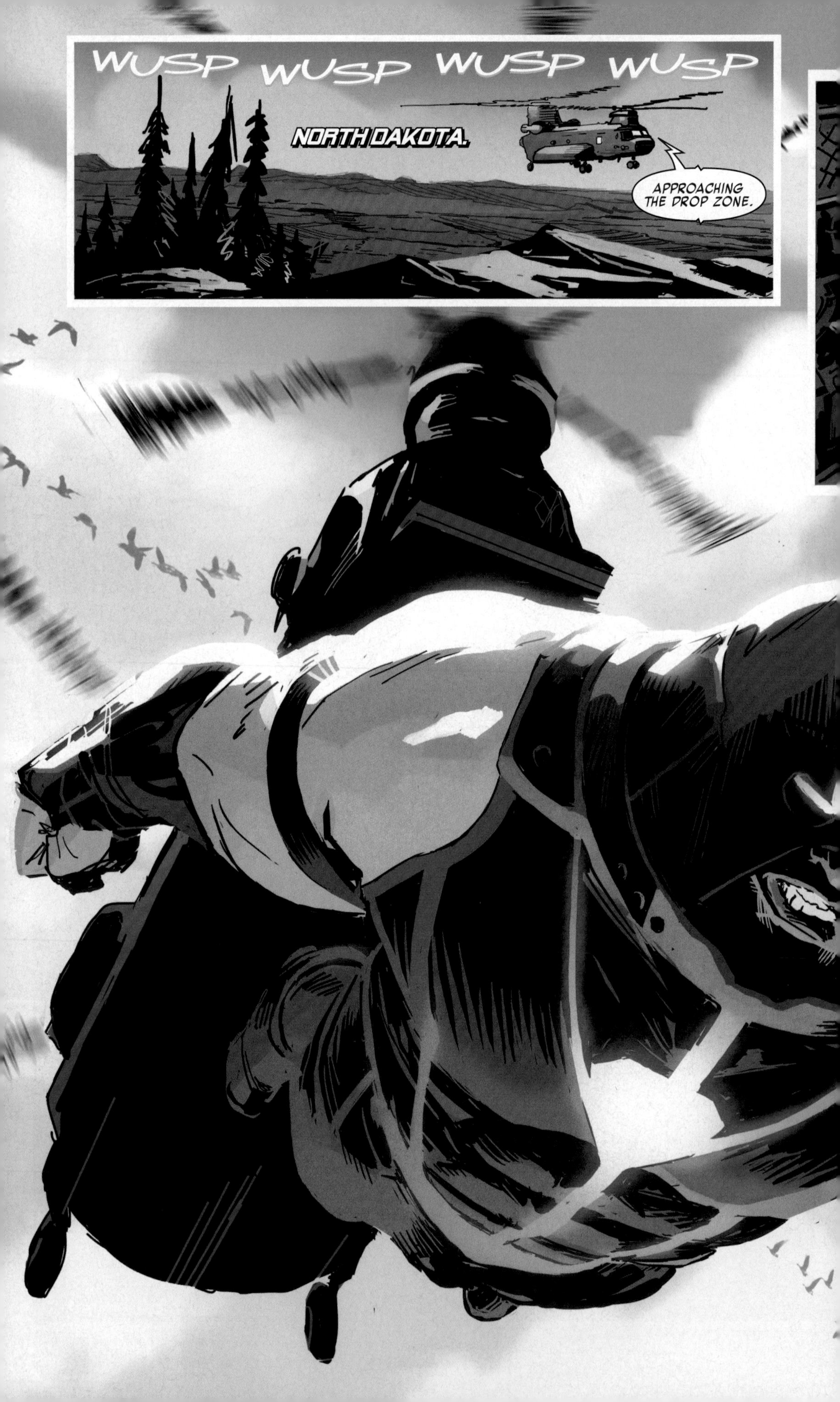
WUSP WUSP WUSP WUSP
NORTH DAKOTA.
APPROACHING THE DROP ZONE.

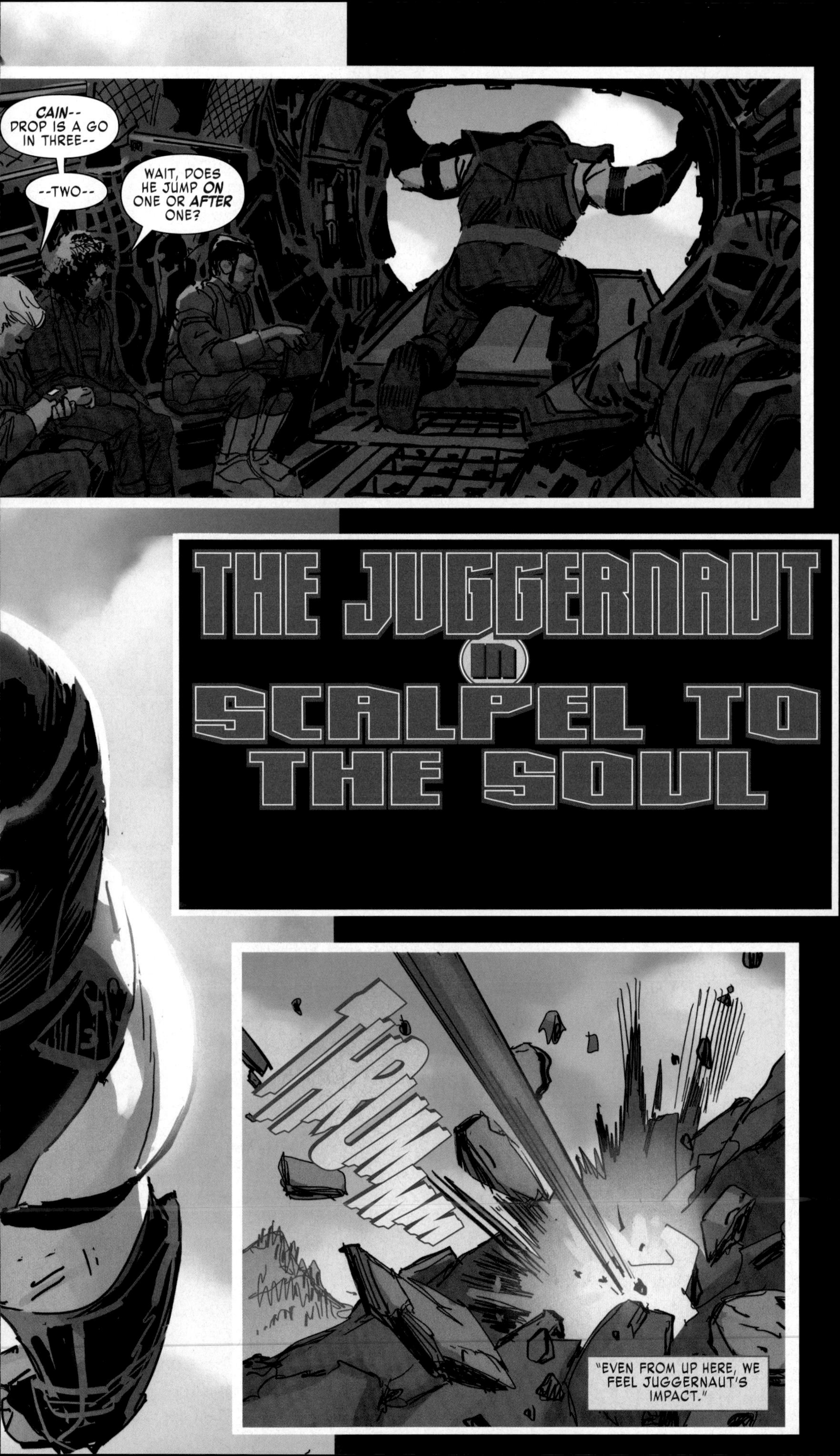

CAIN-- DROP IS A GO IN THREE--
--TWO--
WAIT, DOES HE JUMP ON ONE OR AFTER ONE?
THE JUGGERNAUT
IN
SCALPEL TO THE SOUL
THROOM
"EVEN FROM UP HERE, WE FEEL JUGGERNAUT'S IMPACT."

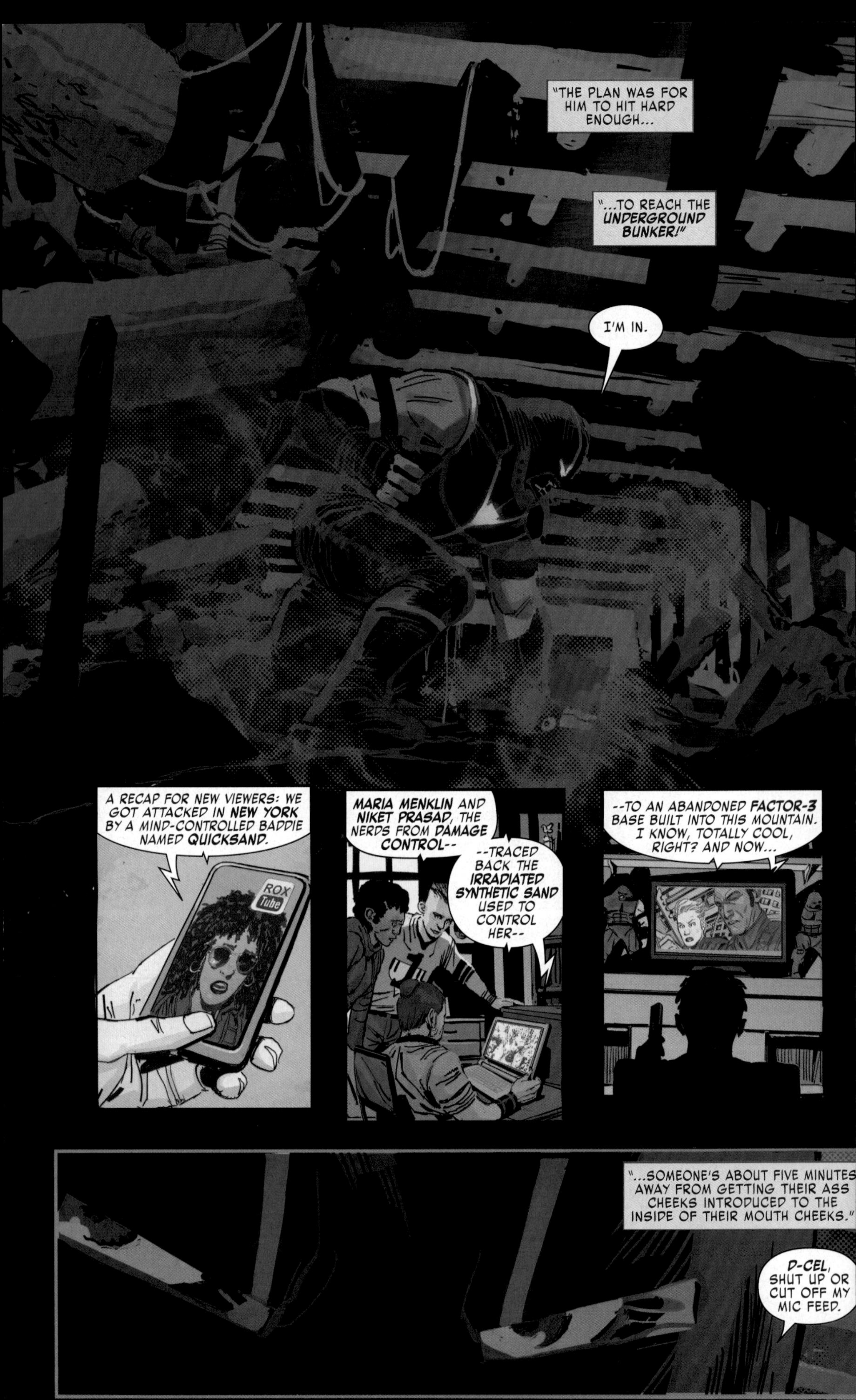
"THE PLAN WAS FOR HIM TO HIT HARD ENOUGH...
"...TO REACH THE UNDERGROUND BUNKER!"
I'M IN.
A RECAP FOR NEW VIEWERS: WE GOT ATTACKED IN NEW YORK BY A MIND-CONTROLLED BADDIE NAMED QUICKSAND.
ROX Tube
MARIA MENKLIN AND NIKET PRASAD, THE NERDS FROM DAMAGE CONTROL--
--TRACED BACK THE IRRADIATED SYNTHETIC SAND USED TO CONTROL HER--
--TO AN ABANDONED FACTOR-3 BASE BUILT INTO THIS MOUNTAIN. I KNOW, TOTALLY COOL, RIGHT? AND NOW...
"...SOMEONE'S ABOUT FIVE MINUTES AWAY FROM GETTING THEIR ASS CHEEKS INTRODUCED TO THE INSIDE OF THEIR MOUTH CHEEKS."
D-CEL, SHUT UP OR CUT OFF MY MIC FEED.

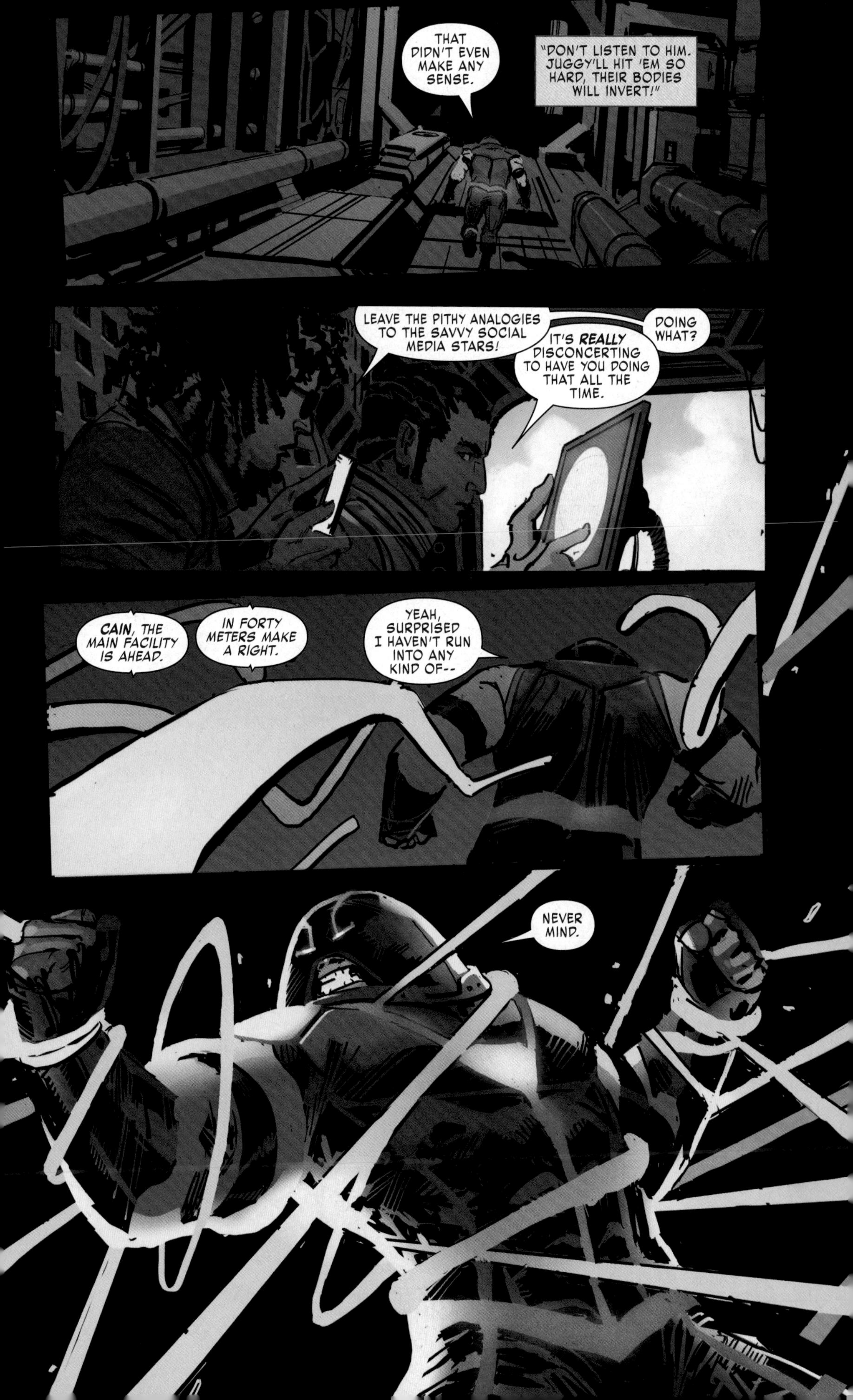
THAT DIDN'T EVEN MAKE ANY SENSE.
"DON'T LISTEN TO HIM. JUGGY'LL HIT 'EM SO HARD, THEIR BODIES WILL INVERT!"
LEAVE THE PITHY ANALOGIES TO THE SAVVY SOCIAL MEDIA STARS!
IT'S REALLY DISCONCERTING TO HAVE YOU DOING THAT ALL THE TIME.
DOING WHAT?
CAIN, THE MAIN FACILITY IS AHEAD.
IN FORTY METERS MAKE A RIGHT.
YEAH, SURPRISED I HAVEN'T RUN INTO ANY KIND OF--
NEVER MIND.

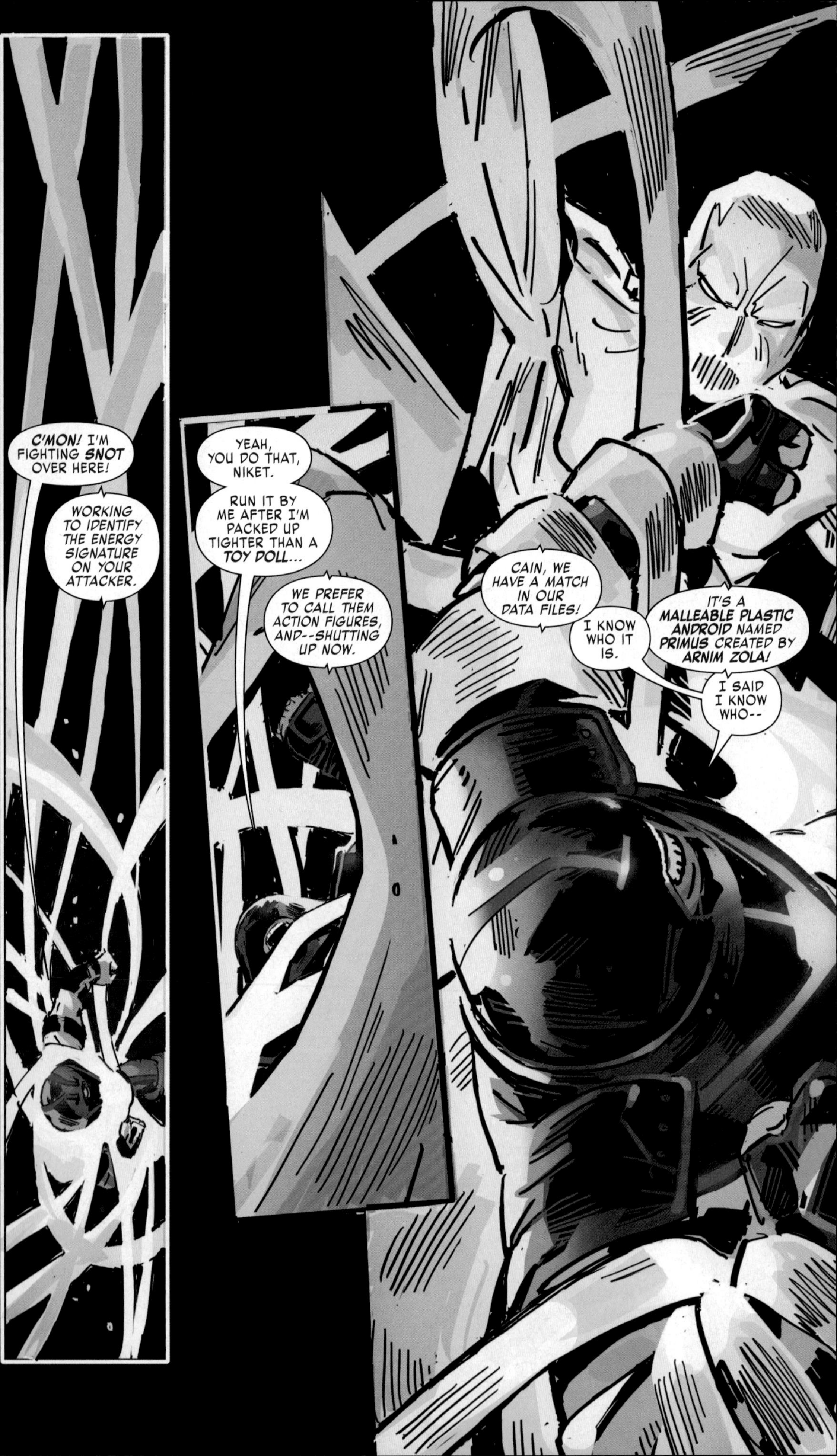

C'MON! I'M FIGHTING SNOT OVER HERE!
WORKING TO IDENTIFY THE ENERGY SIGNATURE ON YOUR ATTACKER.
YEAH, YOU DO THAT, NIKET.
RUN IT BY ME AFTER I'M PACKED UP TIGHTER THAN A TOY DOLL...
WE PREFER TO CALL THEM ACTION FIGURES, AND--SHUTTING UP NOW.
CAIN, WE HAVE A MATCH IN OUR DATA FILES!
I KNOW WHO IT IS.
IT'S A MALLEABLE PLASTIC ANDROID NAMED PRIMUS CREATED BY ARNIM ZOLA!
I SAID I KNOW WHO--

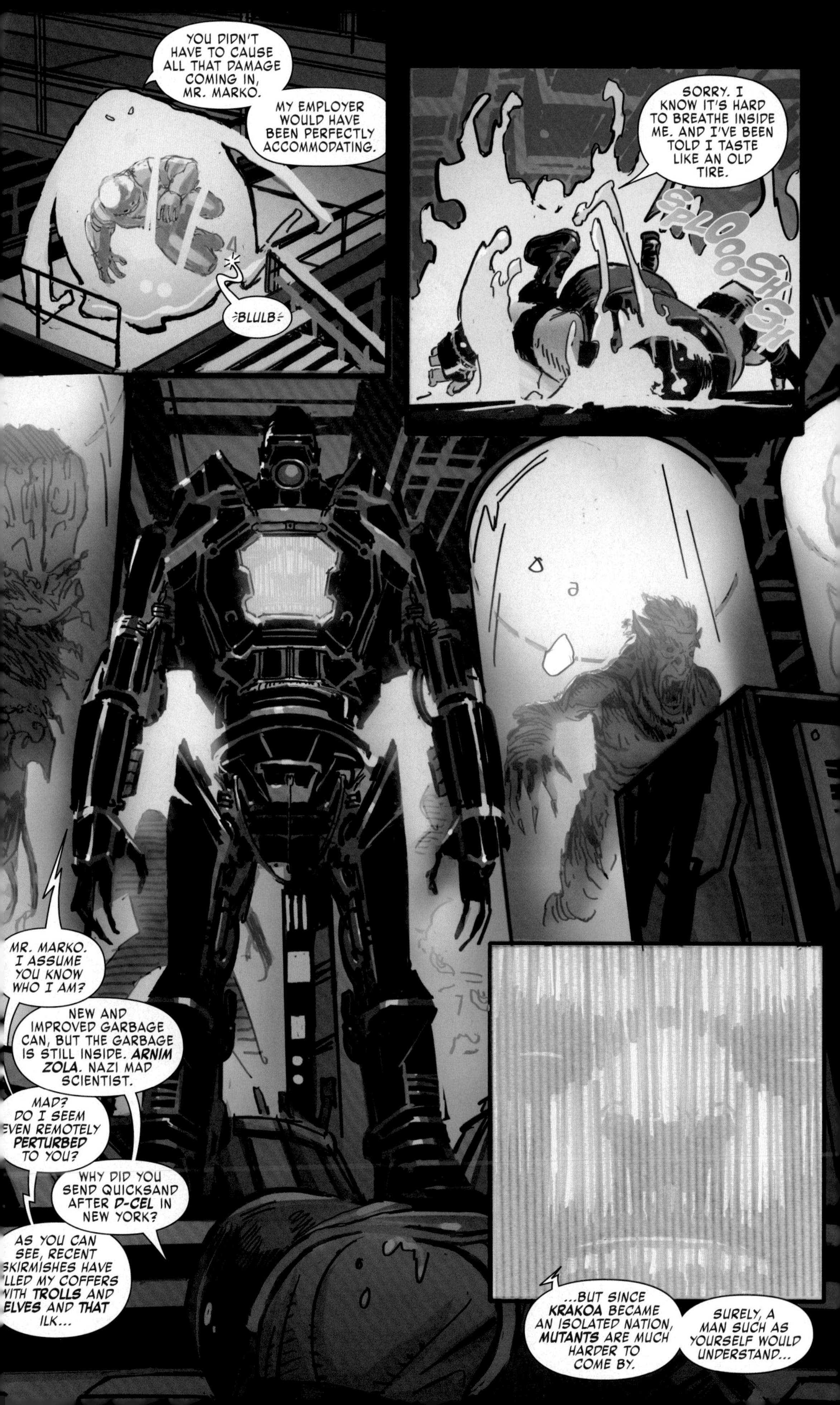

YOU DIDN'T HAVE TO CAUSE ALL THAT DAMAGE COMING IN, MR. MARKO.
MY EMPLOYER WOULD HAVE BEEN PERFECTLY ACCOMMODATING.
BLULB
SORRY. I KNOW IT'S HARD TO BREATHE INSIDE ME. AND I'VE BEEN TOLD I TASTE LIKE AN OLD TIRE.
SPLOOOSHSH
MR. MARKO. I ASSUME YOU KNOW WHO I AM?
NEW AND IMPROVED GARBAGE CAN, BUT THE GARBAGE IS STILL INSIDE. ARNIM ZOLA. NAZI MAD SCIENTIST.
MAD? DO I SEEM EVEN REMOTELY PERTURBED TO YOU?
WHY DID YOU SEND QUICKSAND AFTER D-CEL IN NEW YORK?
AS YOU CAN SEE, RECENT SKIRMISHES HAVE FILLED MY COFFERS WITH TROLLS AND ELVES AND THAT ILK...
...BUT SINCE KRAKOA BECAME AN ISOLATED NATION, MUTANTS ARE MUCH HARDER TO COME BY.
SURELY, A MAN SUCH AS YOURSELF WOULD UNDERSTAND...

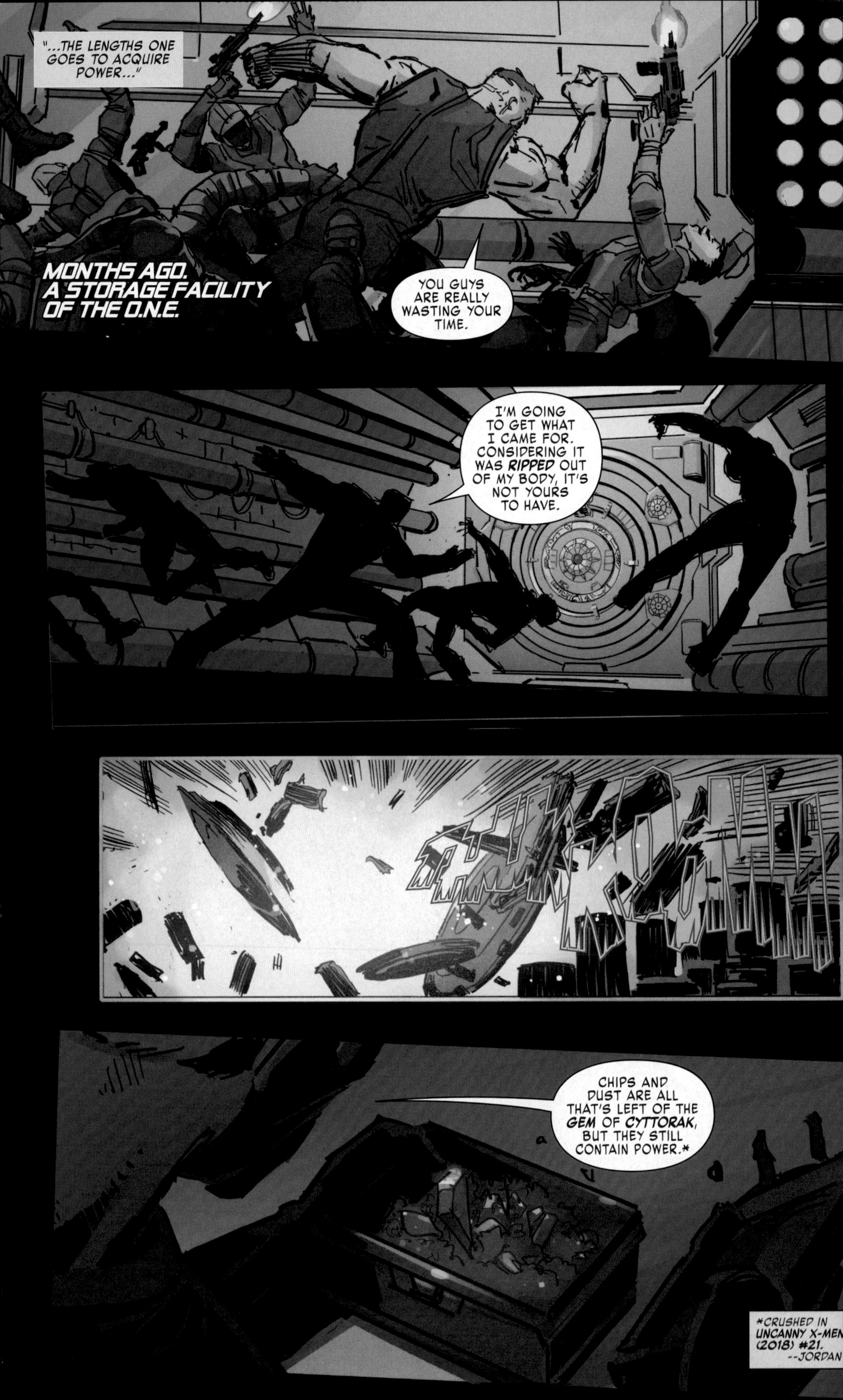

"...THE LENGTHS ONE GOES TO ACQUIRE POWER..."
MONTHS AGO. A STORAGE FACILITY OF THE O.N.E.
YOU GUYS ARE REALLY WASTING YOUR TIME.
I'M GOING TO GET WHAT I CAME FOR. CONSIDERING IT WAS RIPPED OUT OF MY BODY, IT'S NOT YOURS TO HAVE.
CHIPS AND DUST ARE ALL THAT'S LEFT OF THE GEM OF CYTTORAK, BUT THEY STILL CONTAIN POWER.*
*CRUSHED IN UNCANNY X-MEN (2018) #21. --JORDAN

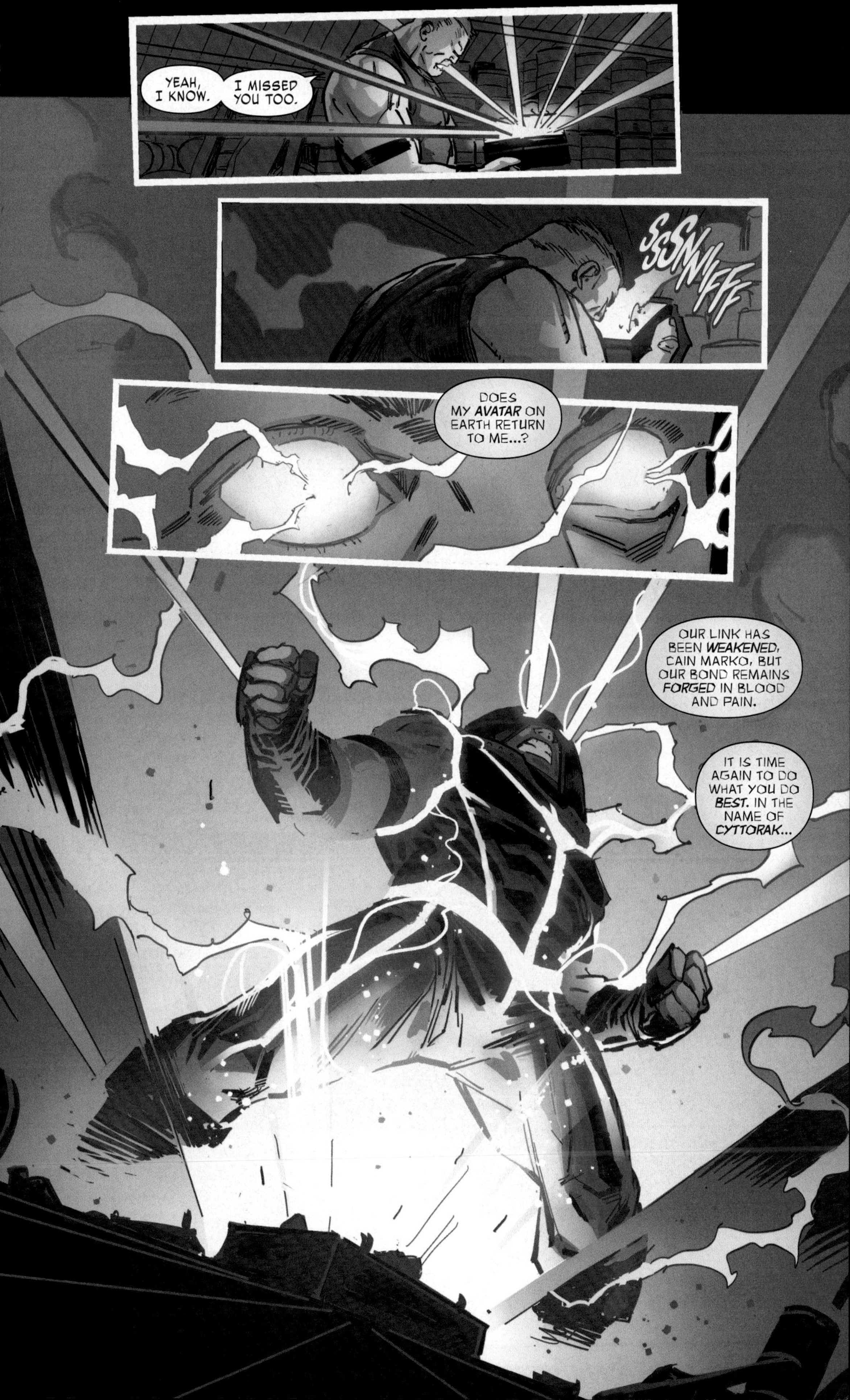
YEAH, I KNOW.
I MISSED YOU TOO.
SSSNIFFF
DOES MY AVATAR ON EARTH RETURN TO ME...?
OUR LINK HAS BEEN WEAKENED, CAIN MARKO, BUT OUR BOND REMAINS FORGED IN BLOOD AND PAIN.
IT IS TIME AGAIN TO DO WHAT YOU DO BEST. IN THE NAME OF CYTTORAK...

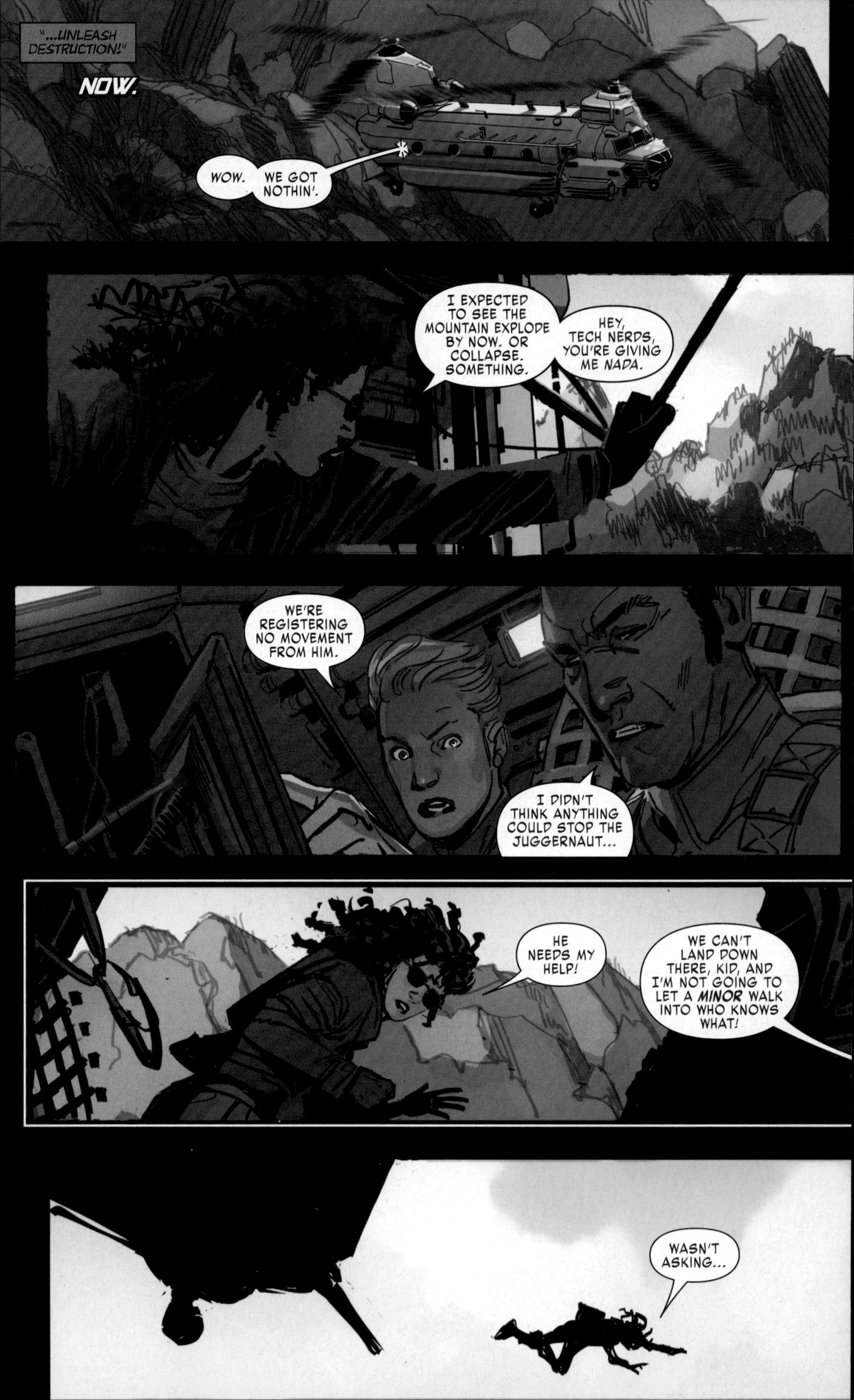
"...UNLEASH DESTRUCTION!"
NOW.
WOW.
WE GOT NOTHIN'.
I EXPECTED TO SEE THE MOUNTAIN EXPLODE BY NOW. OR COLLAPSE. SOMETHING.
HEY, TECH NERDS, YOU'RE GIVING ME NADA.
WE'RE REGISTERING NO MOVEMENT FROM HIM.
I DIDN'T THINK ANYTHING COULD STOP THE JUGGERNAUT...
HE NEEDS MY HELP!
WE CAN'T LAND DOWN THERE, KID, AND I'M NOT GOING TO LET A MINOR WALK INTO WHO KNOWS WHAT!
WASN'T ASKING...

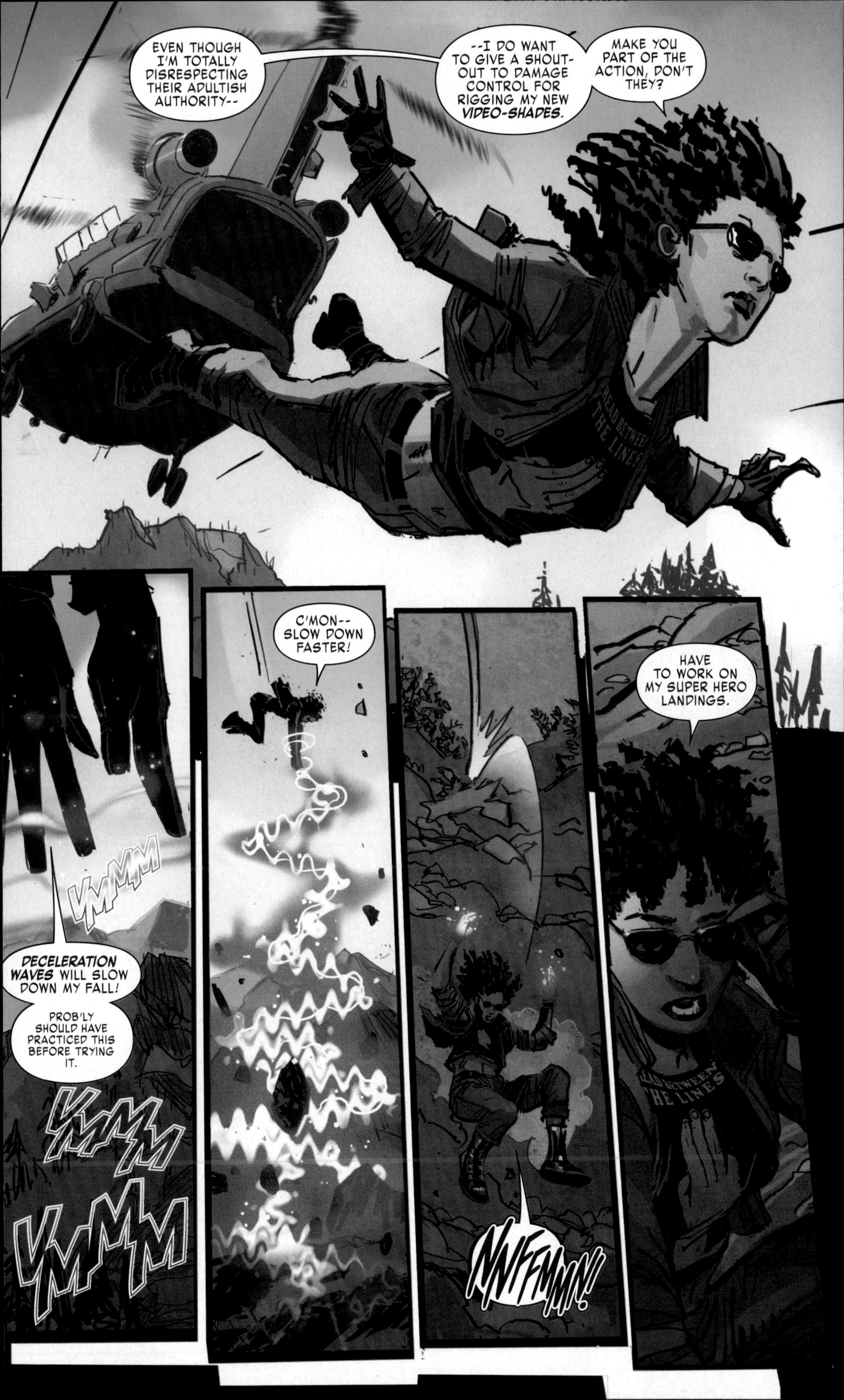

EVEN THOUGH I'M TOTALLY DISRESPECTING THEIR ADULTISH AUTHORITY--
--I DO WANT TO GIVE A SHOUT-OUT TO DAMAGE CONTROL FOR RIGGING MY NEW VIDEO-SHADES.
MAKE YOU PART OF THE ACTION, DON'T THEY?
READ BETWEEN THE LINES
VMMM
DECELERATION WAVES WILL SLOW DOWN MY FALL!
PROB'LY SHOULD HAVE PRACTICED THIS BEFORE TRYING IT.
VMMM
VMMM
C'MON-- SLOW DOWN FASTER!
NNFMMN!
HAVE TO WORK ON MY SUPER HERO LANDINGS.
READ BETWEEN THE LINES

OH, THIS IS DELICIOUS. THE CHILD COMES TO YOUR RESCUE?

I WOULD LIKE TO THANK YOU BOTH FOR MAKING THIS SO EASY.

ME TOO. I REALLY DO ABHOR CONFRONTATION.

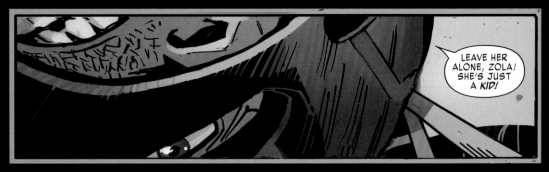

LEAVE HER ALONE, ZOLA! SHE'S JUST A KID!

SHE IS A COMMODITY, MR. MARKO.

AS IS ANYONE WITH POWER, AND INDEED, AS IS THE VERY NATURE OF POWER ITSELF.

WE BOTH KNOW THAT TO BE TRUE.

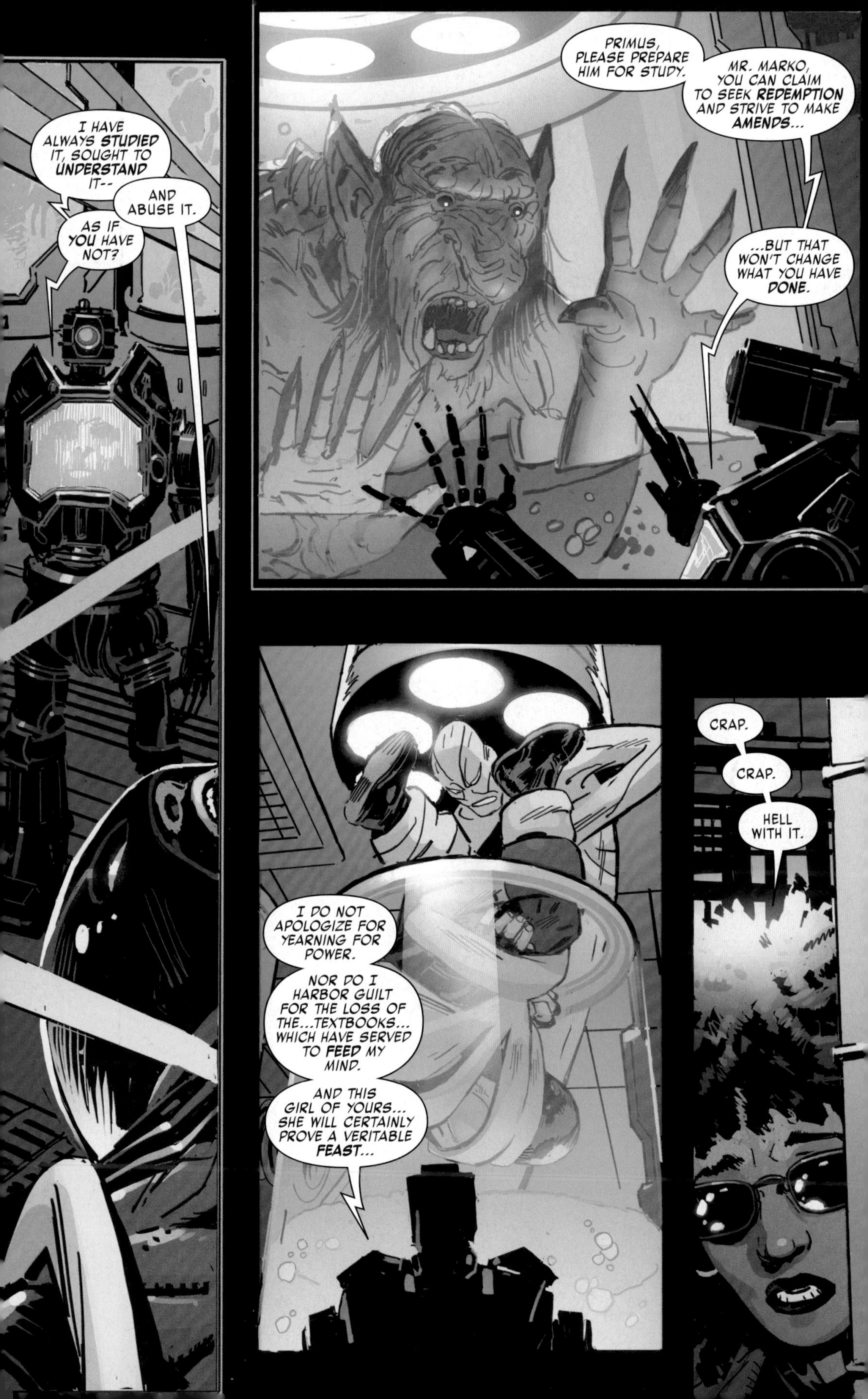
I HAVE ALWAYS STUDIED IT, SOUGHT TO UNDERSTAND IT--
AND ABUSE IT.
AS IF YOU HAVE NOT?
PRIMUS, PLEASE PREPARE HIM FOR STUDY.
MR. MARKO, YOU CAN CLAIM TO SEEK REDEMPTION AND STRIVE TO MAKE AMENDS...
...BUT THAT WON'T CHANGE WHAT YOU HAVE DONE.
I DO NOT APOLOGIZE FOR YEARNING FOR POWER.
NOR DO I HARBOR GUILT FOR THE LOSS OF THE...TEXTBOOKS... WHICH HAVE SERVED TO FEED MY MIND.
AND THIS GIRL OF YOURS... SHE WILL CERTAINLY PROVE A VERITABLE FEAST...
CRAP.
CRAP.
HELL WITH IT.

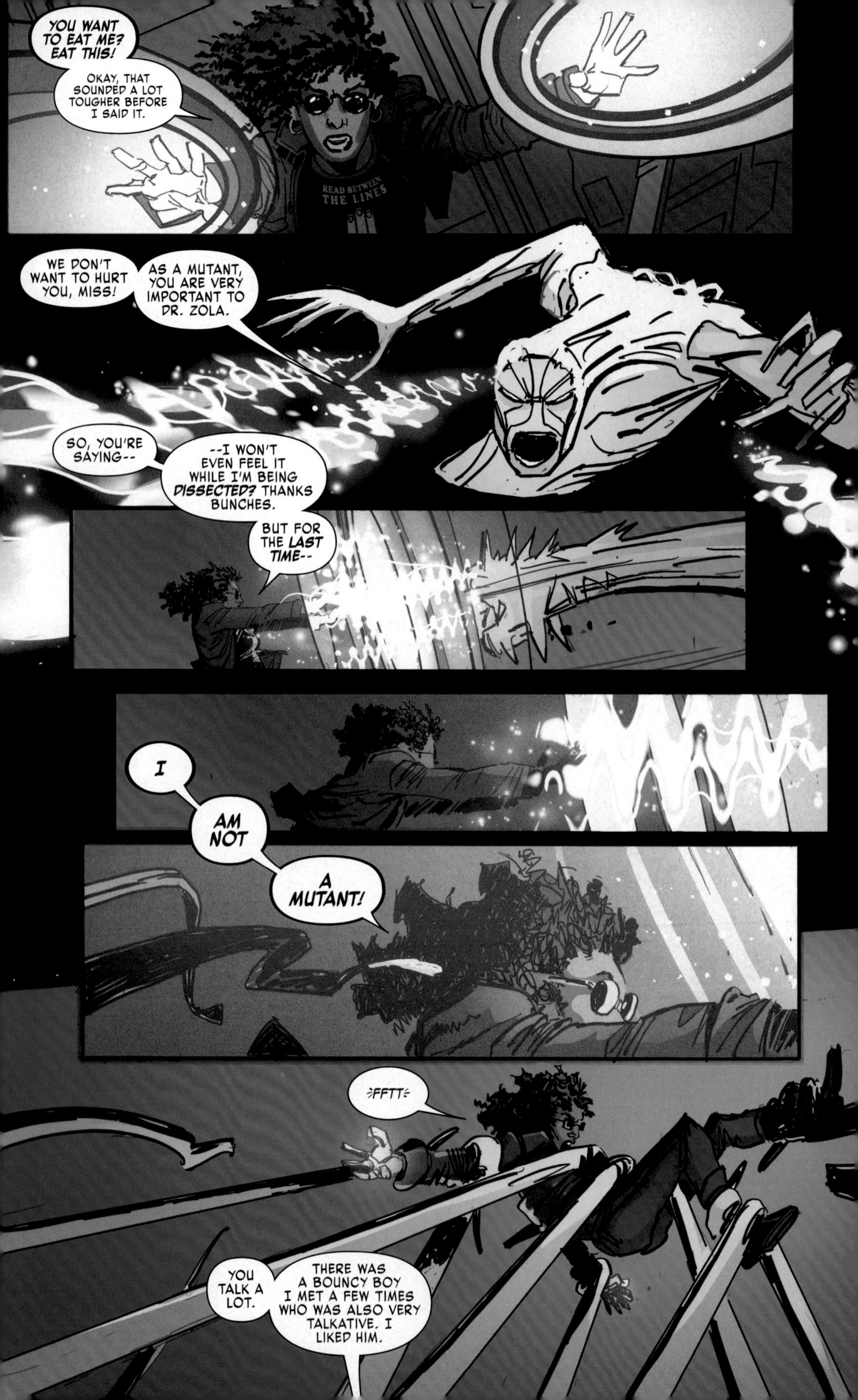
YOU WANT TO EAT ME? EAT THIS!
OKAY, THAT SOUNDED A LOT TOUGHER BEFORE I SAID IT.
READ BETWEEN THE LINES
WE DON'T WANT TO HURT YOU, MISS!
AS A MUTANT, YOU ARE VERY IMPORTANT TO DR. ZOLA.
SO, YOU'RE SAYING--
--I WON'T EVEN FEEL IT WHILE I'M BEING DISSECTED? THANKS BUNCHES.
BUT FOR THE LAST TIME--
I
AM NOT
A MUTANT!
FFTT
YOU TALK A LOT.
THERE WAS A BOUNCY BOY I MET A FEW TIMES WHO WAS ALSO VERY TALKATIVE. I LIKED HIM.

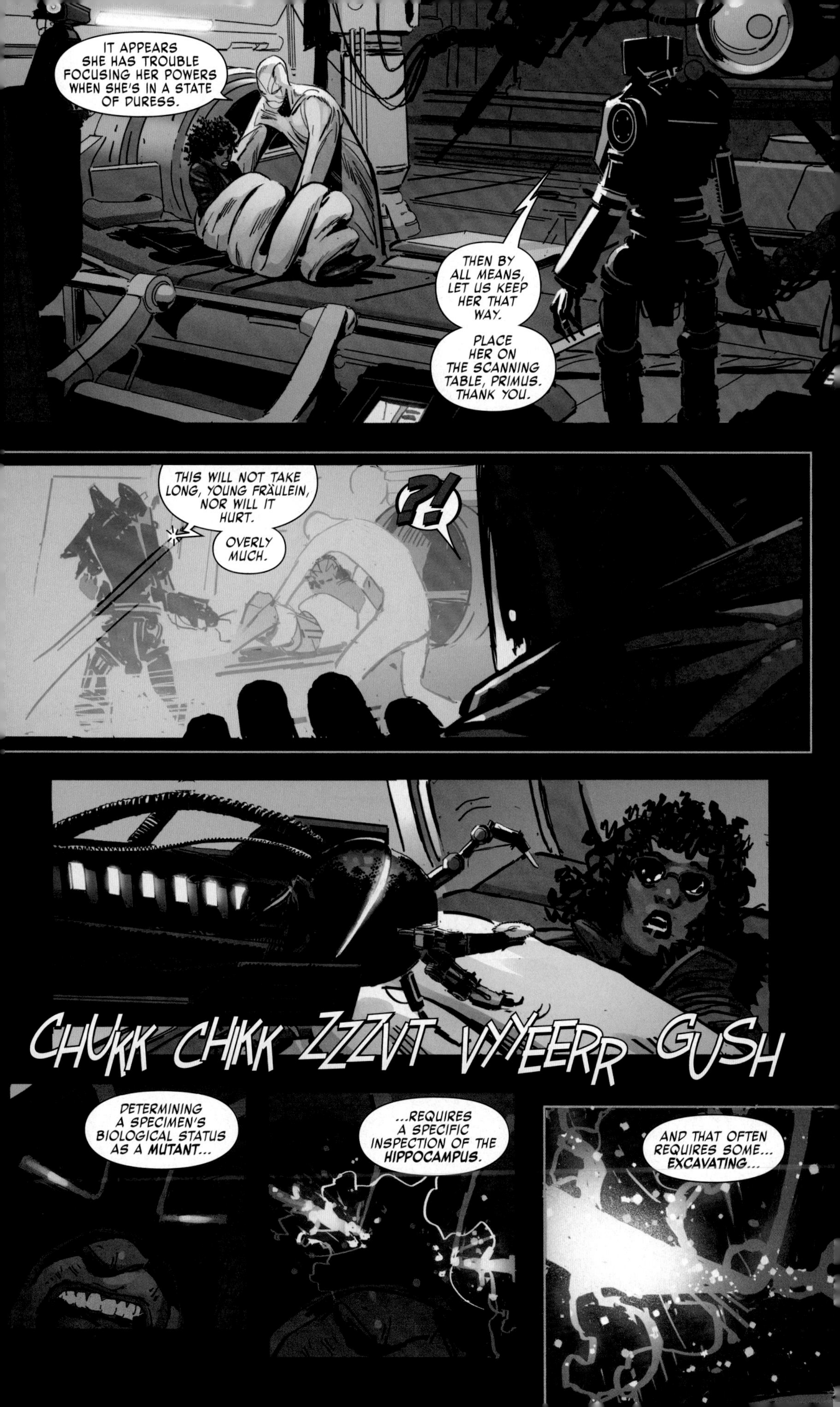
IT APPEARS SHE HAS TROUBLE FOCUSING HER POWERS WHEN SHE'S IN A STATE OF DURESS.
THEN BY ALL MEANS, LET US KEEP HER THAT WAY.
PLACE HER ON THE SCANNING TABLE, PRIMUS. THANK YOU.
THIS WILL NOT TAKE LONG, YOUNG FRÄULEIN, NOR WILL IT HURT.
OVERLY MUCH.
?!
CHUKK CHIKK ZZZVT VYYEERR GUSH
DETERMINING A SPECIMEN'S BIOLOGICAL STATUS AS A MUTANT...
...REQUIRES A SPECIFIC INSPECTION OF THE HIPPOCAMPUS.
AND THAT OFTEN REQUIRES SOME... EXCAVATING...

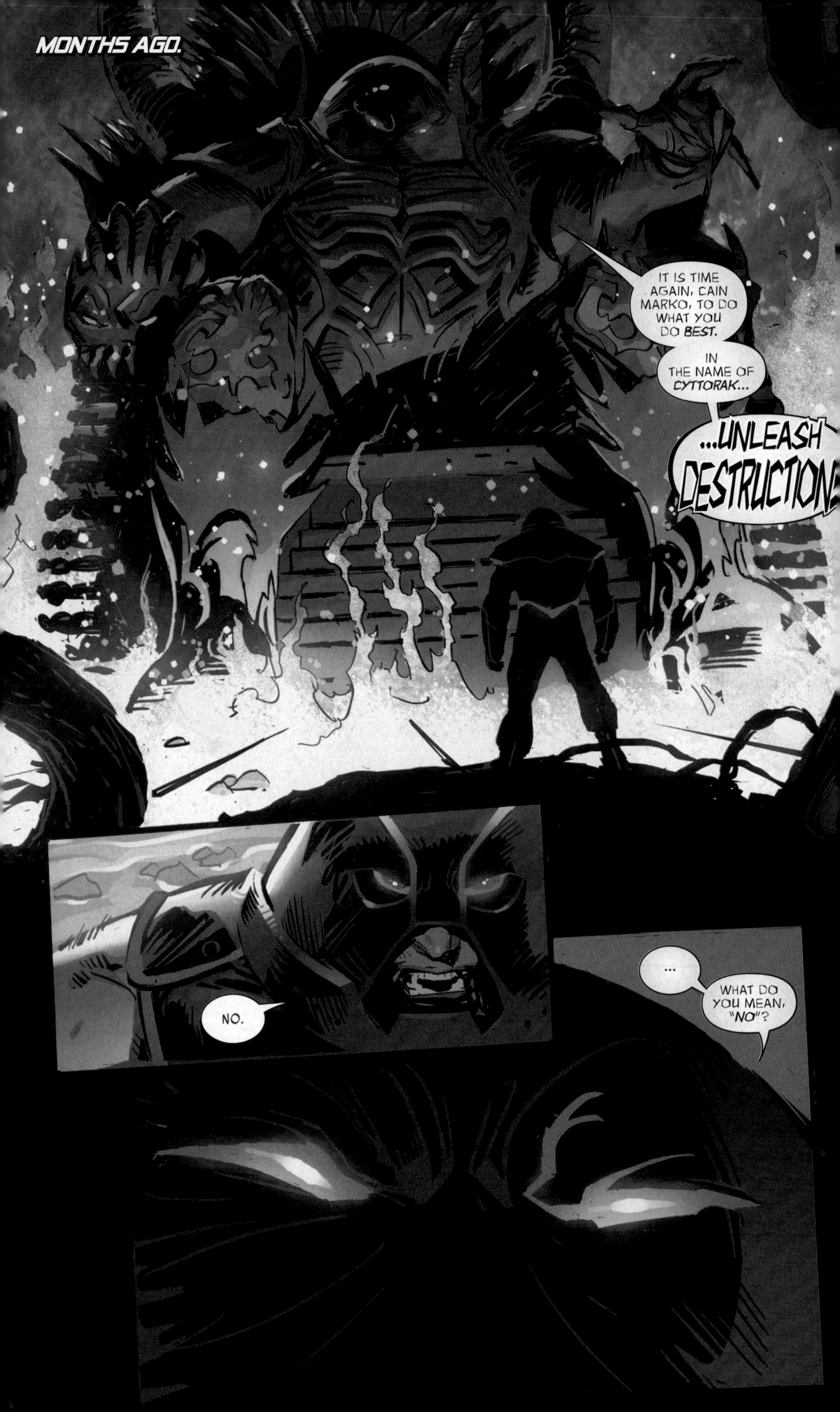
MONTHS AGO.
IT IS TIME AGAIN, CAIN MARKO, TO DO WHAT YOU DO BEST.
IN THE NAME OF CYTTORAK...
...UNLEASH DESTRUCTION!
NO.
...
WHAT DO YOU MEAN, "NO"?

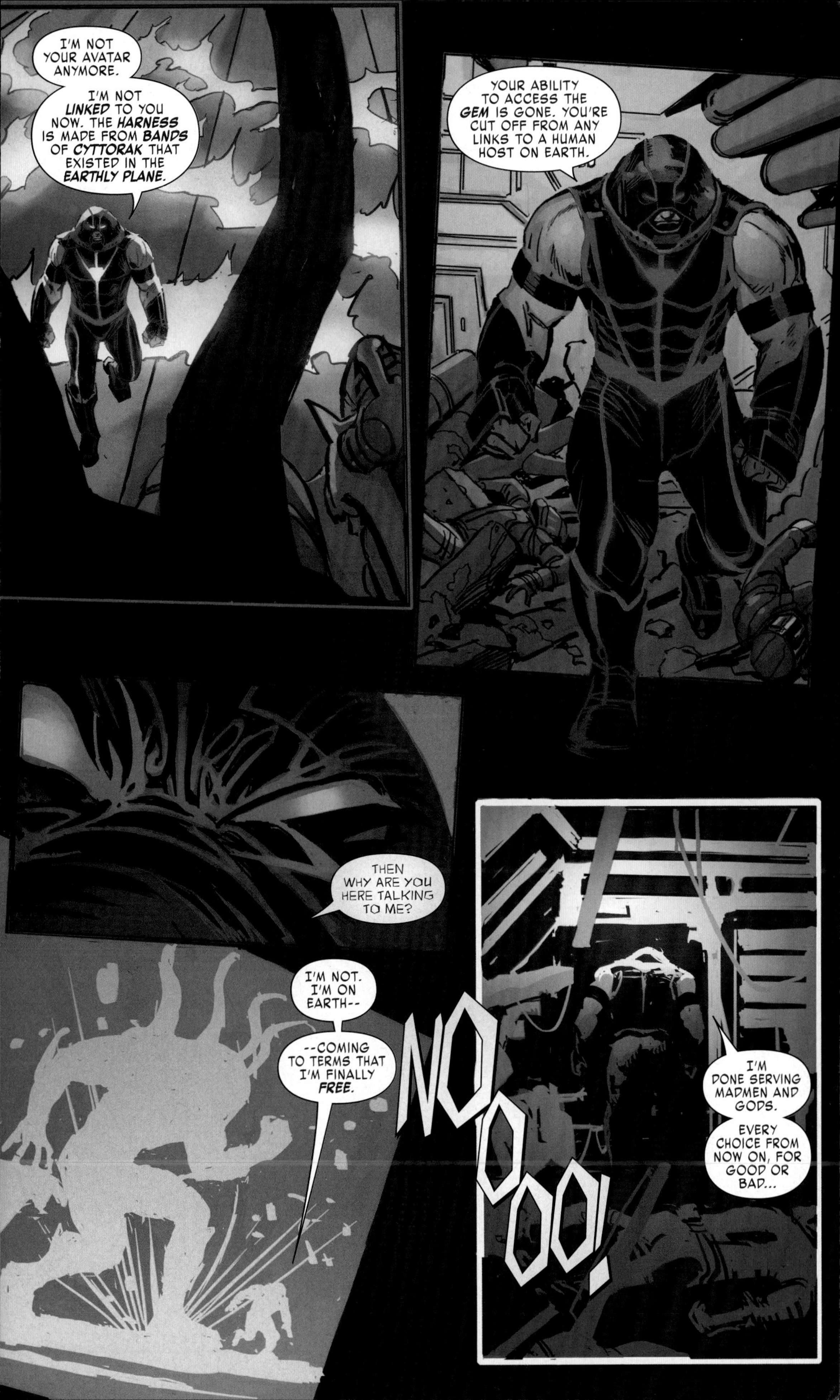
I'M NOT YOUR AVATAR ANYMORE.
I'M NOT LINKED TO YOU NOW. THE HARNESS IS MADE FROM BANDS OF CYTTORAK THAT EXISTED IN THE EARTHLY PLANE.
YOUR ABILITY TO ACCESS THE GEM IS GONE. YOU'RE CUT OFF FROM ANY LINKS TO A HUMAN HOST ON EARTH.
THEN WHY ARE YOU HERE TALKING TO ME?
I'M NOT. I'M ON EARTH--
--COMING TO TERMS THAT I'M FINALLY FREE.
NOOOOO!
I'M DONE SERVING MADMEN AND GODS.
EVERY CHOICE FROM NOW ON, FOR GOOD OR BAD...

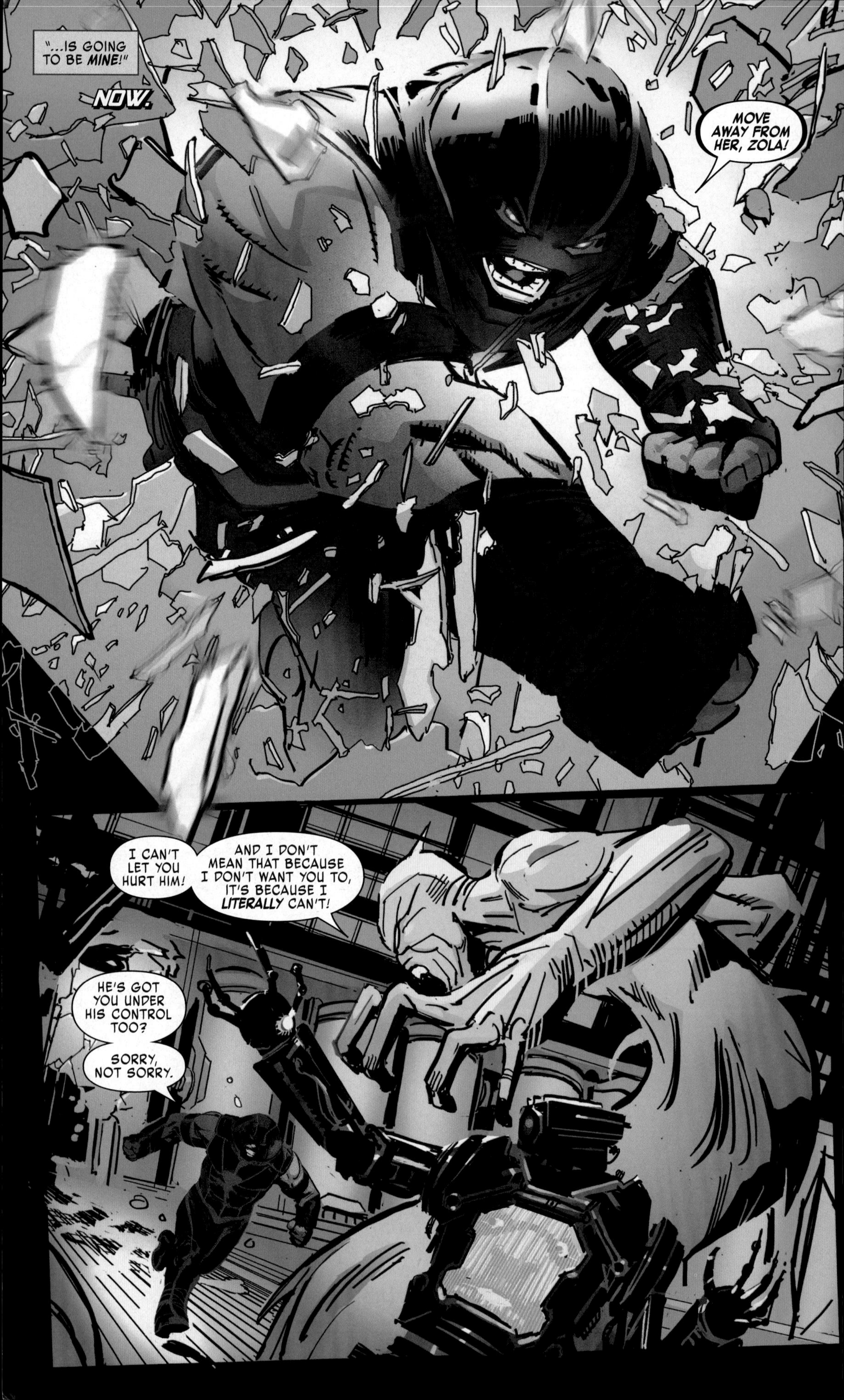
"...IS GOING TO BE MINE!"
NOW.
MOVE AWAY FROM HER, ZOLA!
I CAN'T LET YOU HURT HIM!
AND I DON'T MEAN THAT BECAUSE I DON'T WANT YOU TO, IT'S BECAUSE I LITERALLY CAN'T!
HE'S GOT YOU UNDER HIS CONTROL TOO?
SORRY, NOT SORRY.

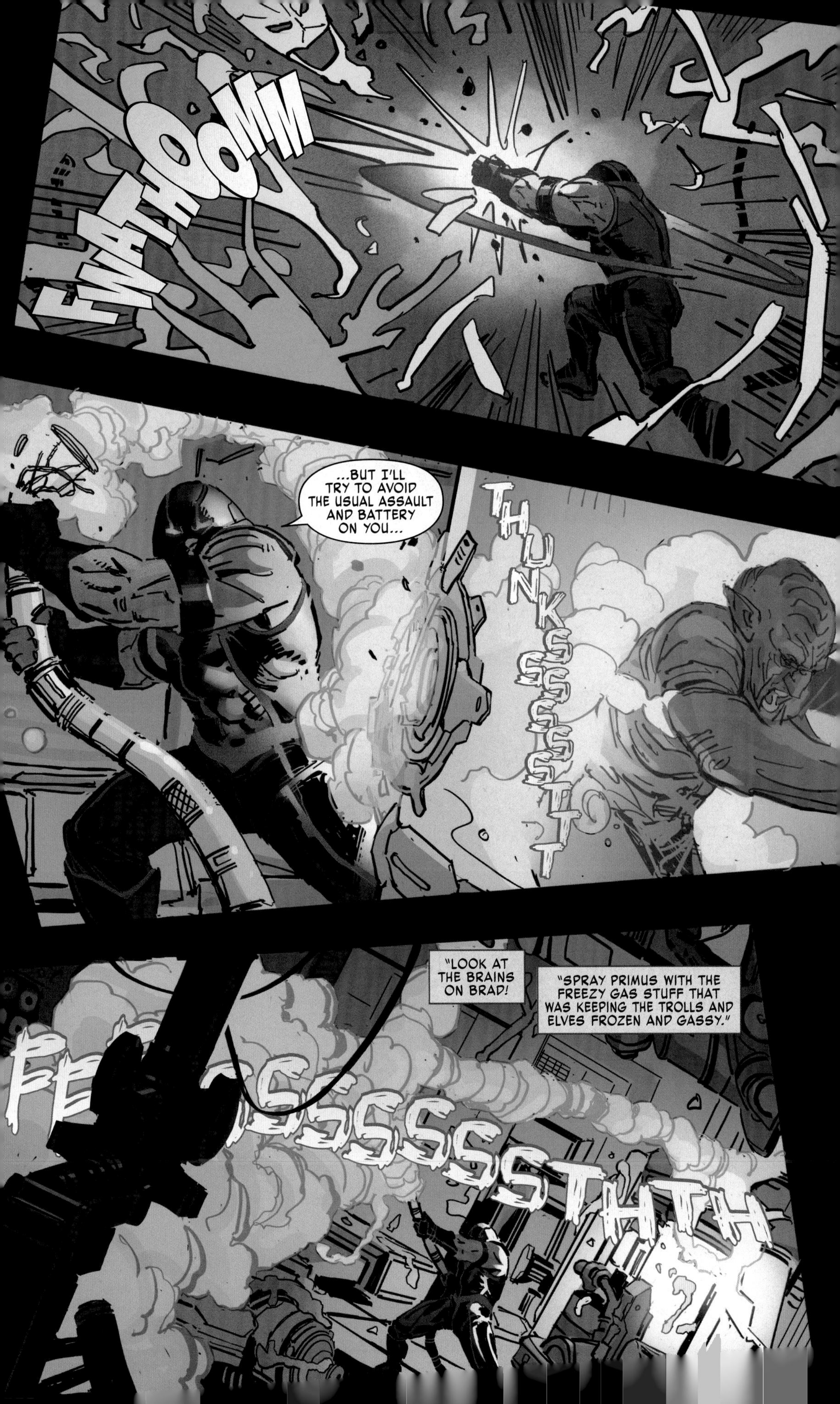
FWATHOOMM
...BUT I'LL TRY TO AVOID THE USUAL ASSAULT AND BATTERY ON YOU...
THUNKSSSSSTTT
"LOOK AT THE BRAINS ON BRAD!
"SPRAY PRIMUS WITH THE FREEZY GAS STUFF THAT WAS KEEPING THE TROLLS AND ELVES FROZEN AND GASSY."
SSSSSSTHTH

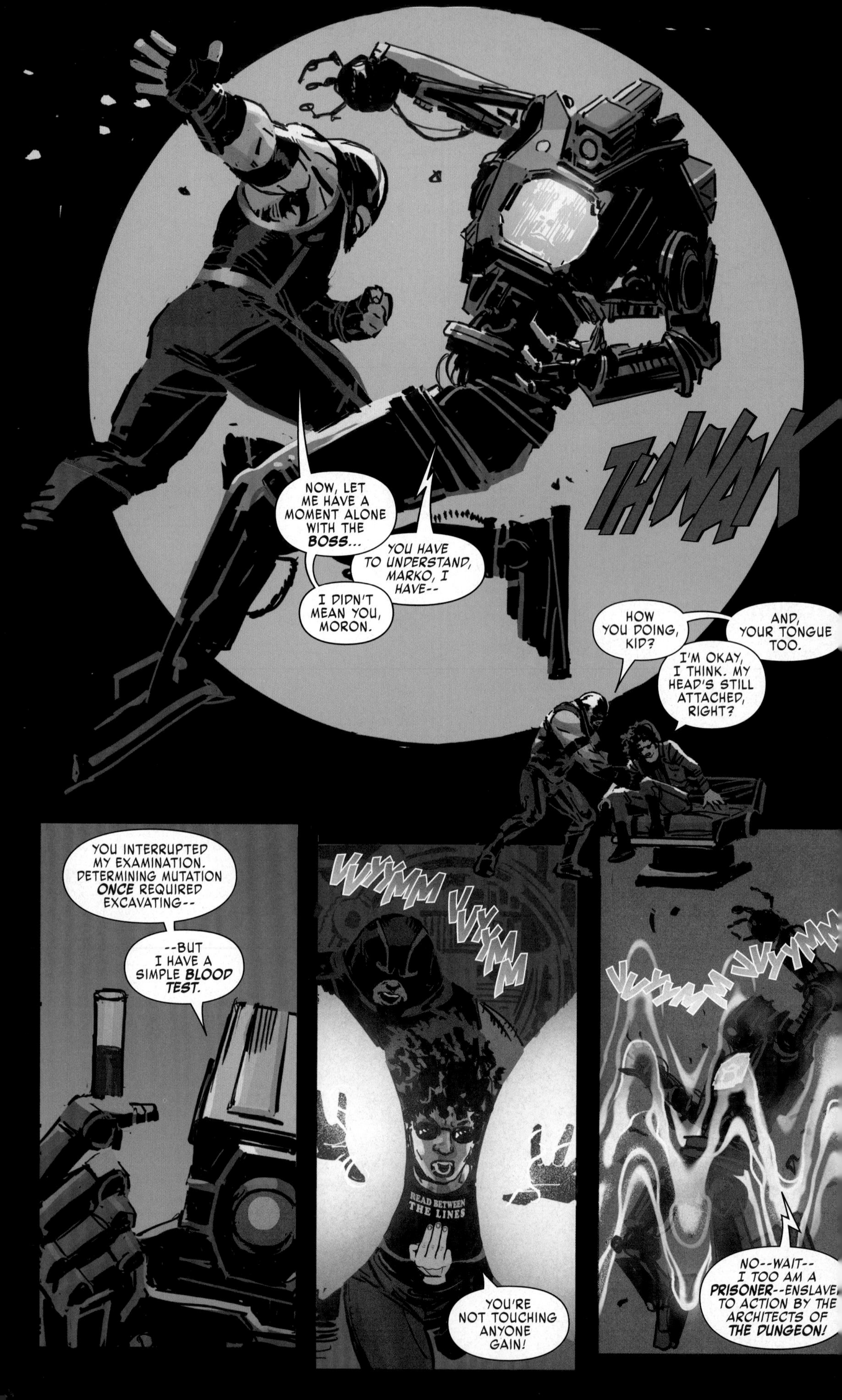
THWAK
NOW, LET ME HAVE A MOMENT ALONE WITH THE BOSS...
YOU HAVE TO UNDERSTAND, MARKO, I HAVE--
I DIDN'T MEAN YOU, MORON.
HOW YOU DOING, KID?
I'M OKAY, I THINK. MY HEAD'S STILL ATTACHED, RIGHT?
AND, YOUR TONGUE TOO.
YOU INTERRUPTED MY EXAMINATION. DETERMINING MUTATION ONCE REQUIRED EXCAVATING--
--BUT I HAVE A SIMPLE BLOOD TEST.
VVYMM
VVYMM
READ BETWEEN THE LINES
YOU'RE NOT TOUCHING ANYONE GAIN!
VVYMM
VVYMM
NO--WAIT-- I TOO AM A PRISONER--ENSLAVE TO ACTION BY THE ARCHITECTS OF THE DUNGEON!

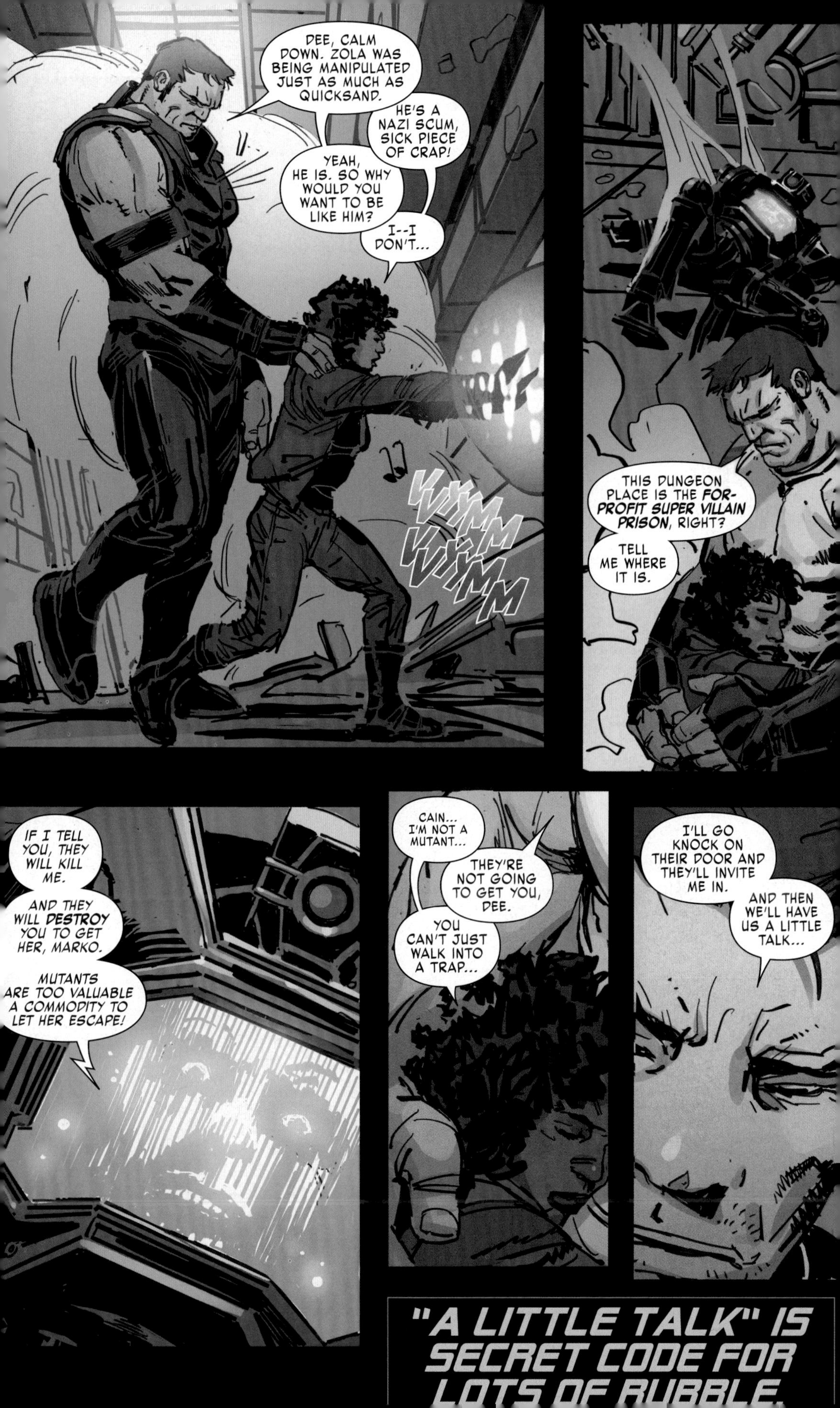

DEE, CALM DOWN. ZOLA WAS BEING MANIPULATED JUST AS MUCH AS QUICKSAND.
HE'S A NAZI SCUM, SICK PIECE OF CRAP!
YEAH, HE IS. SO WHY WOULD YOU WANT TO BE LIKE HIM?
I--I DON'T...
VVVMM VVVMM
THIS DUNGEON PLACE IS THE FOR-PROFIT SUPER VILLAIN PRISON, RIGHT?
TELL ME WHERE IT IS.
IF I TELL YOU, THEY WILL KILL ME.
AND THEY WILL DESTROY YOU TO GET HER, MARKO.
MUTANTS ARE TOO VALUABLE A COMMODITY TO LET HER ESCAPE!
CAIN... I'M NOT A MUTANT...
THEY'RE NOT GOING TO GET YOU, DEE.
YOU CAN'T JUST WALK INTO A TRAP...
I'LL GO KNOCK ON THEIR DOOR AND THEY'LL INVITE ME IN.
AND THEN WE'LL HAVE US A LITTLE TALK...
"A LITTLE TALK" IS SECRET CODE FOR LOTS OF RUBBLE

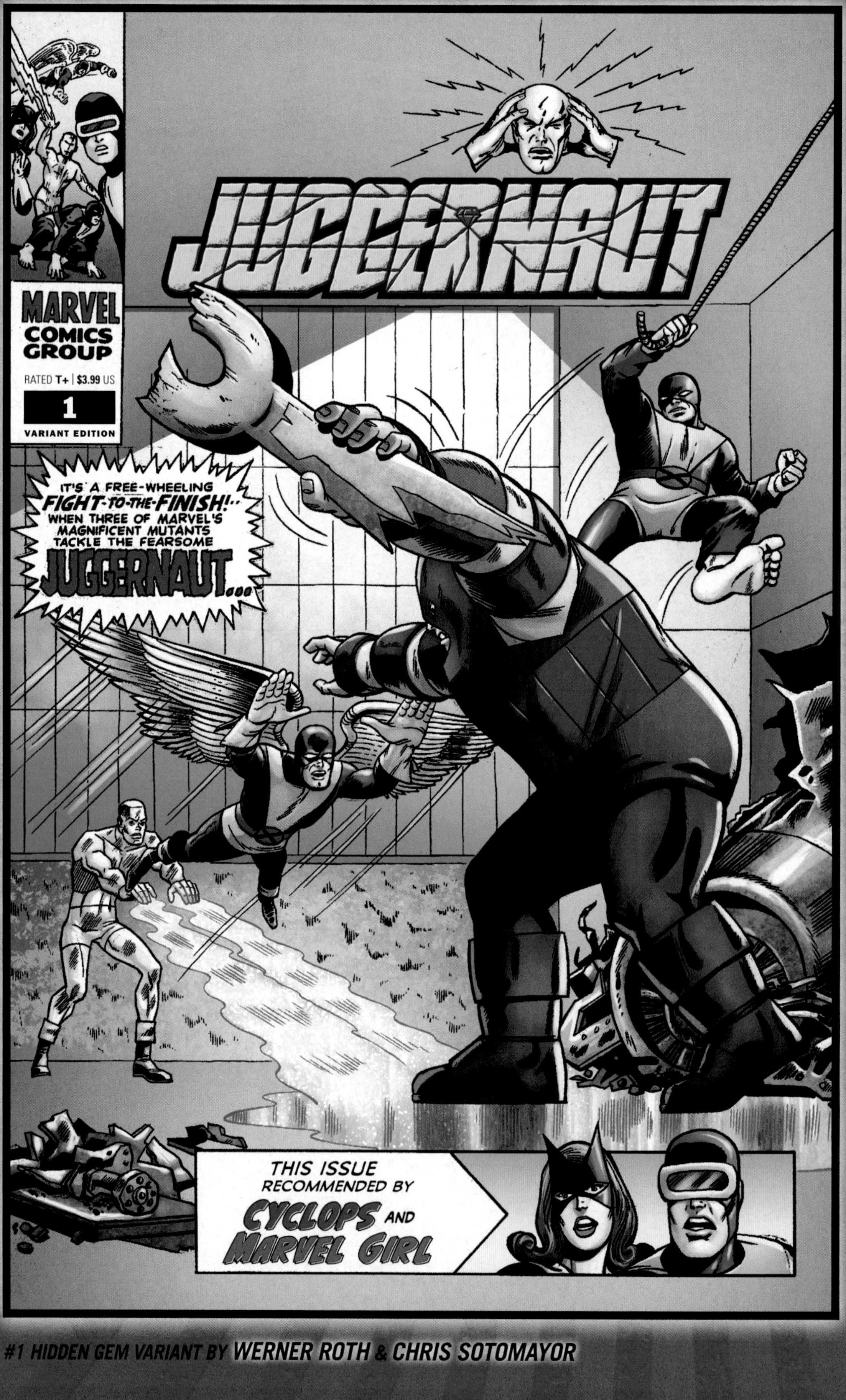

JUGGERNAUT
MARVEL COMICS GROUP
RATED T+ | $3.99 US
1
VARIANT EDITION
IT'S A FREE-WHEELING FIGHT-TO-THE-FINISH!.. WHEN THREE OF MARVEL'S MAGNIFICENT MUTANTS TACKLE THE FEARSOME JUGGERNAUT...
THIS ISSUE RECOMMENDED BY CYCLOPS AND MARVEL GIRL

#1 HIDDEN GEM VARIANT BY WERNER ROTH & CHRIS SOTOMAYOR

5

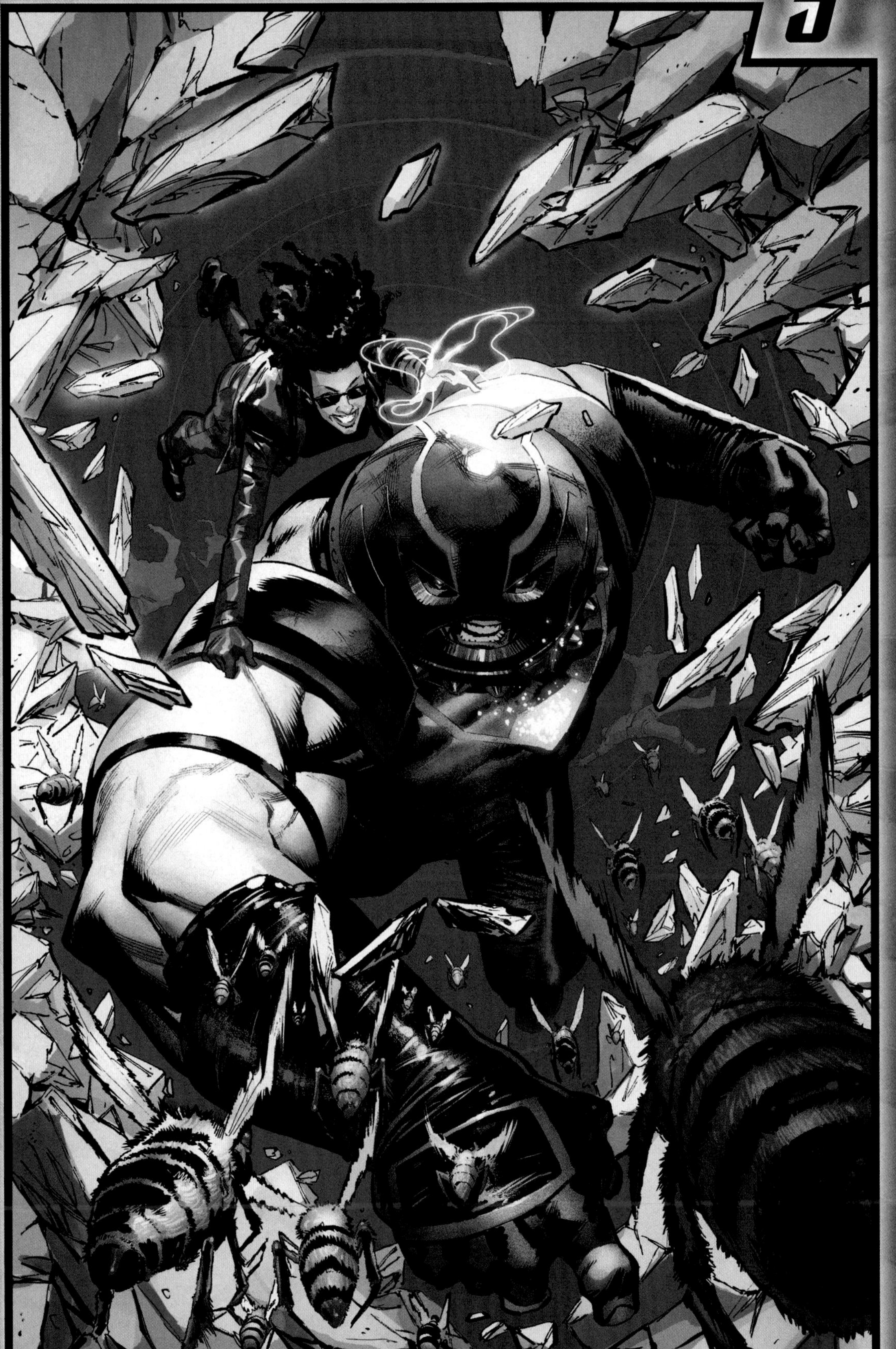

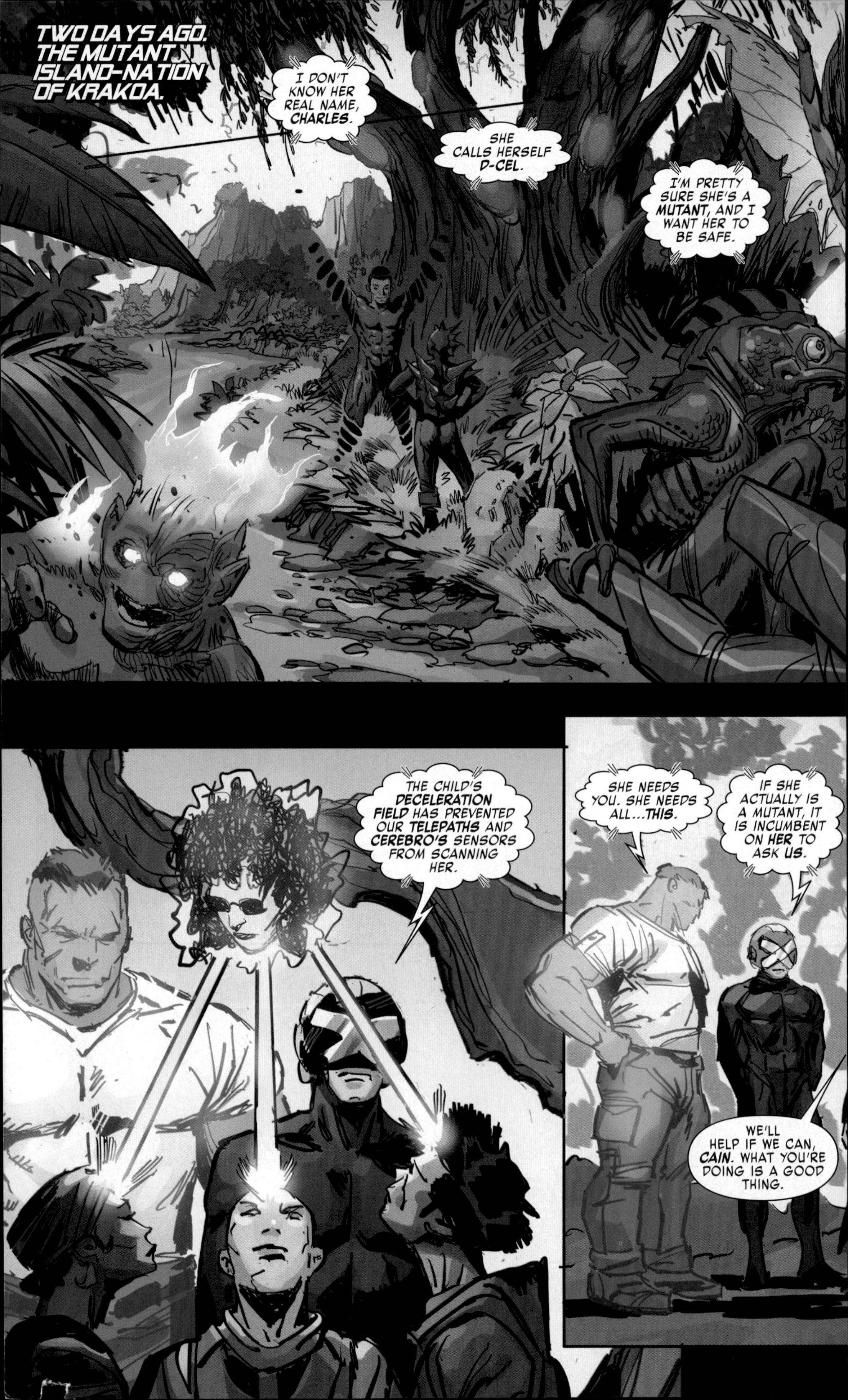
TWO DAYS AGO. THE MUTANT ISLAND-NATION OF KRAKOA.
I DON'T KNOW HER REAL NAME, CHARLES.
SHE CALLS HERSELF D-CEL.
I'M PRETTY SURE SHE'S A MUTANT, AND I WANT HER TO BE SAFE.
THE CHILD'S DECELERATION FIELD HAS PREVENTED OUR TELEPATHS AND CEREBRO'S SENSORS FROM SCANNING HER.
SHE NEEDS YOU. SHE NEEDS ALL...THIS.
IF SHE ACTUALLY IS A MUTANT, IT IS INCUMBENT ON HER TO ASK US.
WE'LL HELP IF WE CAN, CAIN. WHAT YOU'RE DOING IS A GOOD THING.

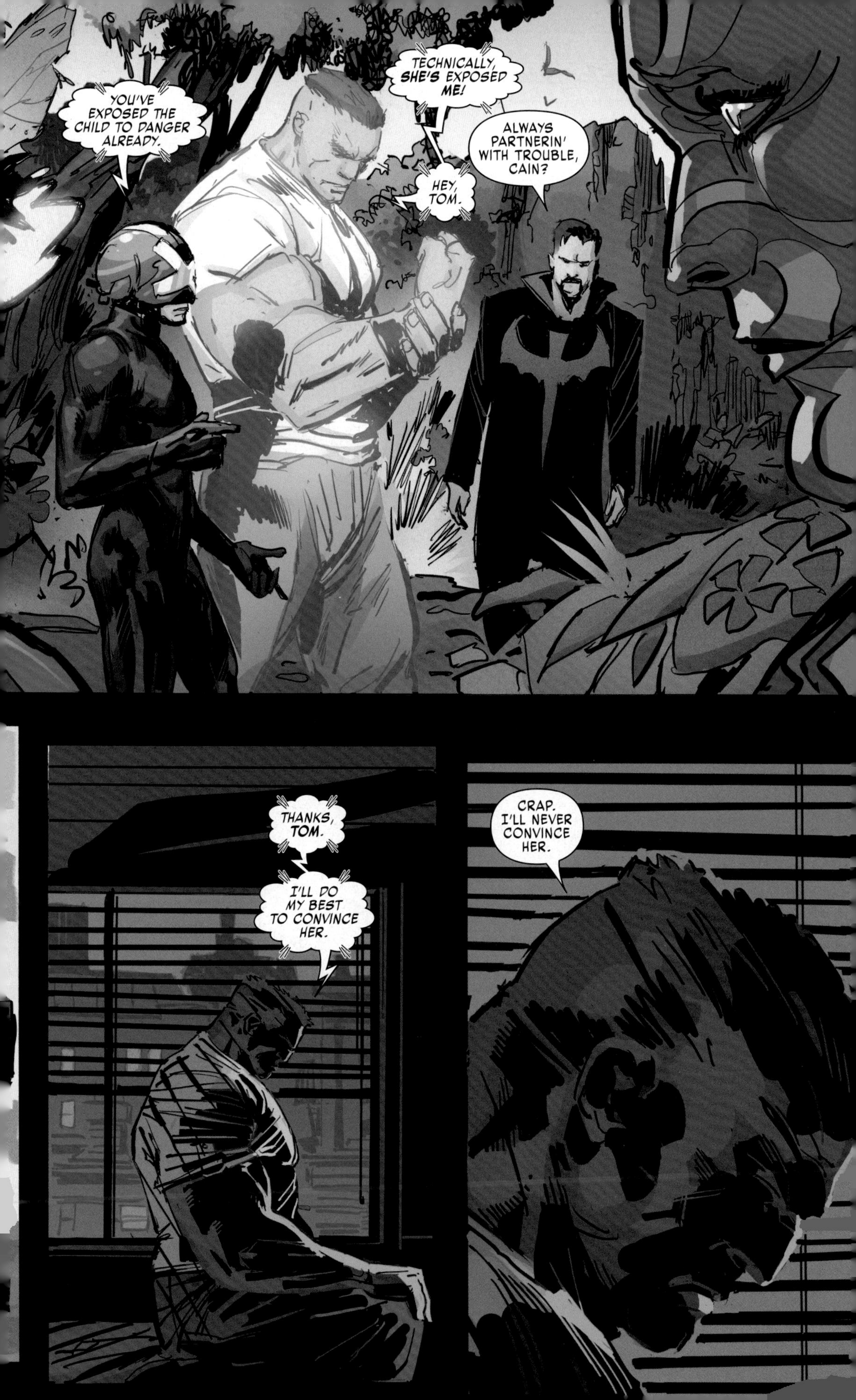
YOU'VE EXPOSED THE CHILD TO DANGER ALREADY.
TECHNICALLY, SHE'S EXPOSED ME!
HEY, TOM.
ALWAYS PARTNERIN' WITH TROUBLE, CAIN?
THANKS, TOM.
I'LL DO MY BEST TO CONVINCE HER.
CRAP. I'LL NEVER CONVINCE HER.

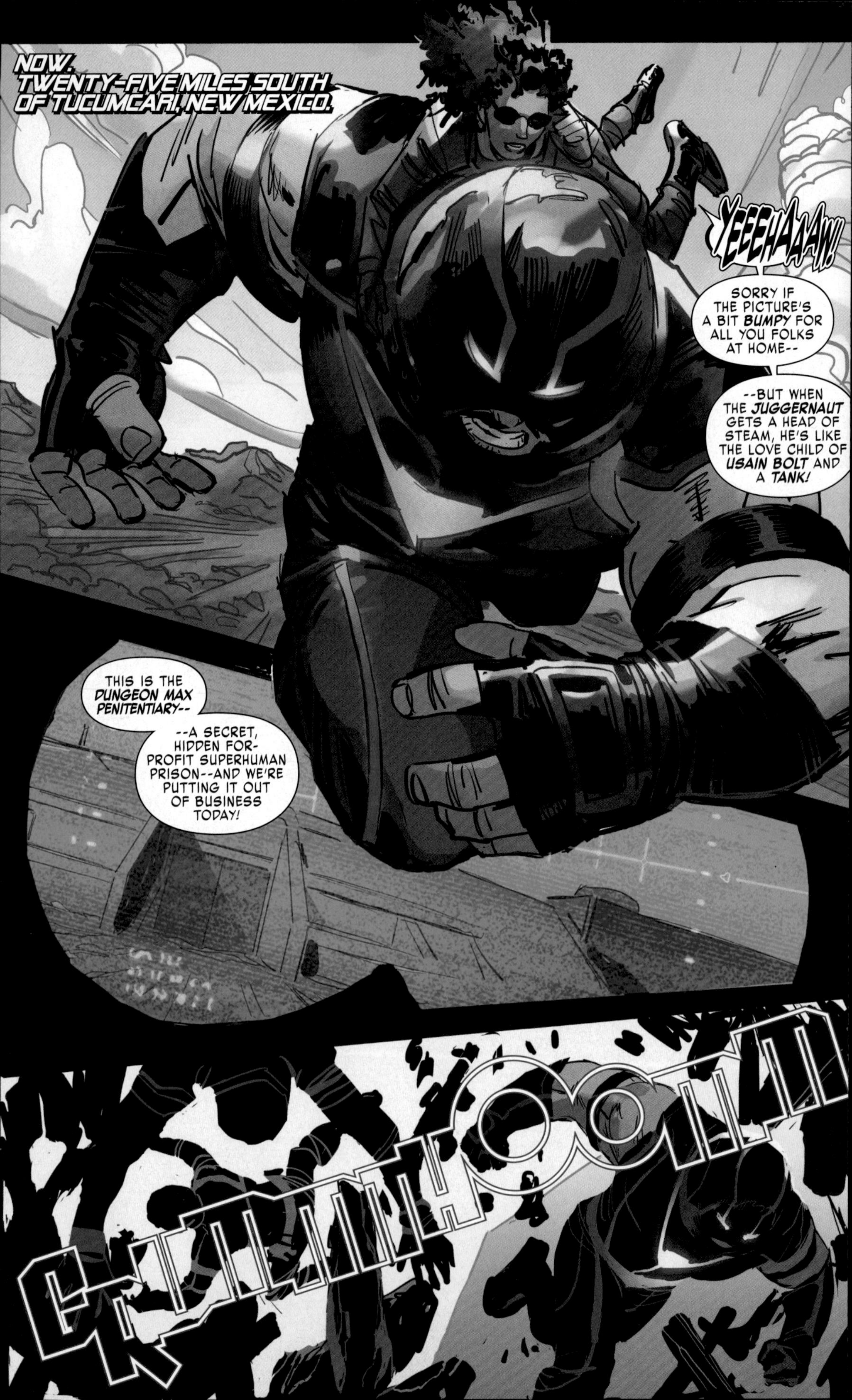
NOW.
TWENTY-FIVE MILES SOUTH OF TUCUMCARI, NEW MEXICO.
YEEEHAAAW!
SORRY IF THE PICTURE'S A BIT BUMPY FOR ALL YOU FOLKS AT HOME--
--BUT WHEN THE JUGGERNAUT GETS A HEAD OF STEAM, HE'S LIKE THE LOVE CHILD OF USAIN BOLT AND A TANK!
THIS IS THE DUNGEON MAX PENITENTIARY--
--A SECRET, HIDDEN FOR-PROFIT SUPERHUMAN PRISON--AND WE'RE PUTTING IT OUT OF BUSINESS TODAY!
CRUUUUHOOOM

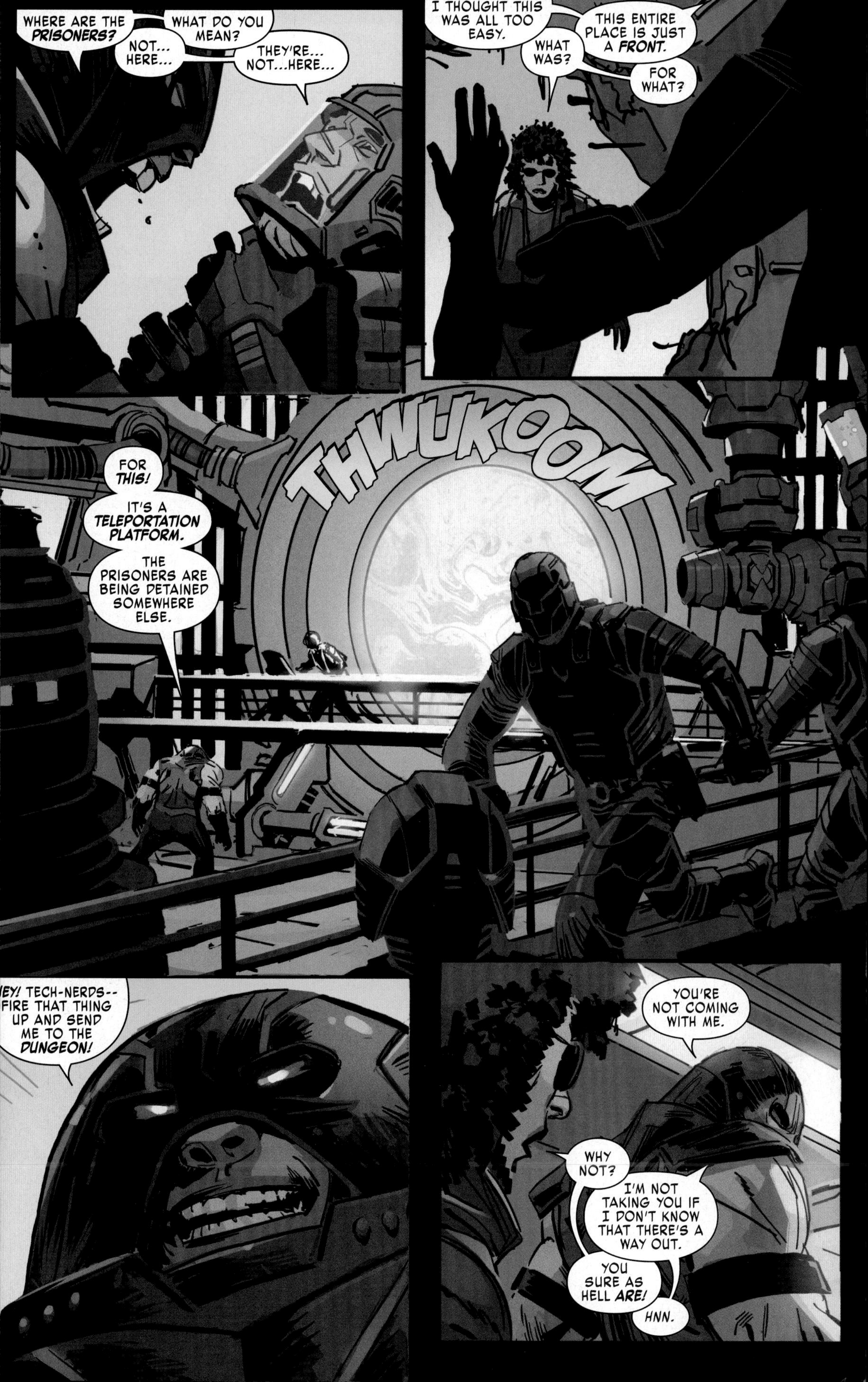
WHERE ARE THE *PRISONERS?*
WHAT DO YOU MEAN?
NOT... HERE...
THEY'RE... NOT...HERE...
I THOUGHT THIS WAS ALL TOO EASY.
WHAT WAS?
THIS ENTIRE PLACE IS JUST A *FRONT.*
FOR WHAT?
THWUKOOOM
FOR *THIS!*
IT'S A *TELEPORTATION PLATFORM.*
THE PRISONERS ARE BEING DETAINED SOMEWHERE ELSE.
EY! TECH-NERDS-- FIRE THAT THING UP AND SEND ME TO THE *DUNGEON!*
YOU'RE NOT COMING WITH ME.
WHY NOT?
I'M NOT TAKING YOU IF I DON'T KNOW THAT THERE'S A WAY OUT.
YOU SURE AS HELL *ARE!*
HNN.

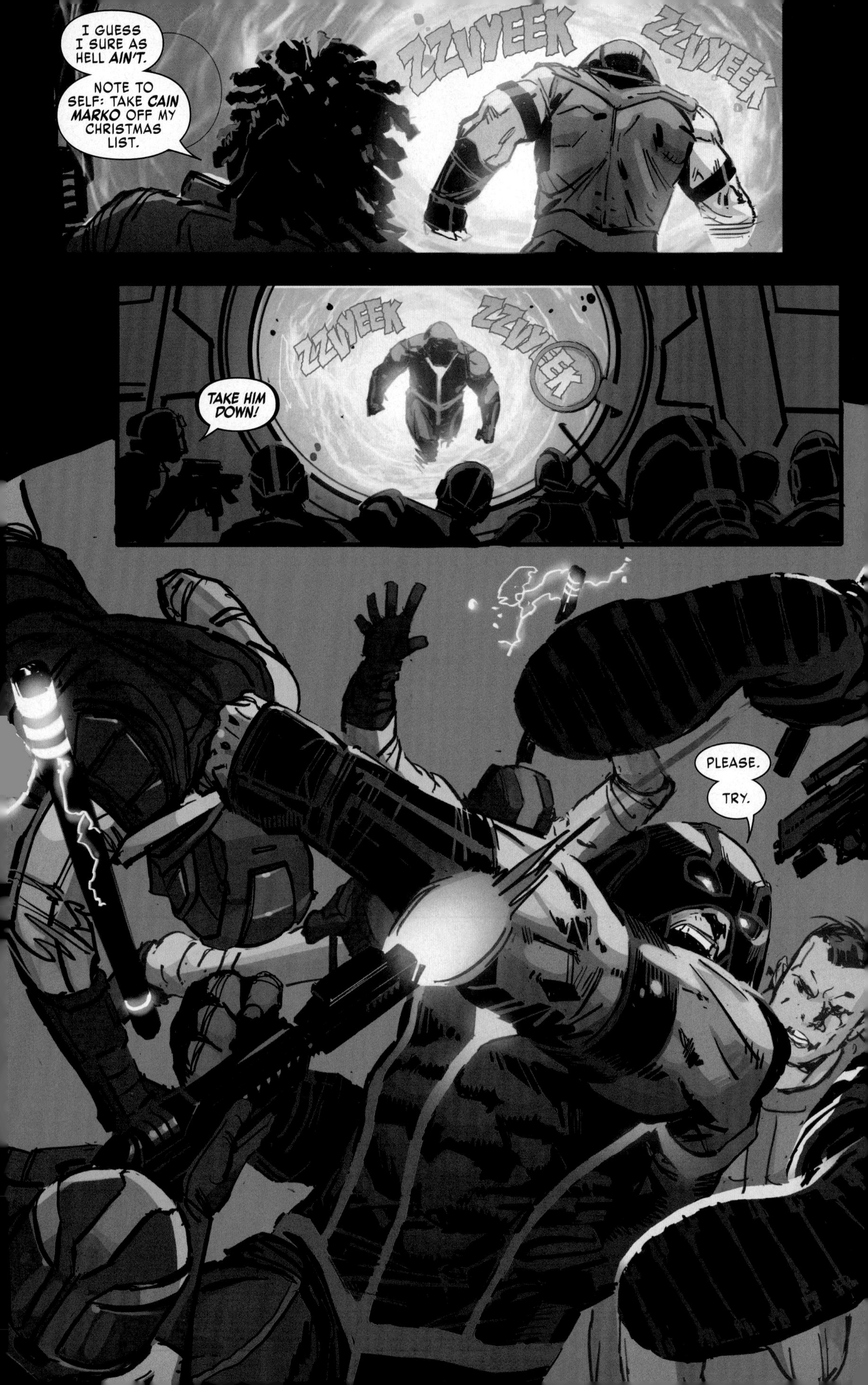
I GUESS I SURE AS HELL AIN'T.
NOTE TO SELF: TAKE CAIN MARKO OFF MY CHRISTMAS LIST.
ZZVVYEEK
ZZVVYEEK
ZZVVYEEK
ZZVVYEEK
TAKE HIM DOWN!
PLEASE.
TRY.

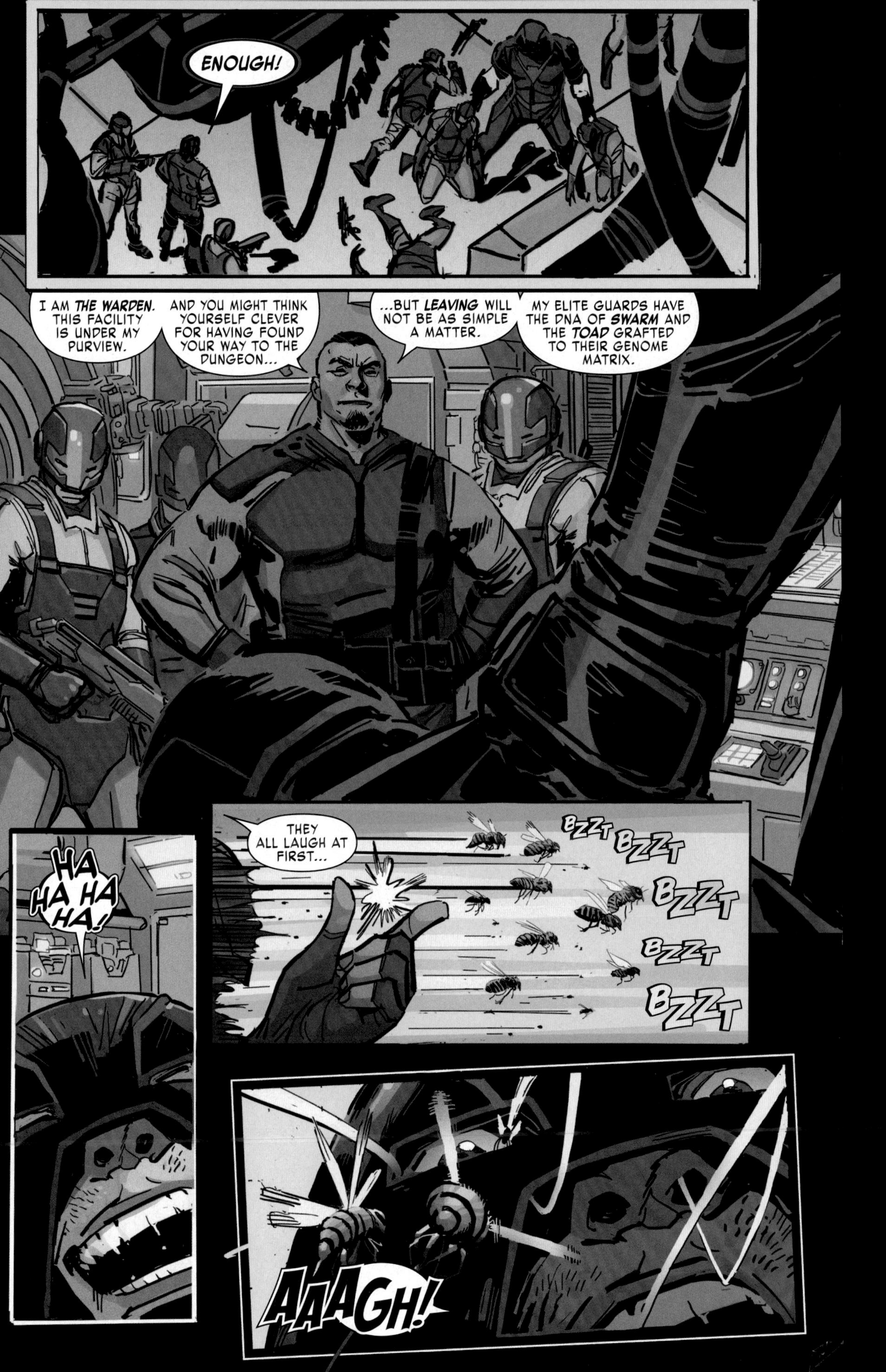
ENOUGH!
I AM THE WARDEN. THIS FACILITY IS UNDER MY PURVIEW.
AND YOU MIGHT THINK YOURSELF CLEVER FOR HAVING FOUND YOUR WAY TO THE DUNGEON...
...BUT LEAVING WILL NOT BE AS SIMPLE A MATTER.
MY ELITE GUARDS HAVE THE DNA OF SWARM AND THE TOAD GRAFTED TO THEIR GENOME MATRIX.
HA HA HA HA HA!
THEY ALL LAUGH AT FIRST...
BZZT BZZT
BZZT
BZZT
BZZT
AAAGH!

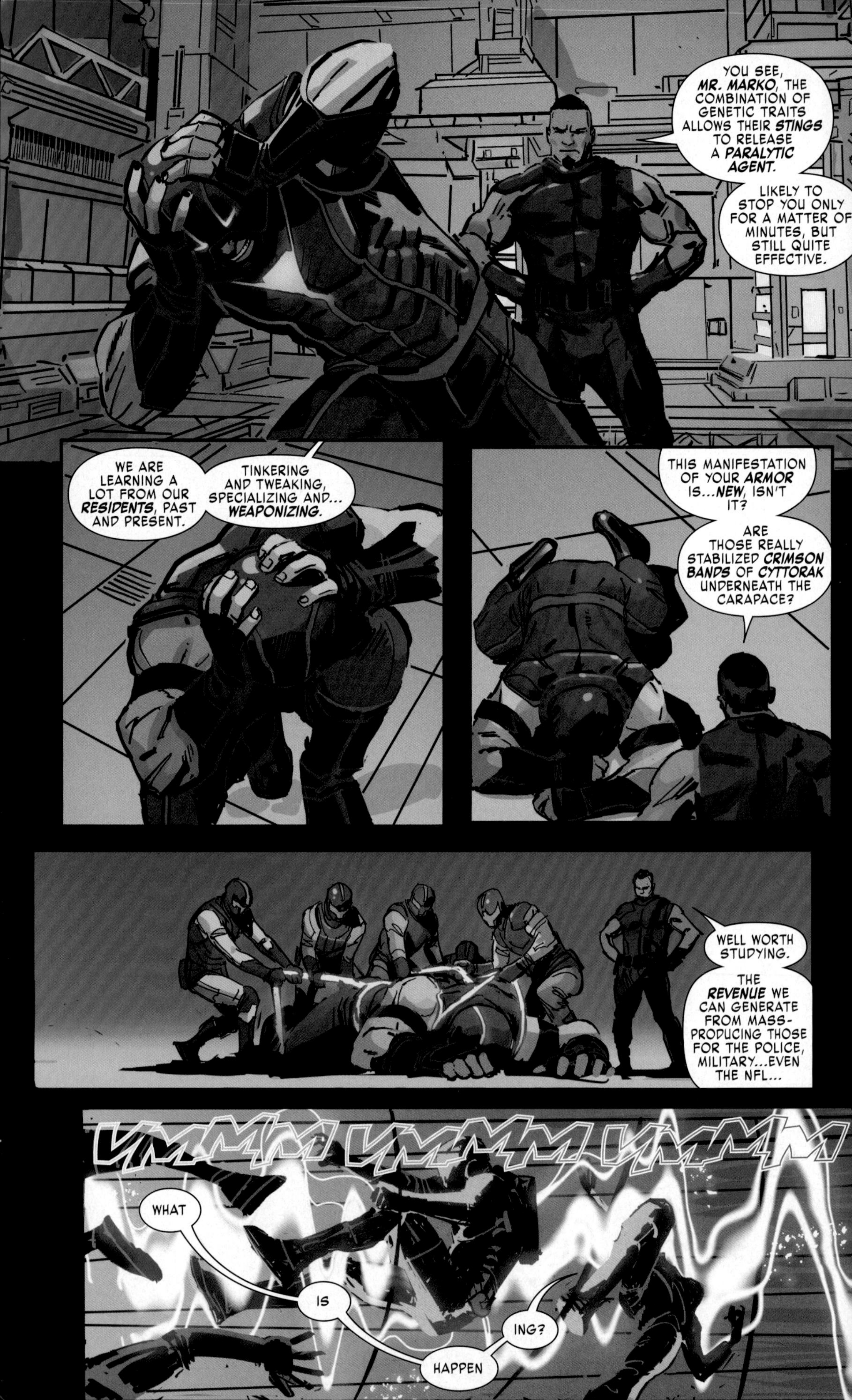
YOU SEE, MR. MARKO, THE COMBINATION OF GENETIC TRAITS ALLOWS THEIR STINGS TO RELEASE A PARALYTIC AGENT.
LIKELY TO STOP YOU ONLY FOR A MATTER OF MINUTES, BUT STILL QUITE EFFECTIVE.
WE ARE LEARNING A LOT FROM OUR RESIDENTS, PAST AND PRESENT.
TINKERING AND TWEAKING, SPECIALIZING AND... WEAPONIZING.
THIS MANIFESTATION OF YOUR ARMOR IS...NEW, ISN'T IT?
ARE THOSE REALLY STABILIZED CRIMSON BANDS OF CYTTORAK UNDERNEATH THE CARAPACE?
WELL WORTH STUDYING.
THE REVENUE WE CAN GENERATE FROM MASS-PRODUCING THOSE FOR THE POLICE, MILITARY...EVEN THE NFL...
VMMMM VMMMM VMMMM
WHAT
IS
HAPPEN
ING?

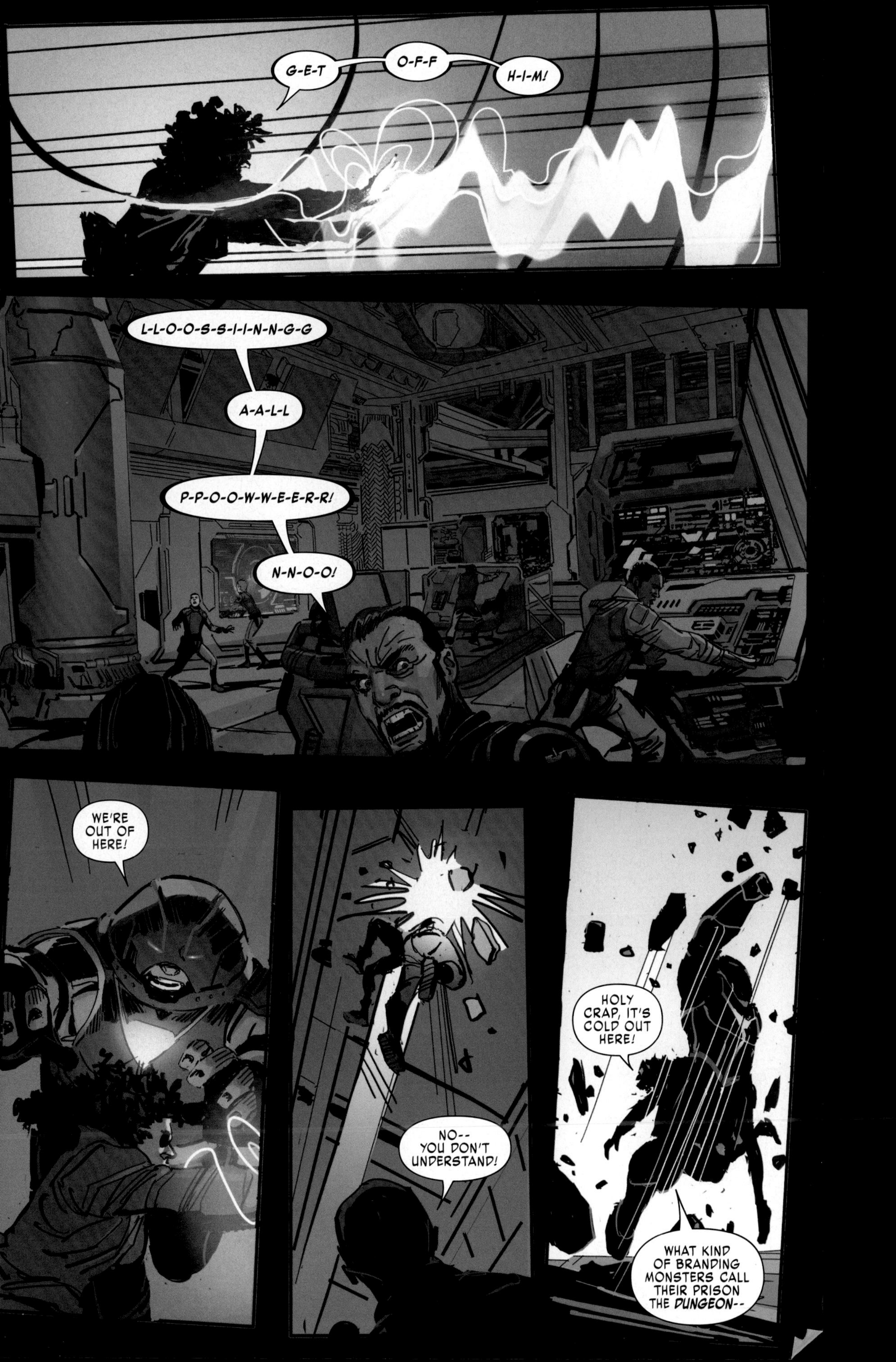
G-E-T
O-F-F
H-I-M!
L-L-O-O-S-S-I-I-N-N-G-G
A-A-L-L
P-P-O-O-W-W-E-E-R-R!
N-N-O-O!
WE'RE OUT OF HERE!
NO-- YOU DON'T UNDERSTAND!
HOLY CRAP, IT'S COLD OUT HERE!
WHAT KIND OF BRANDING MONSTERS CALL THEIR PRISON THE DUNGEON--

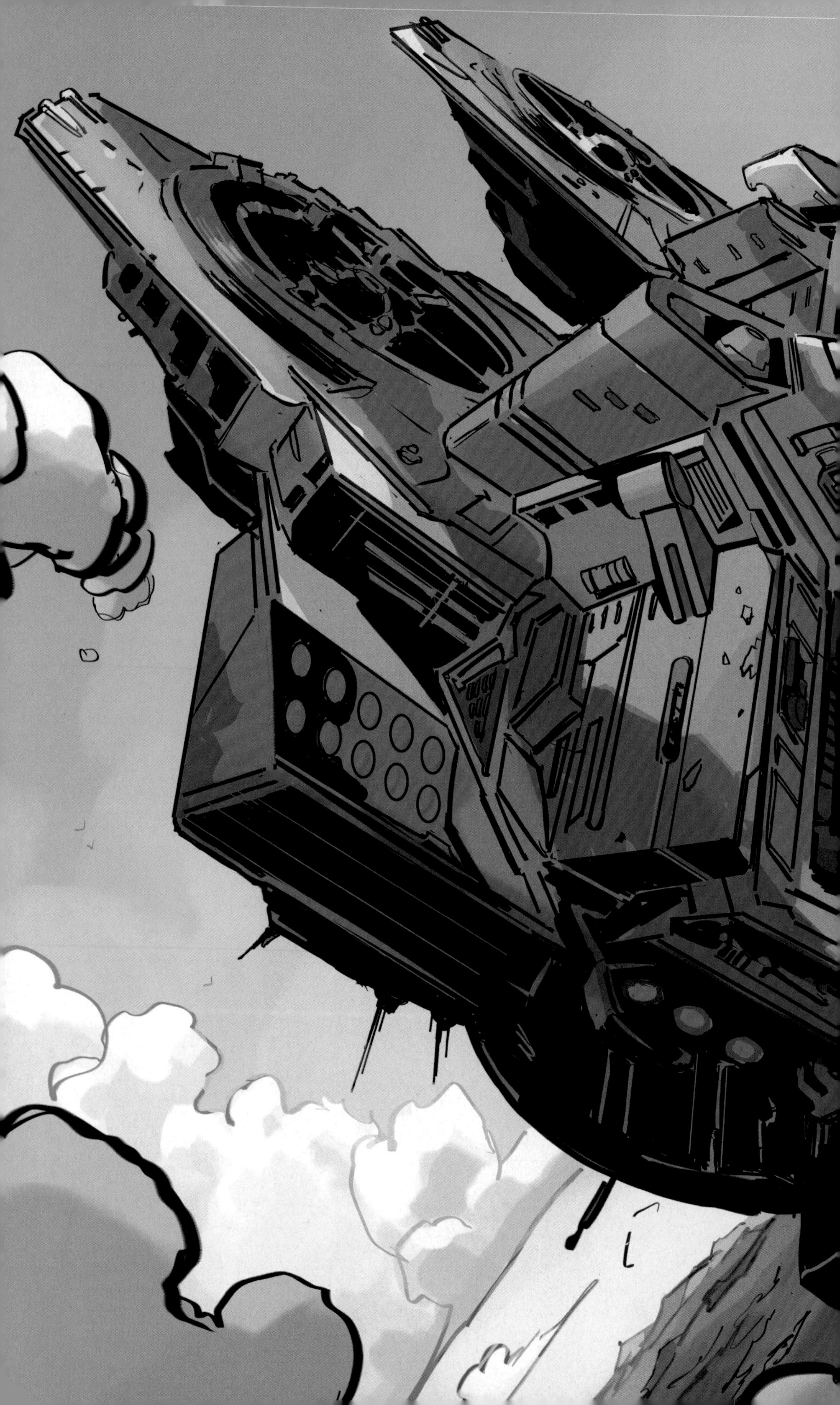

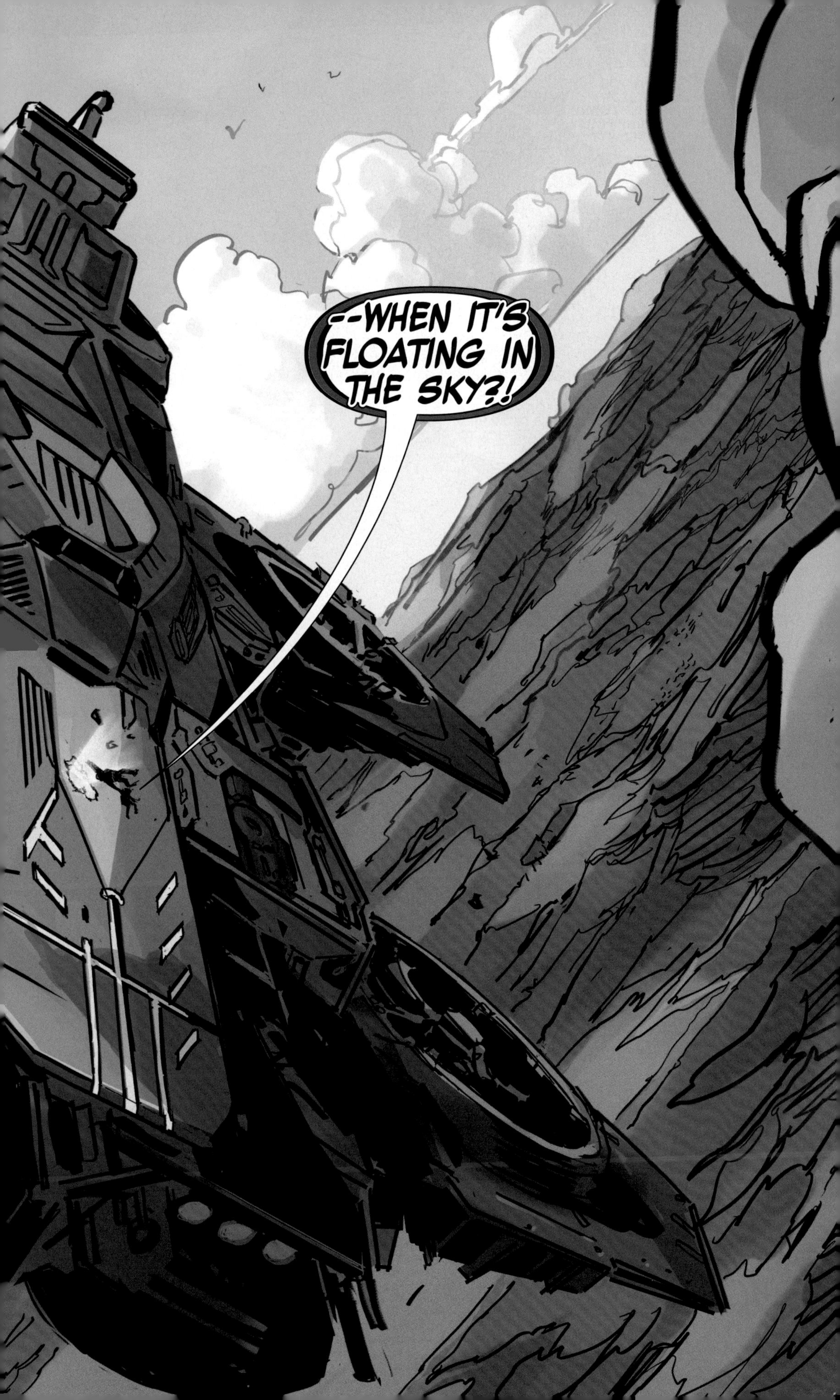
--WHEN IT'S FLOATING IN THE SKY?!

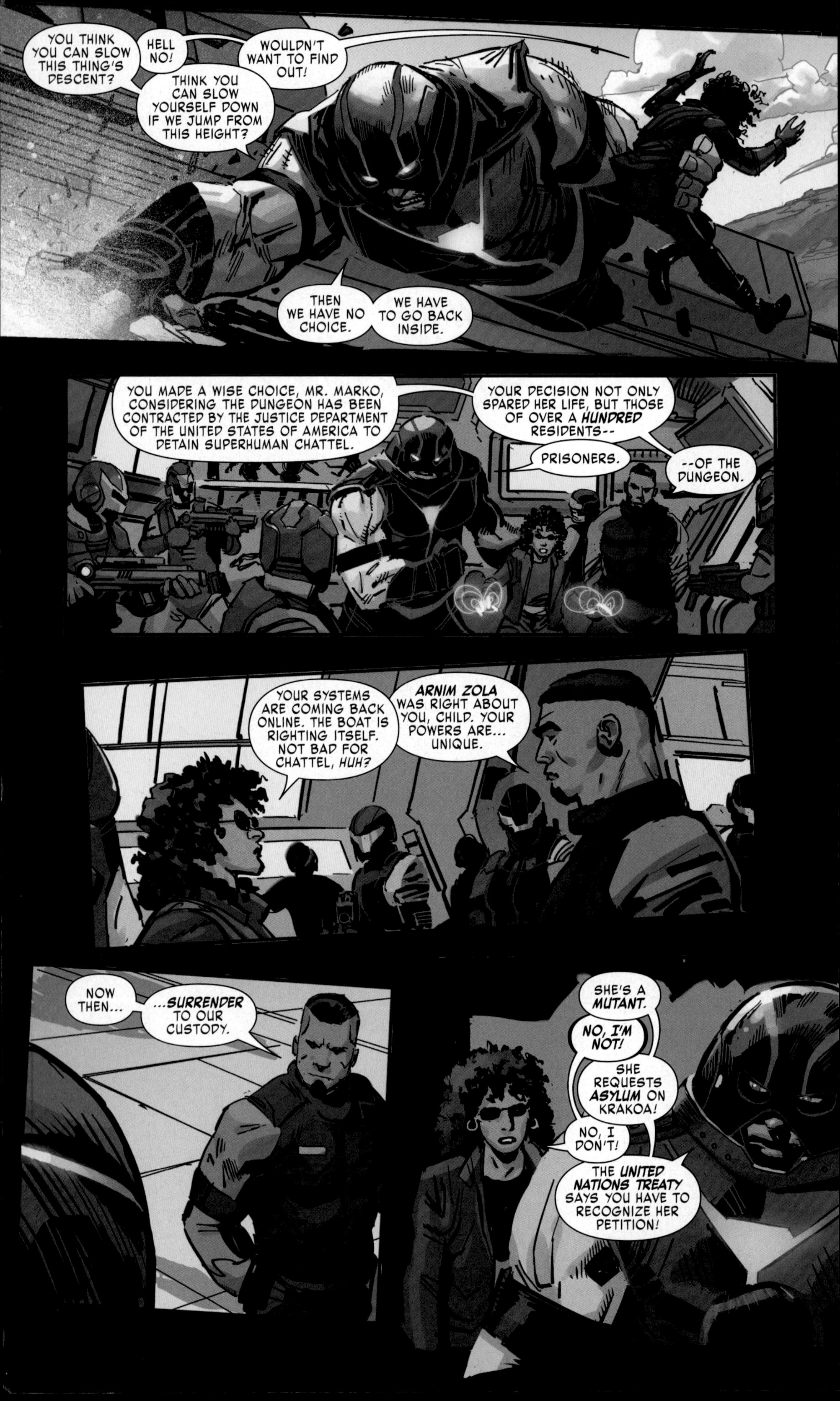

YOU THINK YOU CAN SLOW THIS THING'S DESCENT?
HELL NO!
WOULDN'T WANT TO FIND OUT!
THINK YOU CAN SLOW YOURSELF DOWN IF WE JUMP FROM THIS HEIGHT?
THEN WE HAVE NO CHOICE.
WE HAVE TO GO BACK INSIDE.
YOU MADE A WISE CHOICE, MR. MARKO, CONSIDERING THE DUNGEON HAS BEEN CONTRACTED BY THE JUSTICE DEPARTMENT OF THE UNITED STATES OF AMERICA TO DETAIN SUPERHUMAN CHATTEL.
YOUR DECISION NOT ONLY SPARED HER LIFE, BUT THOSE OF OVER A HUNDRED RESIDENTS--
PRISONERS.
--OF THE DUNGEON.
YOUR SYSTEMS ARE COMING BACK ONLINE. THE BOAT IS RIGHTING ITSELF. NOT BAD FOR CHATTEL, HUH?
ARNIM ZOLA WAS RIGHT ABOUT YOU, CHILD. YOUR POWERS ARE... UNIQUE.
NOW THEN...
...SURRENDER TO OUR CUSTODY.
SHE'S A MUTANT.
NO, I'M NOT!
SHE REQUESTS ASYLUM ON KRAKOA!
NO, I DON'T!
THE UNITED NATIONS TREATY SAYS YOU HAVE TO RECOGNIZE HER PETITION!

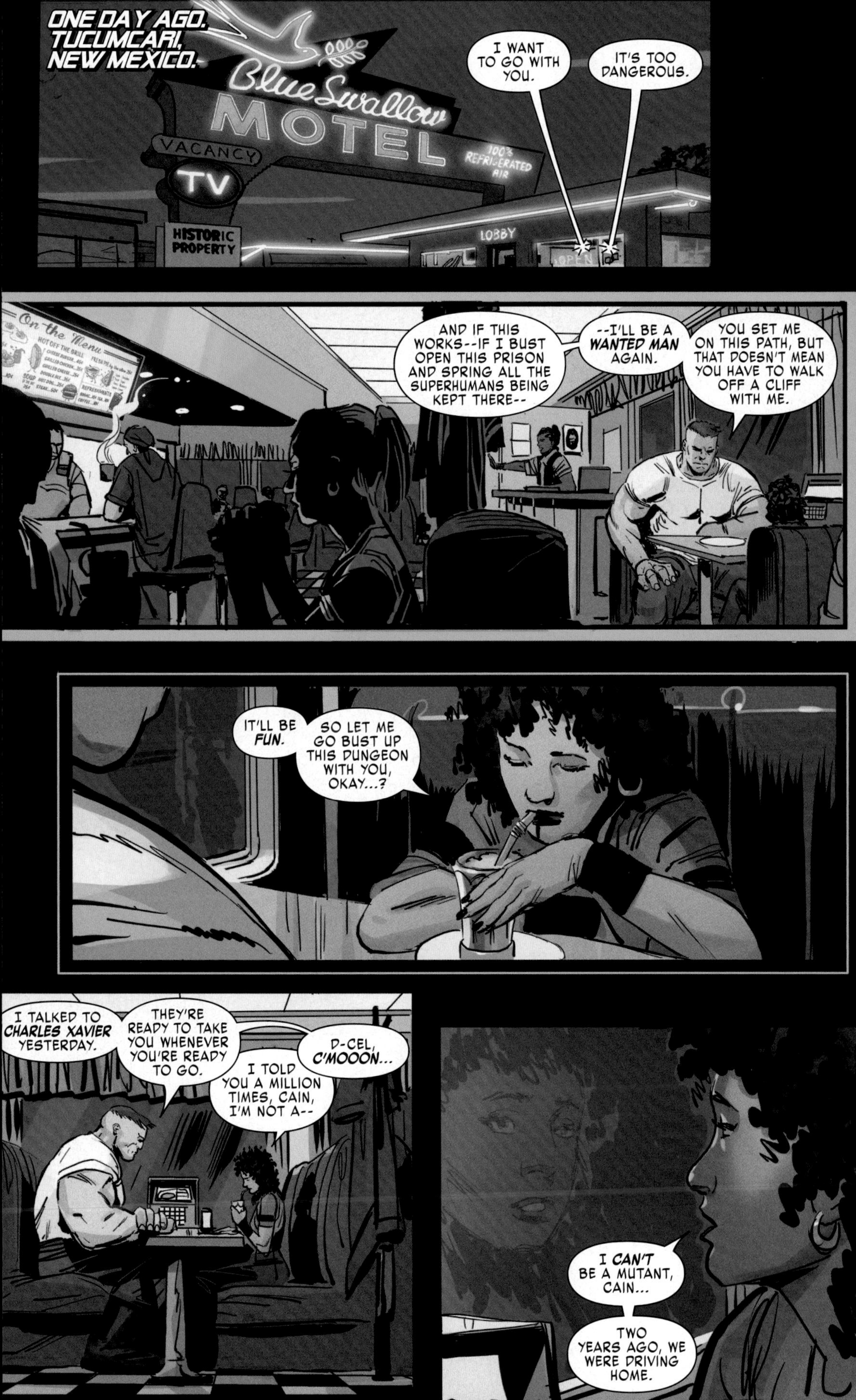
ONE DAY AGO. TUCUMCARI, NEW MEXICO.
Blue Swallow MOTEL
VACANCY
TV
100% REFRIGERATED AIR
HISTORIC PROPERTY
LOBBY
OPEN
I WANT TO GO WITH YOU.
IT'S TOO DANGEROUS.
On the Menu
AND IF THIS WORKS--IF I BUST OPEN THIS PRISON AND SPRING ALL THE SUPERHUMANS BEING KEPT THERE--
--I'LL BE A WANTED MAN AGAIN.
YOU SET ME ON THIS PATH, BUT THAT DOESN'T MEAN YOU HAVE TO WALK OFF A CLIFF WITH ME.
IT'LL BE FUN.
SO LET ME GO BUST UP THIS DUNGEON WITH YOU, OKAY...?
I TALKED TO CHARLES XAVIER YESTERDAY.
THEY'RE READY TO TAKE YOU WHENEVER YOU'RE READY TO GO.
D-CEL, C'MOOON...
I TOLD YOU A MILLION TIMES, CAIN, I'M NOT A--
I CAN'T BE A MUTANT, CAIN...
TWO YEARS AGO, WE WERE DRIVING HOME.

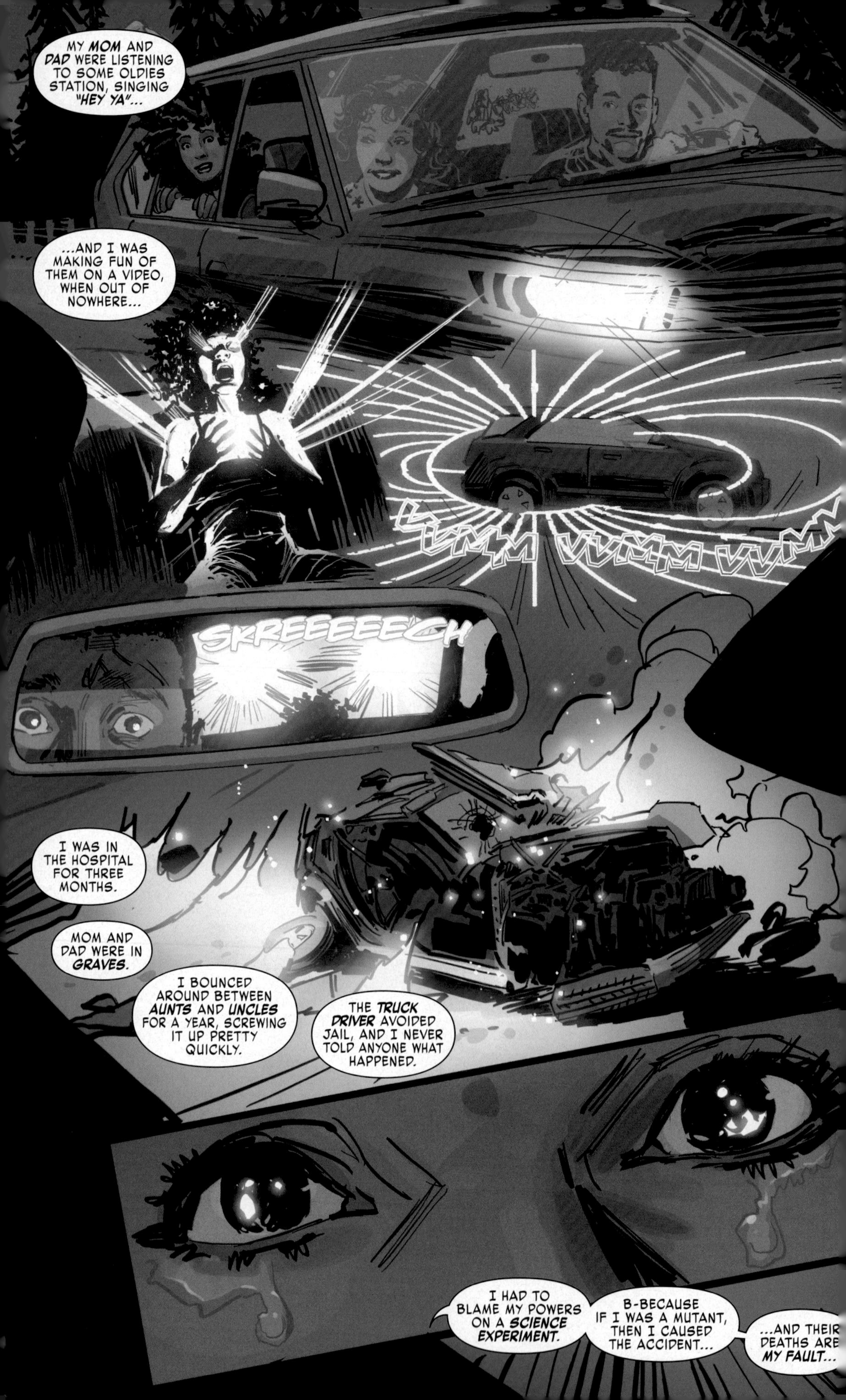
MY MOM AND DAD WERE LISTENING TO SOME OLDIES STATION, SINGING "HEY YA"...
...AND I WAS MAKING FUN OF THEM ON A VIDEO, WHEN OUT OF NOWHERE...
VMM VVMM VVMM
SKREEEEEECH
I WAS IN THE HOSPITAL FOR THREE MONTHS.
MOM AND DAD WERE IN GRAVES.
I BOUNCED AROUND BETWEEN AUNTS AND UNCLES FOR A YEAR, SCREWING IT UP PRETTY QUICKLY.
THE TRUCK DRIVER AVOIDED JAIL, AND I NEVER TOLD ANYONE WHAT HAPPENED.
I HAD TO BLAME MY POWERS ON A SCIENCE EXPERIMENT.
B-BECAUSE IF I WAS A MUTANT, THEN I CAUSED THE ACCIDENT...
...AND THEIR DEATHS ARE MY FAULT...

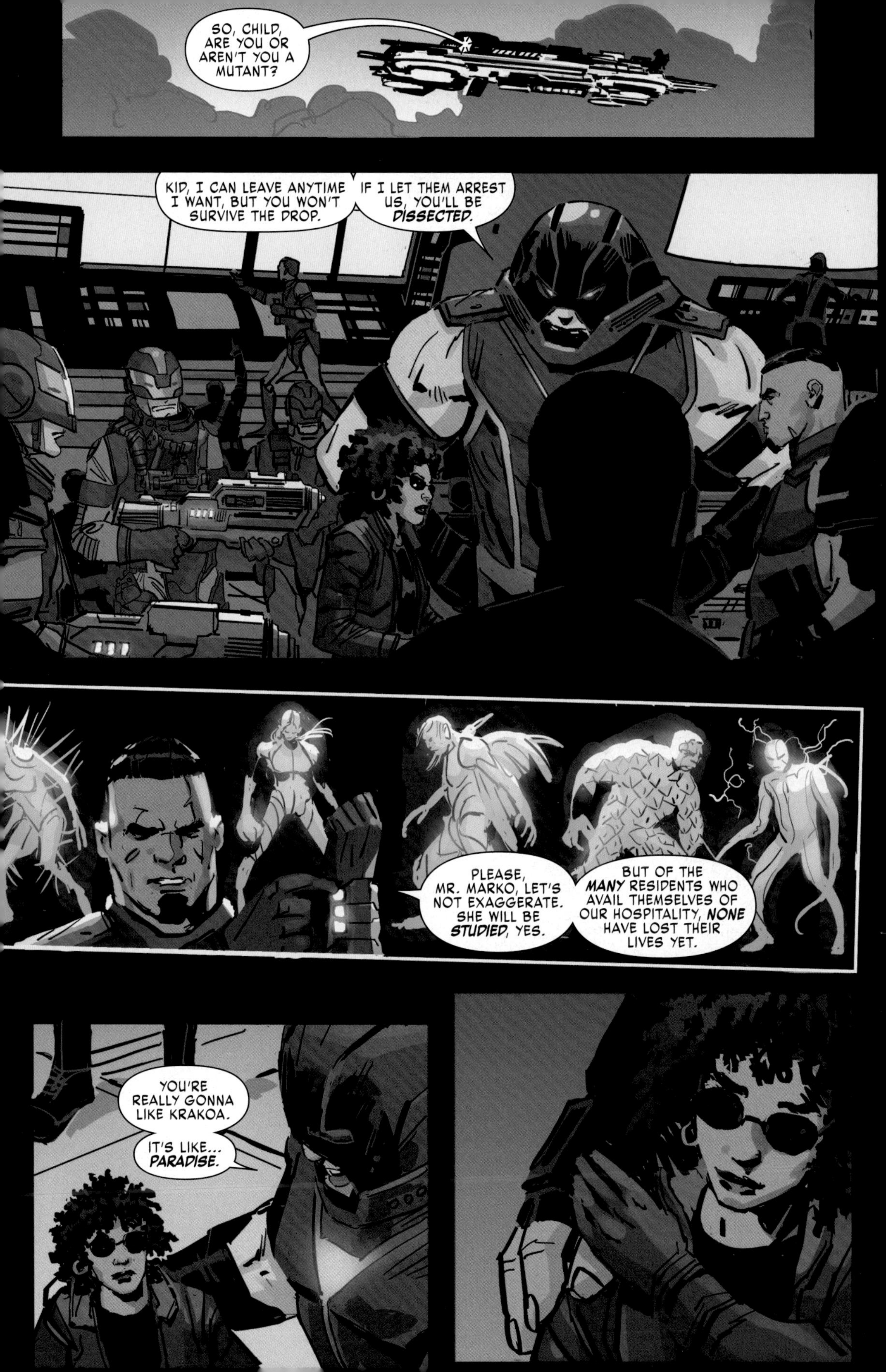
SO, CHILD, ARE YOU OR AREN'T YOU A MUTANT?
KID, I CAN LEAVE ANYTIME I WANT, BUT YOU WON'T SURVIVE THE DROP.
IF I LET THEM ARREST US, YOU'LL BE *DISSECTED.*
PLEASE, MR. MARKO, LET'S NOT EXAGGERATE. SHE WILL BE *STUDIED*, YES.
BUT OF THE *MANY* RESIDENTS WHO AVAIL THEMSELVES OF OUR HOSPITALITY, *NONE* HAVE LOST THEIR LIVES YET.
YOU'RE REALLY GONNA LIKE KRAKOA.
IT'S LIKE... *PARADISE.*

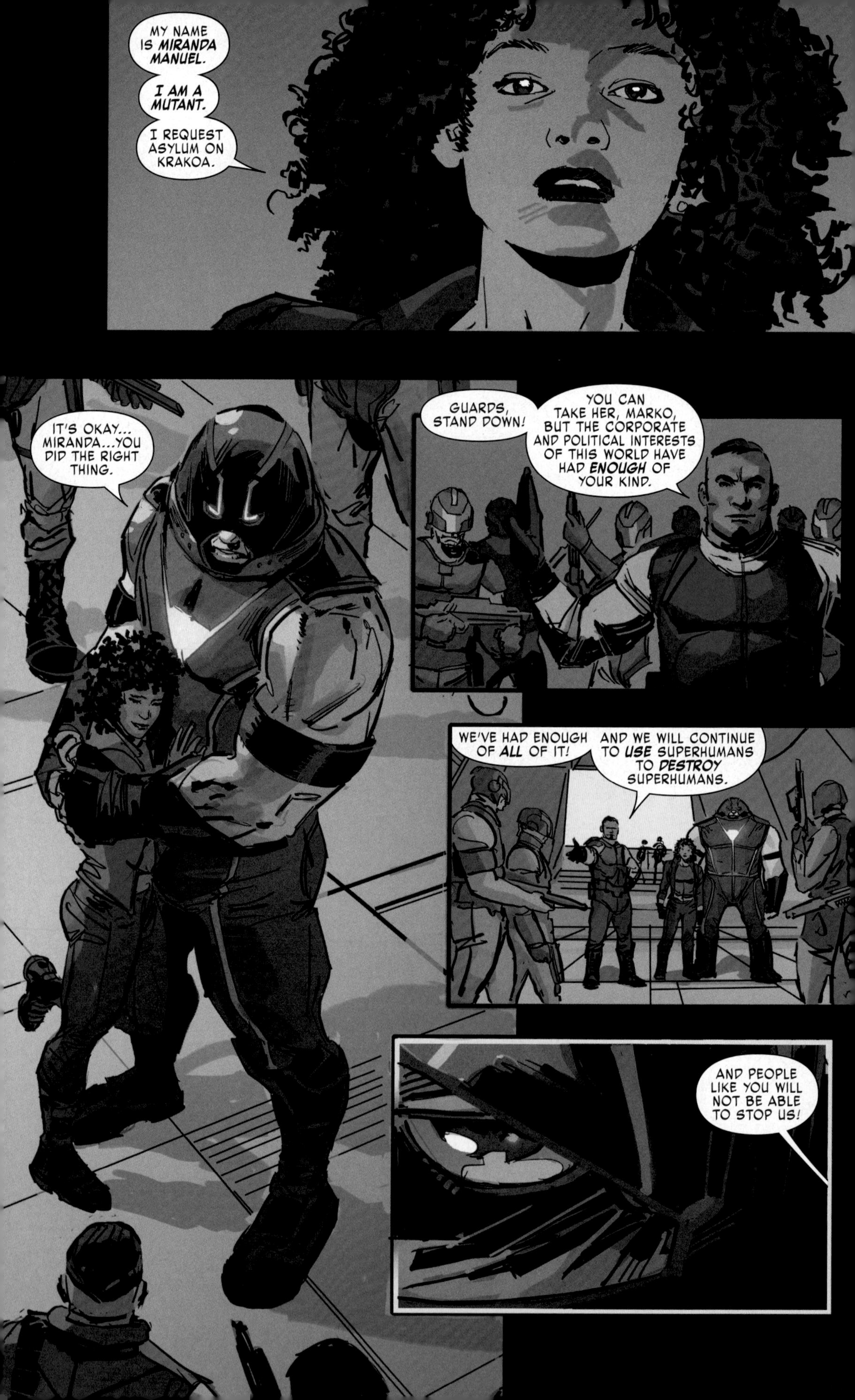
MY NAME IS MIRANDA MANUEL.
I AM A MUTANT.
I REQUEST ASYLUM ON KRAKOA.
IT'S OKAY... MIRANDA...YOU DID THE RIGHT THING.
GUARDS, STAND DOWN!
YOU CAN TAKE HER, MARKO, BUT THE CORPORATE AND POLITICAL INTERESTS OF THIS WORLD HAVE HAD ENOUGH OF YOUR KIND.
WE'VE HAD ENOUGH OF ALL OF IT!
AND WE WILL CONTINUE TO USE SUPERHUMANS TO DESTROY SUPERHUMANS.
AND PEOPLE LIKE YOU WILL NOT BE ABLE TO STOP US!

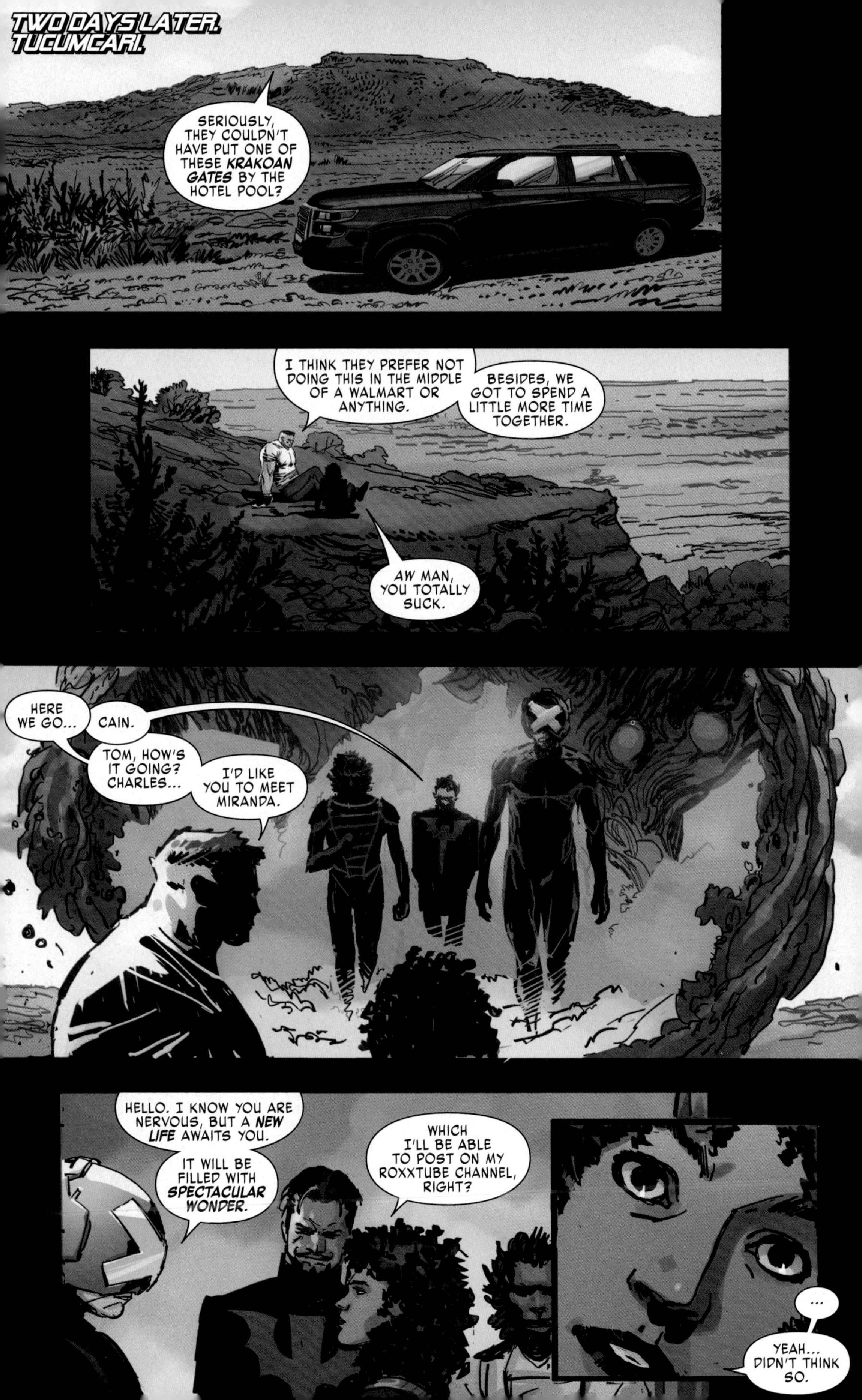
TWO DAYS LATER. TUCUMCARI.
SERIOUSLY, THEY COULDN'T HAVE PUT ONE OF THESE KRAKOAN GATES BY THE HOTEL POOL?
I THINK THEY PREFER NOT DOING THIS IN THE MIDDLE OF A WALMART OR ANYTHING.
BESIDES, WE GOT TO SPEND A LITTLE MORE TIME TOGETHER.
AW MAN, YOU TOTALLY SUCK.
HERE WE GO...
CAIN.
TOM, HOW'S IT GOING? CHARLES...
I'D LIKE YOU TO MEET MIRANDA.
HELLO. I KNOW YOU ARE NERVOUS, BUT A NEW LIFE AWAITS YOU.
IT WILL BE FILLED WITH SPECTACULAR WONDER.
WHICH I'LL BE ABLE TO POST ON MY ROXXTUBE CHANNEL, RIGHT?
...
YEAH... DIDN'T THINK SO.

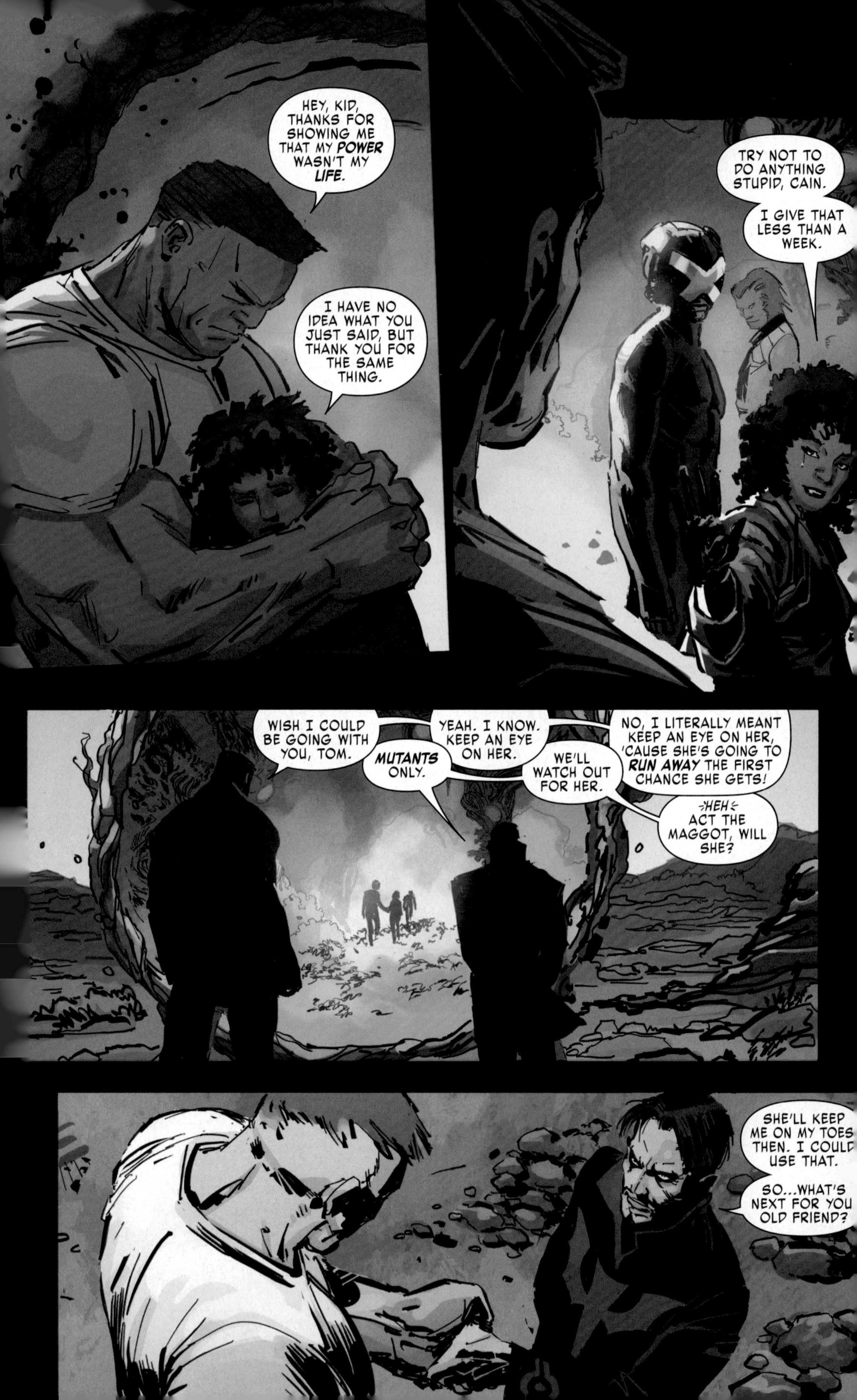
HEY, KID, THANKS FOR SHOWING ME THAT MY POWER WASN'T MY LIFE.
I HAVE NO IDEA WHAT YOU JUST SAID, BUT THANK YOU FOR THE SAME THING.
TRY NOT TO DO ANYTHING STUPID, CAIN.
I GIVE THAT LESS THAN A WEEK.
WISH I COULD BE GOING WITH YOU, TOM.
MUTANTS ONLY.
YEAH. I KNOW. KEEP AN EYE ON HER.
WE'LL WATCH OUT FOR HER.
NO, I LITERALLY MEANT KEEP AN EYE ON HER, 'CAUSE SHE'S GOING TO RUN AWAY THE FIRST CHANCE SHE GETS!
HEH
ACT THE MAGGOT, WILL SHE?
SHE'LL KEEP ME ON MY TOES THEN. I COULD USE THAT.
SO...WHAT'S NEXT FOR YOU OLD FRIEND?

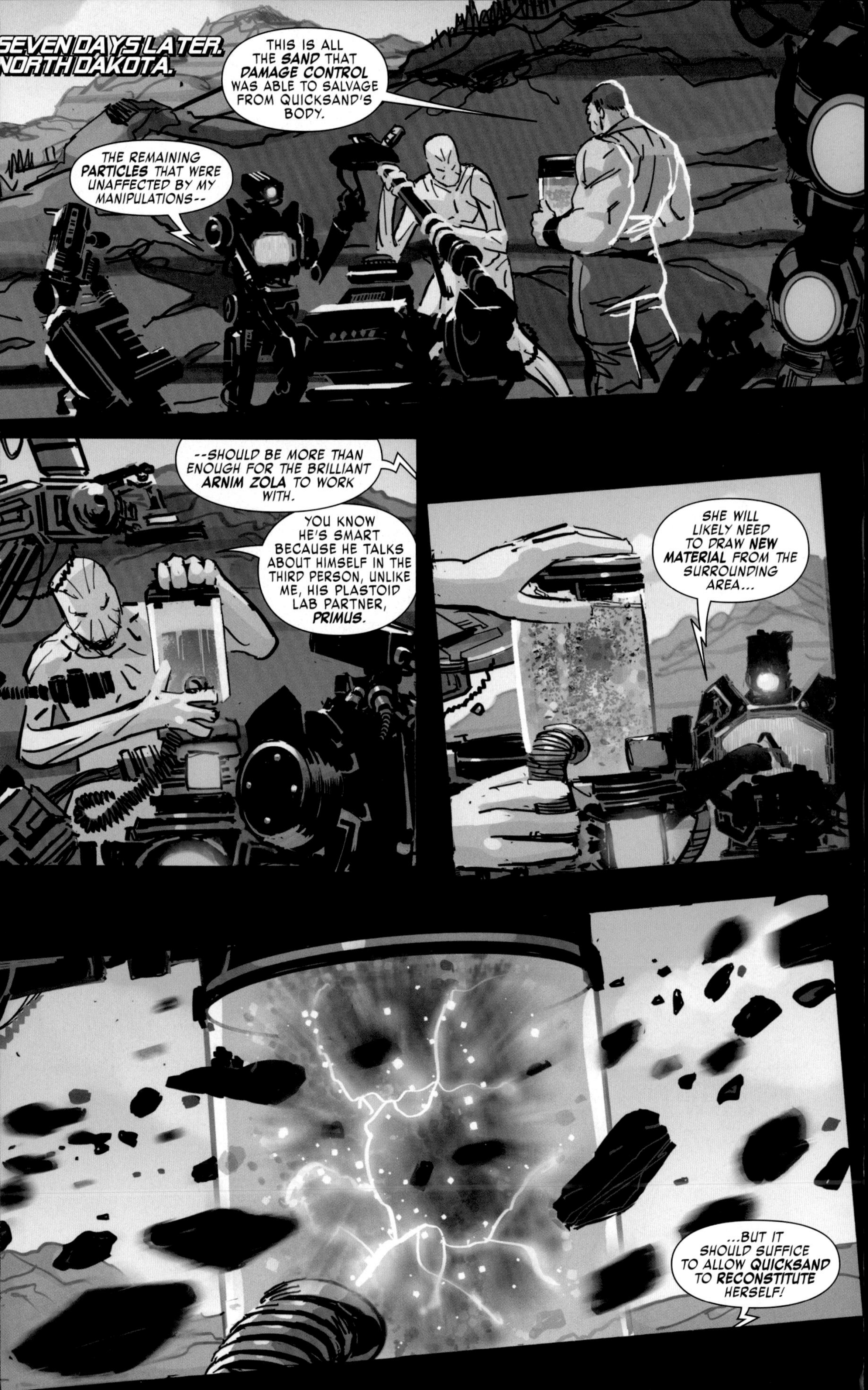
SEVEN DAYS LATER. NORTH DAKOTA.
THIS IS ALL THE SAND THAT DAMAGE CONTROL WAS ABLE TO SALVAGE FROM QUICKSAND'S BODY.
THE REMAINING PARTICLES THAT WERE UNAFFECTED BY MY MANIPULATIONS--
--SHOULD BE MORE THAN ENOUGH FOR THE BRILLIANT ARNIM ZOLA TO WORK WITH.
YOU KNOW HE'S SMART BECAUSE HE TALKS ABOUT HIMSELF IN THE THIRD PERSON, UNLIKE ME, HIS PLASTOID LAB PARTNER, PRIMUS.
SHE WILL LIKELY NEED TO DRAW NEW MATERIAL FROM THE SURROUNDING AREA...
...BUT IT SHOULD SUFFICE TO ALLOW QUICKSAND TO RECONSTITUTE HERSELF!

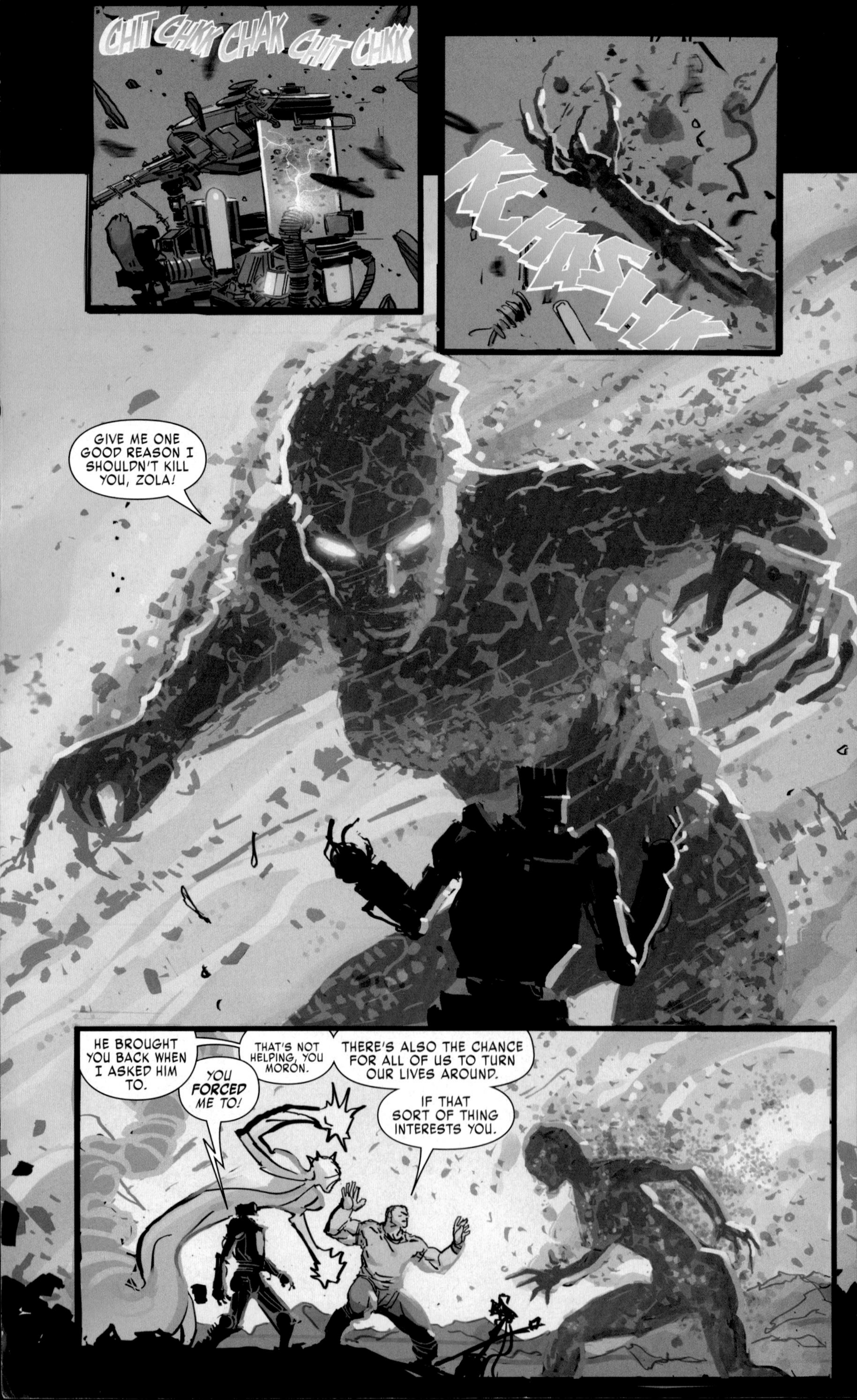
CHIT CHKK CHAK CHIT CHKK
KCHASHK
GIVE ME ONE GOOD REASON I SHOULDN'T KILL YOU, ZOLA!
HE BROUGHT YOU BACK WHEN I ASKED HIM TO.
YOU FORCED ME TO!
THAT'S NOT HELPING, YOU MORON.
THERE'S ALSO THE CHANCE FOR ALL OF US TO TURN OUR LIVES AROUND.
IF THAT SORT OF THING INTERESTS YOU.

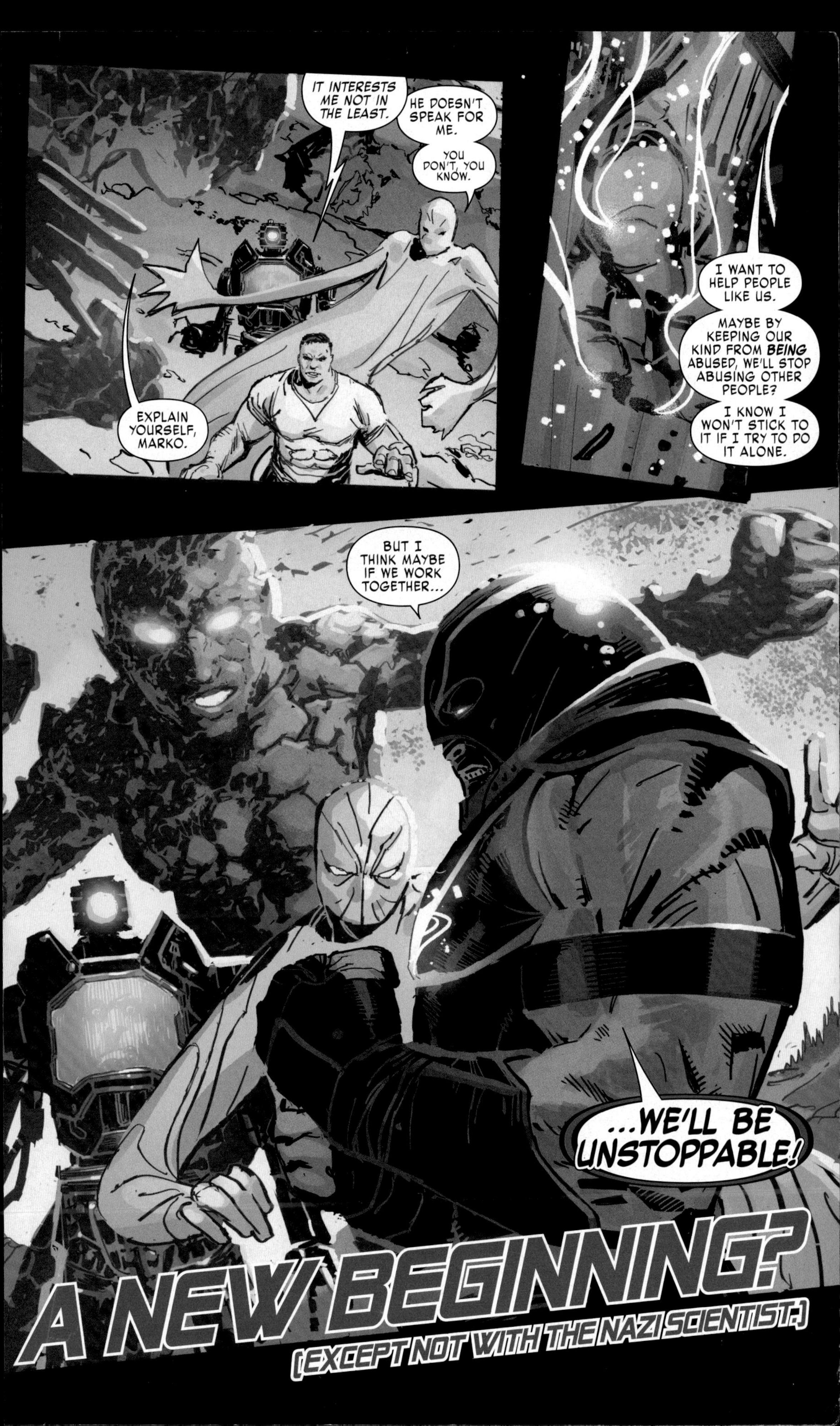

IT INTERESTS ME NOT IN THE LEAST.
HE DOESN'T SPEAK FOR ME.
YOU DON'T, YOU KNOW.
EXPLAIN YOURSELF, MARKO.
I WANT TO HELP PEOPLE LIKE US.
MAYBE BY KEEPING OUR KIND FROM BEING ABUSED, WE'LL STOP ABUSING OTHER PEOPLE?
I KNOW I WON'T STICK TO IT IF I TRY TO DO IT ALONE.
BUT I THINK MAYBE IF WE WORK TOGETHER...
...WE'LL BE UNSTOPPABLE!
A NEW BEGINNING?
(EXCEPT NOT WITH THE NAZI SCIENTIST.)

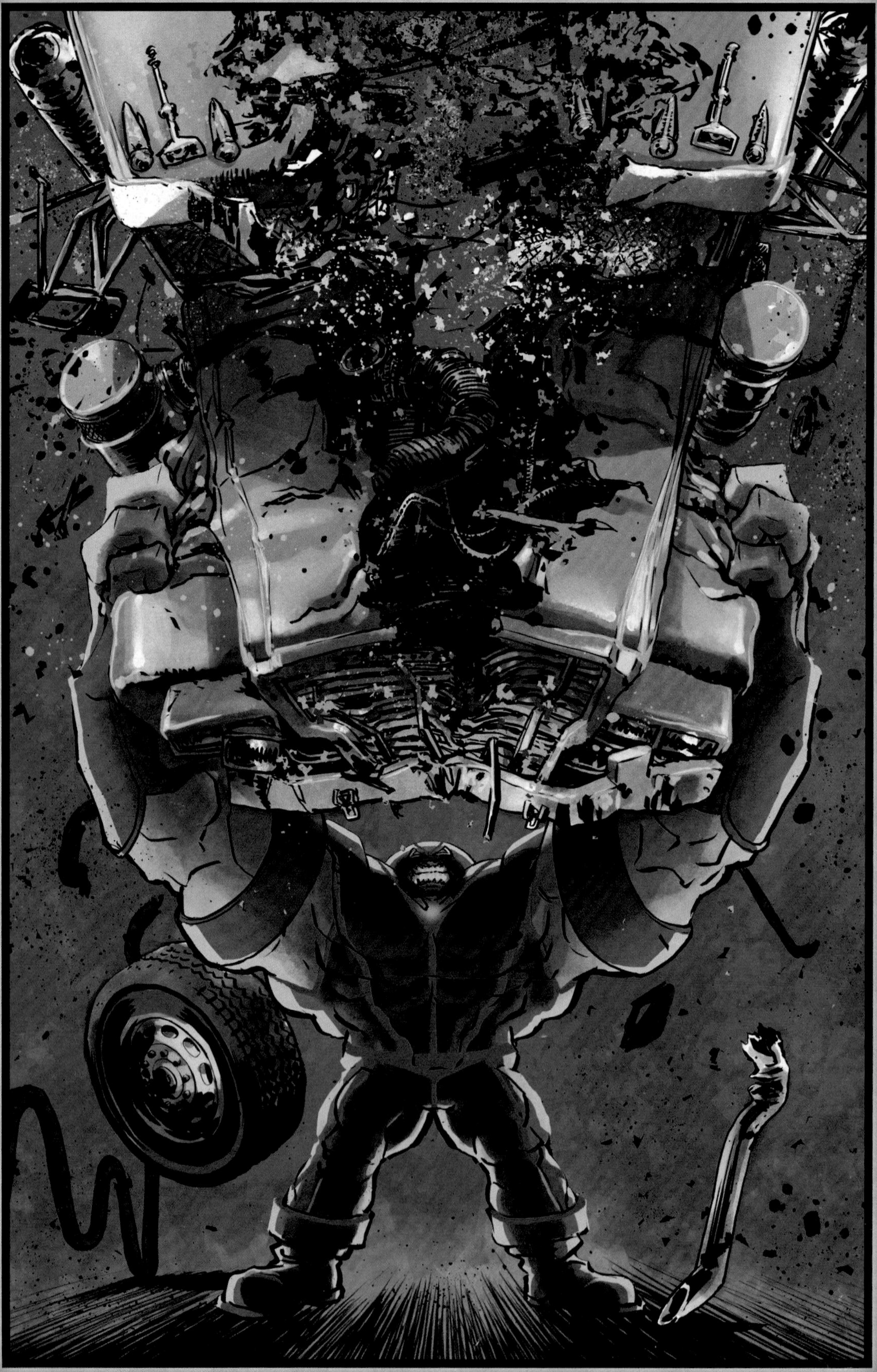

#2 VARIANT BY **SUPERLOG**